KALIGHAT
Its Impact on Socio-Cultural Life of Hindus

KALIGHAT

ITS IMPACT ON SOCIO-CULTURAL LIFE OF HINDUS

INDRANI BASU ROY

GYAN PUBLISHING HOUSE
NEW DELHI-110002

ISBN : 81-212-0401-1

Published in 1993 by
Gyan Publishing House
5 Ansari Road
New Delhi - 110002

Lazer Type Set by Rai Services (P) Ltd., and Printed by
Goyal Offset Printers

CONTENTS

Page No.

Introduction vii

Chapter

1. kalighat and the Kali temple 1
2. Origin and history of the area 15
3. Present day Kalighat 24
4. Regular routine in the temple 63
5. Special Occasions in the temple 72
6. Rcle of the Kali temple in Dasakarma, Sraddha and other Rites 99

Conclusion 116

Appendix 123

Index 154

Maps and Illustrations 159

LIST OF ILLUSTRATIONS

MAPS

S.No

1. Position of Kalighat within 100 Wards of Calcutta
2. Area of present day Kalighat
3. 'Kali Temple' within its Campus
4. Kalikshetra (Calcutta : 12th Century)

5a. Calcutta (middle of 17th. Century)

5b. Calcutta (middle of 18th. Century)

5c. Calcutta (middle of 19th. Century)

CHARTS

1.a Remarkable Spots inside The Campus

1.b Remarkable Spots outside The Campus

2. Background of Bhawanidas Chakraborty
3. A Profile on Temple Personnel
4. Resource Pattern of The Temple
5. Remarkable activities at a Glance
6. Forms of Special Occasions
7. Chief occasion of "Shebait" and the normal routine
8. "Broto"- The Nature and Features
9. Hindu Rites of Passage at Kalighat

INTRODUCTION

Since ancient times, the vast expanse from Himalayas to Kanya Kumari has been known as 'Bharat-Varsha'. We find references in the Vedas, the Puranas, the Epics and the writings of foreigners about the boundaries of the Indian Subcontinent → the great Himalayas in the north and other three sides are encircled by ocean. If we look into religious Constitution of India, we find the bulk of the population as Hindus. Indian Civilization refers principally to the Hindus, the genesis of which lies in the synthesis between Aryan and non-Aryan cultures. Aryans, the carrier of Sanskritic tradition were not only highly intellectual people, they used to hold a very rich religious philosophy which had been reflected in the works - 'Vedas'. When they invaded India and settled themselves in Indian soil, their powerful religion engulfed the baffling variety of local beliefs, cults and ritualistic practices. The diverse cultural traditions gradually crystallized into a single system. It is interesting to note that the evolved Hindu culture was nothing but a compromise and co- existence of both the Sanskritic (Sastriya) and native (Loukik) traditions. For example, it is seen that every rite and ritual of Hindu possess two distinct parts - The 'Sastriya' part where Sanskritic hymns are essentially spelt by the help of Brahmin (Religious specialist) and the 'Loukik' part where non-Brahmins or females perform the regional norms. The Sanskritic part is usually short and necessarily same for all the Hindus irrespective of their dissimilar geographical placement and linguistic difference. On the other hand, 'Loukik' performances follow no uniform pattern and vary greatly. This fulfils the concept of Great and little tradition as shown by Robert Redfield in the field of Civilizational study. According to Redfield, continuity of civilization is handled in terms of the notion of 'Cultural Structure'. The cultural structure of a particular civilization consists of the structure of its cultural traditions and the structure of its thought and values. The structure for any civilization is always compounded of 'Great' and 'little' dimensions in mutual interaction and influence. The great tradition is cultivated in schools or temples; the little tradition itself out and keep going in the lives of unlettered in the village communities. The tradition of philosopher, theologian and literary man is a tradition consciously cultivated and handed down; that of the little people is for the most part taken for granted and not submitted to much scrutiny or considered refinement and improvement. This great and little traditions are actually two currents of thought and action, distinguishable, yet ever flowing into and out of each other.

Worship of the goddess Kali can be said a continuation of native (Loukik) tradition. Because evidences of Indus Valley Civilization (a civilization of non-Aryan people in ancient India which was perished with the advent of Aryan people) tell that worship of mother goddess Sakti and Siva was popular at that time. 'Kali' is one of the forms of 'Sakti' - worship of which is still very popular among the Hindus. The traditional centres of Sakti worship are extremely divine and regarded as 'Pitho-sthan' to the Hindus. Although there is a great deal of disagreement regarding the actual number of 'Pitho-sthan', but it is commonly believed that fifty-one(51) such devine places are scattered all over the India. According, to the standard Hindu almanac 'Gupta Press Panjika. (See *Appendix*) People from all Castes and Sects, economic, ethnic and linguistic sectors are united at these centres due to a coherent feeling of common identity which ultimately means an identical consciousness works in thought and action of each and every Hindu and so they wish for visiting and performing workships in those sacred centres. Thus, cultural continuity is maintained against all other disintegrating urban and modern forces.

Kalighat is considered as one of the traditional centres of Sakti worship (Pitho-sthan) at the heart of the city, Calcutta. A large number of Bengali Hindus and Hindus from other states also visit the temple regularly for religious purposes. Different categories of Brahmin (the special class of literati who are supposed to transmit the elements of great tradition) serving the deity and pilgrims in usual as well as in special occasions evoke interest since the god is originally a folk one used to be worshipped by the lay people with idols and without any specialized sacred formula. The spot is again interesting against the current thought which advocates that, traditional religious beliefs and practices have been degenerating among the Hindus, particularly among those who are living in Cities and urban spots because of the impact of industrialization, urbanization and western education. But in fact it is found that not only the uneducated or poor but the western educated and also the rich people visit the spot quite frequently. Finally, this religious spot is typically important in estimating its accurate influence on the social life of the contemporary people.

The work is the outcome of the thesis submitted by me for Ph. D. Degree which was awarded to me in 1990. I started field-work in February 1981 and the primary data collection ended in March 1983. I kept close connection with field upto middle of 1984 for further verification of facts.

The method of social-cultural anthropology emphasized in my work was essentially 'Intensive Observation'. That was of course, supplemented by collection of concrete case- histories by interviews. Fortunately, as a Hindu, I was allowed to enter in each and every sacred spot in this centre and witnessed all happenings there. Those direct observations helped me to comprehend the implication of each sacred performance of Shebaits and devotees throughout the year. The specific role, relationship and interaction of the persons unveiled the on-going process of cultural heritage.

My approach was purely qualitative. Special interview techniques such as Repeated (Panel) interview[1] and interview in depth[2] were adopted in verifying the facts. Structured open-ended questionnaires were employed. To trace the office in relation to worship, I used 'Genealogical method'. Official records from committee and other old records in the form of book or booklet were also obeyed. Rapport was established prior to selection of informants. Basing on the nature of my requirement, I selected appropriate persons. Beside the key informants, supplementary informations were collected from other individuals, chosen among the willing persons-*Shebait*, temple personnel or devotee.

I am extremely grateful to my respected teacher Biswanath Banerjee, Reader in Dept. of Anthropology, Calcutta University whose guidance enabled me to reach my goal. I am also indebted to a number of teachers,

---

[1] A group of people were subject to repeated interviews at various intervals' (Duverger.M.- Introduction to the Social Sciences, P.183)

[2] The procedure is for an investigator to obtain permission from a person to see him regularly over a period of time to question him on events in which he has been involved'. (Duverger. M.__Introduction to the Social Sciences, p. 187).

informants and friends who not only helped or cooperated but also encouraged and inspired me in course of work. I should not forget the authority of U.G.C. who financially supported me with 'Junior' as well as 'Senior' Research Fellowships (from 19-3-80 to 18-3-82 and from 19-3-82 to 19-9-84) for the particular work.

CHAPTER 1

Kalighat and the Kali Temple (Structural Aspect)

The central figure of Kalighat Kali temple is obviously the goddess Kali herself. According to Hindu mythology, it is one of the fifty-one *Pitho-sthan.* Whole Kalighat area, more particularly the area around the Kali-abode exhibits a huge number of small temples of different allied deities. Even within the boundary (demarcated by the cemented wall, with entrances) of the Kali temple, some other temples and sacred spots are found. This total encircled area of the main temple (Kali-abode) is designated as 'Kali temple' by the local people.

Local Haldar family claims to be the original owner of the temple property but it was disputed by the Chowdhurys of Barisha (District 24-Parganas, south-west of Calcutta). In nineteen sixties the Government intervened and a Committee was formed for administrative management of the temple with representatives of both Government and Haldars.

The duty and responsibility of conducting worship totally rests over the Haldars and their heirs, generally known as *shebaits.* Following the traditional order, they still serve in the temple by turn and receive the respective income. The system is termed as 'Pala' (ref: Chapter III, p.32).

It is interesting to note that, not only tha main Kali temple but also the *Saimbhu*[1] Siva at 'Nakuleshwar-tala' and the 'Sosthi-tala'/'Monosha-

1. It is believed that, in each place where mutilated part from the body of Soti (a mythical figure) had fallen, there Siva has automatically revealed himself. Such self-originated Siva is called 'Saimbhu' i.e. not installed by man.

tala' (abode of the goddesses named Sosthi and Monosha) are served at the same time as a part of 'Pala'. As a counterpart of goddess Kali, self-originated Nakulesh draws equal attention of *shebait* in Kalighat. The seat of goddess Sosthi below a cactus plant is important as it is believed that the great goddess Kali appeared there by the prayer of one devotee, in ancient time. The cactus plant itself locally represents the goddess Monosha, the authority of the snakes.

1. THE MAIN-TEMPLE i.e. THE KALI ABODE

It is the oldest as well as the biggest temple in the locality. Centering this temple, the whole complex has been developed in course of time. It is ninety feet (90') in height and twenty-five feet (25') x forty - six feet (46') in breadth. The temple area (i.e. the land inside the boundary wall) covers one (1) *bigha*, eight (8) *cottahs*, and nineteen (19) *chhataks*. The lower level is about fifteen feet (15') high from the sea-level. Present address of the temple is 9, Bhagabati Lane, Calcutta-700 026. In design, the temple follows the 'Atchala'[1] (eight-roof) hut pattern-the traditional thatched roof pattern of West Bengal.

Old book references point out that in past the area was inhabited by the *kapaliks* who used to worship the goddess with human sacrifices. There is a popular story that the goddess became fed up with the barbarity of human sacrifices and so once, she wished for the worship by the domestic people. In her desire, a female child was born by the union between a *Brohmochari* and a *Vairavi.* Thereafter that girl got married with a Brahmin named as Bhawanidas Chakraborty of Jassore District (for details vide Chapter II). In a later phase the descendants of Bhawanidas Chakraborty acquired the title Haldar and with that reputation they still pursue their service towards the goddess, generation after generation.

At present the temple attracts people from all over India-it has become a source of immense income. At the same time the number of Haldar family member (i.e. the successors) are growing fast. Intra-family conflicts arose time to time with this source of income and those disputes

1. History of religious architecture in Bengal may be conveniently divided into three periods: (1) Early Hindu (upto the end of 12th. Century, Alater in western areas). (2) Sultanate (14th.to early 16th. Century). Muslim came at the beginning of the 13th. century and that created a sharp break in relation to the past tradition. (3) Hindu revival (16th. to 19th.century). Most of the temples of pre-Muslim period have disappeared. The 'Atchala' temples belong to the post-Muslim tradition.

reached upto the yard of Court. Finally a scheme was sanctioned by the Government with the consent of the *shebaits*. Present rules and regulations which are maintained in the temple, follow that scheme.

Besides a long historical background (ref: Chapter II), the Kali temple possesses a complicated operative network (ref: Chapter III). The worship activities too, offer an elaborate framework as it consists of routine as well as special pattern (ref: Chapter IV and V respectively) both for the *shebaits* and public. Not only for ordinary types of worship, but also for various other sacred performances, Hindus of different Castes, Sects, economic and linguistic groups come to this temple. All these are critically important.

Inspite of controversy, it seems to me more reliable that the present temple was erected by the initiative of Zamindar Santosh Kumar Roy Chowdhury (1710 -1799), Barisha. He started the erection but could not finish. After his demise his own son Ramnath Roy and brother's son Rajiblochan Roy supervised and ultimately the temple was completed in 1809. Altogether thirty thousand rupees was spent. This was actually the third time erection because at the beginning the goddess was worshipped within a wretched hut. After that a small temple was erected at the expense of King Mansingha in the early sixteenth century (probably 1606/7). Next to that on the same place Santosh Kumar Roy Chowdhury constructed the present temple. The dome of the temple has been decorated in colour. The top-stick is believed to be made of gold. There is a verandah encircling the temple. Of the two doors of the temple-room, the south door is not supposed to be used but remain open and the east door (locally called *khirki darwaja*) is used for entrance as well as for exit. On the east, from varandah an over-bridge is found upto the kitchen *(bhog-ghar)* of the goddess Kali. This is used to take cooked food carefully inside the temple avoiding the crowd.

Inside the temple-room *(nijo-mandir)*, stairs are found to climb down. There the image is placed which is highly ornamented and south facing. This specific spot is called *Garva griha.* The image is protected by iron railing and it's gate is used to regulate the crowd. A red canopy is found just over the image. There are arrangements of light and fan inside the temple-room but the room is devoid of window.

The face and the four hands of the image are only exposed. The face is presumably made up of touch-stone. Local rumours say, it was engraved by the god Biswakarma and originally found floating in the Ganges but old book record is different (Vide Chapter II, p.26). However, adding four arms made of gold, the engraved stone-piece was enshrined. The uppe: arm of the right side denotes assurance, the lower one of the same side denotes blessings. The left upper hand is with a large falchion (*Khara*) and the lower one holds a decapited head. Inner structure of the body is in secret and on each night the image is clothed with a new sari. All clothes are changed at a time and usually this happens twice a year. But there is no fixed date for it. When the exposed parts of the image tend to be covered by the load of the clothes, the old clothes are removed. Meanwhile the cloth-materials too get rotton and fetid due to constant overflow of milk, water, juices of fruits and sweets. The act of clothes- changing is a very time consuming task; it involves removing of all saris one after another, preparation of the inner frame with fresh precautionary measures (to protect against insects) and finally wearing a new expensive sari. Every-thing is done behind the public-eye by the specialized associates.

The legendary mutilated body fragment of the goddess (*soti-ango*) is said to be preserved within the temple-room which is bathed once in a year on the auspicious day, *Snanjatra*. It is absolutely a secret affair, restricted to few of the *shebaits* only. As a result, many *shebaits* are confused in identifying the exact place where the *soti-ango* is kept. Perhaps it is placed just beneath the image, within a small iron chest.

A big rectangular platform called *Natmondir* is found adjacent to the temple, from where the face of the image is seen (vide Map. 3).Stairs are found on two sides (east and west) to climb up the platform. This *Natmondir* was built by the Zamindar Kasinath Roy in 1835.

There are six entrances along the boundary of temple. In the north, the big decorated gate made by a donar from well-known 'Birla' family is commonly referred as 'Birla Gate'. It remains usually closed and on special occasions (for instance, first day of Bengali new-year) it is kept open. The east gate towards 'Kali Temple Road' and the west gate towards the Ganges are maximum used by the public. The campus includes some flower shops, *pera* (sweet) shops, four Siva temples, Radha -Krisna temple with *Dolmancho*. *Sosthi* / *Monosha* abode, *Hom-bedi*, two *Harikath* and *Tahobil*. There are also the kitchens of the goddess Kali and Radha Krisna, *Vien-ghar*, Store-room, Committee-office and *Nahobatk-hana*. Entrances of Committee-office and Nahobatkhana are same from outside of the campus and both are on the first floor.

The southern spacious varandah of the main temple, facing the image is called *Jor-bangla*. Performances occurring inside the temple-room are visible from *Natmondir*, through the *Jor-bangla*. Besides, the performances like worships for *Manosik* (ref : Chapter VI, p.117), Broto celebrations (ref : Chapter v, p.90) Upanayans (ref: Chapter VI.p.119), reading of the famous Hindu scriptures e.g.'Gita','Chondi' etc. are performed on the *Natmondir*, keeping the image in front.

2. NAKULESWAR-TALA

The Siva named Nakulesh or Nakuleswar is present at north-east direction about three hundred feet (300') away from the main temple. Address of this temple is 23, Haldar para Road, Calcutta - 700 026.

The legend behind Nakuleswar-tala is that, a devotee of remote past (Brahmananda) discovered this phallic Siva, spontaneously originated in the spot. The month was *Chaitra* (Mar- April). He went to pluck flowers for the goddess Kali. A few standing cows came into his notice whose milk were falling over a black piece of stone. Returning home, in meditation he came to know that the stone-piece is the 'Nakulesh'.

The spot was within the forest, under a banyan tree. After that discovery a hut was made and Siva worship started by Brahmananda. When the authority of worship shifted to the hands of the Haldar family, they also used to worship this Siva along with the mother goddess Kali. In the mean time, a devoted Brahmin named Sudarshan Panda came in Kalighat from 'Jhajha' village of the State Orissa and selected a spot at the bank of the Ganges (now the place is called as *mayer-ghat*, cemented by a Punjabi soldier named Hujurimalla in 1770/71) for meditation. Incidentally Haldars picked him to give appointment as a Priest for Siva (Nakulesh) worship. Since then his descendants act as priest of Nakuleswar temple. They are locally known as *Ure-Panda.*

In 1854, a Punjabi merchant named Tara Singh made the present temple for 'Nakulesh' in Gurudwara[1] style. Here lies another myth. Tara Singh was a Saiva. Once he was able to make immense profit in business and decided to erect a Siva temple in Benaras (State, Uttar Pradesh). Therefore, he sailed for Benaras with the required building materials. But the sailors could not anchor the ship at the bank of Benaras. The tide dragged them in a different track and ultimately arrived at Kalighat. Tara Singh noticed the miserable condition of Nakuleswar-abode, while wandering in Kalighat. Therefore he made the present temple with the same devotion.

---

1. It refers to the specific architecture pattern followed among the Punjabi people, connected with their religion.

So far as the administration is concerned, all money and loose coins which is offered to the idol goes to the *paladar* (i.e. the *shebait* of the great goddess Kali); only the fee or the gift for the performance (*dakshina*) is received by the attendant Priest. (vide Chapter III). No separate *Misra* rank exists for this temple.

Inside the temple, an image of Siva is found facing west, attached to the wall. The temple-door is in west. This temple possesses a *Natmondir* also, from where the image and internal performances are seen. In front of the image Siva, the self-originated phallic Siva is present, over which water can not be poured without stooping downwards. Two seats (*ason*) are found on two sides of the image, where at a time two Priests sit for worship on behalf of the public. The right seat is termed as *danason* and the left one as *bamason*. At present the Oriya Priests are seven in number who follow the priest-hood for Nakuleswar temple(vide Genealogy.1).They maintain a systematic rotation pattern (*pala*) of their own to avoid conflict. According to the informant Shesdev Panda (locally famous in the name Babaji), enjoyment of shares by present day Priests run in the following manner.

WORSHIPPERS OF RIGHT SEAT	WORSHIPPERS OF LEFT SEAT
1. Nidhiram Panda (for three months)	1. Akkhoy Kumar Panda (for six months)
2. Madhusudan Panda (for three months)	2. Ganesh Panda (for three months)
3. Mayadhar Panda (for three months)	3. Pitambar Panda (for three months)
4. Dukhishyam Panda (for three months)	

Among other descendants of this lineage, some supervise properties of their native village and receive income from those. Others are engaged as Priests in local temple. Shesdev himself is the Priest of the local Nabogroho[1] temple, just opposite of the Nakuleswar temple.

The account of *pala* completes in a year. Proportions, as said before are determined by the number of heirs. But due to the presence of some idle months (when earnings fall short), they have settled the rotation of

1. The governing deities of nine planets e.g. Sun, Moon, Mars, Mercury, Jupitar, Venus, Saturn, Dragon's head or ascending node (formerly identified as 'Rahu') and Dragon's tail i.e. the descending node (formerly identified as 'Ketu').

service day-wise. In this fashion the turns rotate after two days and finally coincide with the total number of scheduled days.

Three generations back, one uncle (mother's brother) was introduced in *seva-pala*. His share is now divided into two parts. Ganesh Panda and Pitambar Panda are enjoying that. Their *gotro* is 'Bharadwaj' whereas the *gotro* of the original stream is 'Batswa'.

The temple opens at 4 a.m. Before *mongolaroti*, last night's dress and decoration is removed and on the bow of Siva, *sankho* (conch), chakro (wheel), *goda* (club) and *padma* (lotus) are drawn with white sandal-paste. A snake and a trident made up of flower are also affixed over the head. The image is dressed in *dhuti-chador* and that is put off after *mongolaroti*.

Public are allowed to enter into the temple after the performance of *mongolaroti*. At about 12 a.m. the *bhog* (only *payesh*) is taken from the kitchen of the goddess Kali. It is the responsibility of *paladar* to keep it prepared in time. At about 1.30 p.m. the temple is closed and reopened in the afternoon at about 5 p.m. Final closing is around 10 p.m. Of course there are seasonal variations and on special occasions e.g. *Sivaratri*, *Nil* etc. (ref: Chapter V) the temple remains closed for a minimum time in the day. Saturdays are the crowded days, so in such days the temple remain open for more than the usual time.

In the evening after *sondhyaroti*, sitol is arranged. Sixteen *luchis* and some saltless fried potato-chips come from the kitchen of Radha-Krisna temple. Salt is prohibited in the potato because with salt these are considered as orts. Of the sixteen *luchis*, *paladar* gets twelve and rest four are received by the Priest on rotation. Milk and sweet (*sandesh*) for *sayan* are arranged and taken by the same Priest.

The Oriya Priests (*urepanda*) of this spot generally buy the spot from *paladar* as a regular phenomenon (vide Chapter III, p.34).

3. SOSTHI / MONOSHA ABODE

This is a rectangular altar about three feet (3') high bearing a small cactus plant. Beneath the tree, on an altar three stones are placed side by side - left to right representing as the goddesses 'Sosthi', 'Sitola', and 'Mongol Chondi'. The spot is very sacred and locally known as *Sosthi-tala* or Monosha-*tala*. The altar was constructed by a person named Govinda Das Mandal in 1880.

Public offer their worships in the name of *Sosthi,Sitala* or *Chondi* in the same altar. The place of the altar is actually the *samadhi*[1] of Brahmananda Giri (a keen devotee of past, vide Chapter II).

In this sacred spot, all Priests are female i.e. Priestess. A man named Sudhanshu Banerjee acts as the incharge of the spot - he governs over those Priestesses. This spot as a part of *pala* is regularly sold (vide Chapter III, p.34). Banerjee buys it against a lumpsum money. Hence, the profit or loss is a matter of his luck. He appoints the Priestesses and by himself supervises them except two for hours in the noon when he goes home for lunch. *Paladars* can deprive him by selling the spot to somebody else or treating the *pala* as *khaser-pala.*[2]

Usually, *Sosthi-tala* is sold along with *Nakuleswar-tala* to the Oriya Priests of *Nakuleswar-tala.* Banerjee has grown such a reputation that he is able to buy *Sosthi-tala* regularly. Even when the *pala* is treated as *Khaser pala* (vide Chapter III, p.33) he acquires the charge of supervision. He is working in this spot for a long time.

Price of the spot varies on the basis of date and occasion. For example, it increases on Tuesdays, Saturdays, Sundays, holidays and also on special occasions because of greater assemblage of public. The transaction-price usually remains within Rs. 80/- to Rs. 150/-. Sometimes it reaches upto Rs.500/-. Sudhanshu Banerjee buys in advance (the day before the particular day) calculating the expected income and he has to bear all costs of administration.

All operative rules for this spot are created by Banerjee. Normally four Priestesses work on rotation. Duty continues for successive three days and rotate after nine days. Occasionally (on special occasions like *Monosha-puja,Sitola-puja* etc. i.e. when public concentration increase) two Priestesses are needed at a time. Remuneration of a Priestess is Rs.15/- for three days. Flexibility is very negligible. If there is heavy income, they get Rs.16/- or Rs.17/-. Working hours are from 4 a.m. to 11 p.m. i.e. from the opening to closing of the temple. The Priestesses have to collect the offered coins and submit those to the incharge. They have also to look-

1. The burial place of a self-absorbed spiritual meditator who gave up his life through profound meditation.

2. Its refers to that system where *paladar* does not sell any portion of his area but appoints some faithful persons to look- after the spots.

after, clean and decorate the altar, attend the public by serving *charunamrito, dio-phota* etc. and above all help them in their worship. Neither daily worship is done, nor a *bhog* is offered in this altar because the goddesses remaining here are considered as parts of the great goddess Kali, only with functional speciality.

Priest-hood are not hereditary. Faithfulness is the prime criterion of this job. Personal acquaintance is required for judging the efficiency and thus, new persons enter into the job.

Although the spot is meant for the females but males are not at all restricted. Some people come for simple worship and some come with specific prayers. People of latter category have to tie small bricks with the branches of cactus plant by thread. After fulfillment of the particular desire the brick is supposed to be un-tied. Both time (to tie and to un-tie) Rs. 1.25/- is charged. Moreover, at the time of untying, the Priestess over there claims Rs. 2/- to Rs. 10/- (any amount, whatever she wishes), cloth, sweets etc. in the name of the deity. Normally, after fulfillment of desires people become so happy that they do not hesitate to please the Priestesses. The forms of desires are as follows:

MALE DESIRES	FEMALE DESIRES
1. To get promotion in the service.	1. To get alive child.
2. To get a suitable job.	2. For quick marriage.
3. To pass in the examination.	3. To pass in the examination.

There is also a convention of keeping a small portion of hair in *Monosha-tala*, when the head-hair of a child is shaven for the first time (ref: Chapter VI, p.). A tax of one rupee and nine annas (Rs. 1.55/-) is levied, out of which five annas (30 paisa) is the gain of *Monsha-tala* and rest one rupee and four annas (Rs. 1.25/-) reaches to the *paladar*. Practically, when such tax is collected in absence of *paladar* or his representative, then the total amount remains in *Monosha-tala*.

A large number of ladies are assembled here at different dates of *Sosthi-puja* and *Monosha-puja* as per the respective lineage-norm and regional culture pattern. The *Durga- puja* which is conducted in the temple, starts from this spot through the invocation of the goddess (*bodhon*).

Many a *Sathi-brahmans* (vide Chapter III) are found to utilize this spot. Unfamiliar visitors and worshippers are often trapped by them. Their method of exacting money is an open secret in the temple. When Sathi-brahmans take the pilgrims in *Sosthi-tala*, worship is offered by themselves; Priestess only serve *charonamrito* and *doi-phota.*

When I first visited *Sosthi-tala* for my field-work, it was a roofless altar. At the end of 1983, it had got a new shape, by the initiative of a donar from Birla family.

Two stories about *Sosthi-tala* are in vogue. The first one advocates that the goddess Kali appeared in this particular spot. Long long ago, a devotee became very eager to see the goddess by his mortal eyes. He was continuously praying for that with hard meditation. At last he could be able to see the goddess on that very spot. The second one is completely different. In ancient time when the *Kapaliks* used to perform their bloody rites, once a small boy was spotted as subject of their sacrifice. The boy was the only child of a widow. Somehow the widow came to know the motive of the *Kapaliks*. She began to cry piteously and prayed to the goddess to save her son's life. The goddess became perplexed with the plaintive cry of the widow mother. So she wished for a disaster in nature. Incessant rain with heavy storm started. The boy tried to hide himself under a bush of cactus plants. (It is said that at the place of present altar, that cactus bush was present). The situation was so calamitous that the *Kapaliks* did not find out the proposed boy. Thus, the boy got a shelter and his life was saved. It is well-known that a form of Kali is identified as *Sosthi*, the goddess of child welfare. As the mother Kali has responded to the doleful utterance of a helpless lady and saved her only son, since then the very spot has been known as '*Sosthi-tala*'.

The other sacred spots which deserve to be mentioned in this context, are as follows:

(a) HARKATH-TALA

Animal sacrifice is intimately associated with Kali worship. There are two specialized stands for animal sacrifice, kept side by side. Both the stands are locally called as *Hari- Kath* and the area as *Harkath-tala.*

The spot is adjacaent to *Natmondir*, southwards. Of the two stands, the bigger one is for buffalo sacrifice and the smaller one for goats and sheep. For continuous use, the original small stand had decayed. According to Bhola Haldar, that was replaced about fourteen years ago by a expert carpenter with a great care. Material was the timber from 'Sal' tree. A worship was done by the chief Priest before setting the new one.

In Kalighat the act of immolation is associated with the caste 'Kamar' (black-smith), traditionally. Male members of the caste 'Bagdi' are supposed to help the immolator at the particular time. The total proceedings are as follows. At first, *sankalpo* is done by a *Sathibrahman* and a flower garland is put on the neck of the proposed animal. At this time a male *Bagdi* bathes the animal in the Ganges-water. (A main hole opening is found inside the campus, near *Harkath-tala.*). Next to that, the animal is placed on *Harikath* in proper position; the *Bagdi* pulls the legs. On that moment the immolator is supposed to behead the animal by single stroke. Smooth immolation depends on the degree of pulling.

It is believed that dangers, more particularly life crises (*fara*) can be avoided or minimized by the act of *pronam* to *Harikath.* So many people rush to salute and in course of their salutation they touch the blood and flowers lying around. Some people also break coconut over the spot, with the same belief.

Animal sacrifice is often criticized by those who do not believe in its inner theory. According to Sri Pulin Haldar, once (40/45 years back) a strong debate was held on *Natmondir* between late Madan Mohan Malabya[1] and late Gurupada Haldar, with the issue of animal sacrifice. Late Gurupada Haldar, the most educated and renowned scholar of Haldar-lineage of those days could be able to prove its significance with reasons. He also convinced that the system should not be criticized because it bears some real value. Since then the practice has not been seriously challenged and continued to remain as before.

(b) RADHA-KRISHNA TEMPLE

This temple is locally known as 'Shamo-ray temple' and is situated at the west of the main temple, within the temple campus.

Bhawanidas Chakraborty, the progenitor of Haldar- lineage at Kalighat was initially a Vaisnava by sect (for details vide Chapter II). When he became a Sakta starting Kali worship, his mental attitude did not change totally. He could not wash off his old bearings. So he placed a Basudev idol and Radha-Krishna idols in the same temple and began to worship all together. Present Radha-Krishna temple, *Dolmancho,* separate kitchen for Radha-Krishna are the gradual additions by different devotees. Now the vegetarian *bhog* of Radha -Krishna is prepared in that separate kitchen.

---

1. A well -known national leader and a great patron of learning.

In 1723, a settlement officer of District Murshidabad first erected a separate temple for Radha-Krisna. After that in 1843, one Vaisnavite Zamindar named Udoy Narayan Mandal made the present Radha-Krisna temple on the same place. The Dolmancho was founded in 1858 by Madan Koley of 'Saha-nagar', Calcutta.

Administration of this temple is somewhat different. It is not under the main *pala* - system and *shebaits* do not claim its income. Because when this temple was erected first, its income was meagre, *Shebaits* appointed a Brahmin named Durga Charan Chakraborty to look-after the temple with an agreement that he will receive the total income. Accordingly, Durga Charan Chakraborty with his brother took the entire responsibility of that temple. Till now their successors are engaged in the same service, by rotation. *Shebaits* choose Durga Charan as he belonged to the same *gotro* as that of the *shebaits* to avoid the faults and defects in worship.

At present there are four parties among whom the responsibility rotates. The turn for a party comes after twenty four days and exists for eight days. These Priests are called as *Radha-Krisna mandirer misri-masai.*

In fact a few of such Priests of this temple are found to hold different titles. They are appointed persons by the original lineage successors to serve on their behalf. The appointed persons stay for the stipulated period and the rest of the month they spend in their home-land pursuing other occupations. Swapan Mukherjee is such an appointed *misri masai*, whose residential district is Midnapur. He performs agricultural work there, when the turn of his authority is over.

Shebaits still do not claim any income from this temple, though it is their deity within the *devottar* land. But as the income of the temple has increased a lot, a wooden box has been kept at the door of the temple where public puts coins as *pronami.* Only the accumulated coins in that box is credited in the Committee fund.

The *misri masais* of this temple undertake the responsibility of preparing *sitol* for the goddess Kali- *luchi* and saltless potato-chips. They have to carry it to the main temple at the particular time (after evening-*aroti*) with sweets and milk. Similarly they send *sitol* to *Nakuleswar-tala.*

Expenditure of *bhog* (noon) *sitol* and *aroti* (evening) for this Radha-Krisna temple are met from the personal fund of the *misri-masais.* A special type of lamp (*pancho- pradip*), a conch for blowing (*sankho*), a cloth (*Kapar*) and a fly-whisk (*chamor*) are the requirements of *aroti*.

Another Radha-Krisna temple is found nearby but that is outside the temple campus. Name of the image over there is 'Govinda'. It is heard that the image was situated in 'Govindapur' i.e. where the present Fort Willium stands. (That area was named after the image) *Borgis* at the time of plunder touched the image and spoilt its sanctity. Raja Basanta Roy brought it to Kalighat to protect from destruction. But as the sanctity was already lost, so the image did not get any place within the campus. This Govinda temple has however no connection with the Haldars.

(c) KUNDUPUKUR

It is the cement-floored sacred tank situated at the south-east of the temple, outside the boundary. At present the tank is well protected under the supervision of great donar business family, 'Birla'. It remains open from 6 a.m. to 12 a.m. and again from 5 p.m. to 8 p.m. In February 1981, when I first visited the spot, it was merely a dirty tank. At the end of 1981, cleansing began. As the original water could not be pumped out totally, so inspite of filling water by deep tube-well, the water of the tank remains turbid. (The well-known 'Birla' - family has also renovated the Committee-office during the same period).

Prior to this cleansing, efforts were made twice for improving the tank- firstly in 1871 by the contribution of all *shebaits* and secondly, in 1887 by the initiative of Alipore Municipality. But in none of the cases, the tank could be emptied. This indicates that there might be any subterranean connecting link with the Ganges.

Present area of the tank is approximately ten *cottahs*. In past it was more wide and called as 'Kaku-Kunda'. In sixteenth century *soti-ango* was discovered from its water (ref : Chapter II, p.26).This tank was of great importance in past to the devotees. There was a well-known proverb - 'Even if a barren women takes bath in the tank after maintaining certain specific norms, she should definitely bear a child', Moreover, water of this tank was regarded as sacred as that of the water of the Ganges. But at present the attention of the public to Kumdupukur has dwindled.

(d) HOM-BEDI

It is a small roofed altar set up by a donar from 'Birla' family, few years back. This altar is situated in south of the main temple, within the campus. It has no connection with *pala* of the *shebaits* but as placed on the *devottar* land so a sort of monthly rent has to be paid by the incharge to the Committee.

Bhusan Tiwari, a Brahmin of Bihar State is the incharge of this altar. The altar is extremely important to the Hindusthani and Marwari people. They consider it as an abode of the great god Brahma. The pit over the altar is known as *Hom-Kundu* where performance named *hom* is found.

Normally incharge's presence is noticed from dawn to noon (upto 1 p.m.). At the time of *navoratri* in the month of *chaitra* (Mar-April) and of *Aswin* (Sept-Oct),the *hom* performance continues throughout the day upto evening.

Public (as said, Hindustanis and Marwaris) come with ingredients like *belpata*, sandal-wood dust, ghee etc. Incharge helps them keeping the flame continuous by adding 'sal' wood pieces into the fire. Ideology of public behind this performance is to please the creator of the world for well-being.

(e) SIVA-TEMPLES

Of the four Siva temples two are joined (south-west corner of the campus). Rest two are in northern and south-western side along the boundary of the temple.

Each of these Siva temples is an autonomous body as founded by different families of Haldar lineage at different times. Respective successors are liable for the supervision and worship management. Naturally income runs to the respective proprietor.

The area outside the boundary also shows an influx of Siva temples since it is an important *pith*.

CHAPTER 2

Origin and History of the Area

Early history of Kalighat is purely conjectural based on myth, legend and hearsay. To achieve a more or less reliable history, the textual as well as the contextual sources have been explored. Comparing both the data, new informations (obtained from the contextual data) have been added in some places and presented in the following way.

Antiquity of Kalighat can be logically traced from the 'Puranic age',[1] because we get the legendary reference about the creation of *pitho -sthans* from the ancient Hindu text namely 'Kalika Puran' and 'Mahabhagbat Puran'. Soti (said as one of the ten manifestations of the goddess Kali), the daughter of the King Daksha and wife of the lord Siva, though uninvited, went to participate in the *Yajna* (a pompous vedic sacrifice) arranged by her father. She was insulted there and could not stand husband's upbraiding. With the terrible shock she died ultimately. Hearing this sudden news, Siva bursted into anger. He rushed to the spot, spoilt the yajna and killed Daksha. After tremendous turmoil, taking the body of Soti upon his shoulder, he began to wander the whole universe. He was so excited that nobody could dare to reach close to him. Gods trembled. Indra, the King of the gods being afraid sought protection from Visnu, who finally with his flashing disc ('Sudarshan Chakra') cut the dead body into fragments. Those fragments dropped in different places making each place a holy *pitho-sthan.*

1. It refers to a historical period when the sacred Hindu texts entitled as 'Puran' were written. The period may dated as sixth Century approximately.

As per the orthodox Hindu belief Daksha's *Yajna* was a true incident and that has been ascribed to Satya Yuga',[1] dating of which is impossible. Kalighat is now a well-known *pitho-sthan* as one of the fragments containing little four toes of right foot dropped here.

On the other hand, geologists confirm that in remote past this region of Bengal was under water- gradually with alluvial deposition (probably from 7th to 16th Centuries) the area developed to a firm earth. The exact time from when Kalighat got it's recognition as *pith* is still unknown. Our great epics never referred any places named Kalighat. *Purans* though started to furnish the *pith* legend, but there also, among the list of pitho-sthans the name of Kalighat was totally omitted. Most of the *Purans* mentioned a place named 'Samotat' to mean the forested south Bengal; present day 'Kalighat' was possibly included there. Among the *Tantras*, some highly- esteem *Tantras* do not recognise Kalighat as pith. In 'Pithamala Tantra' and 'Nigam Tantra', reference of a place named Kalikshetra[2] was found which is somewhat bow-shaped and extended about sixteen miles from Bahula (present day Behala, located at District 24- Parganas, south-west of Calcutta) to Dakshineswar (District Howrah, north-west of Calcutta). It was believed that, a portion from the mangled corpse of Soti had fallen centrally within that arched area. However, 'Tantra Chudamani' acknowledges fifty-one *piths* and mentions this as 'Kali-pith'. From 'Acharanirnaya Tantra' we get the name of *Vairav* as Nakulesh in this particular area. As per 'Mahanil Tantra' the presiding deity at Kalighat has been named as 'Guhya Kali' i.e., the Kali who is not revealed. Gourdas Basak, one of the old inhabitants of Calcutta has correlated the conception of 'Guhya Kali' with fifteenth Century.

Allusions of the shrine are present from the period of Hindu King Ballal Sen (middle of the 12th Century). At this time many pilgrims used to have their bath in the Ganges of 'Kalikshetra' to get recovery from sin; merchant ships passing by used to wait awhile near its bank before their journey to distant lands. As per the Bengali book 'Kalighater Oitihasik Katha' (p.64), 'Kalikshetra' existed about two thousand years ago but no other historical evidence could be cited in its support. Further, when it had achieved the particular name 'Kalighat' is in obscure. 'Ghat' in Bengali

1. According to Hindu mythology, the external time can be divided into four periods or Yugas-Satya, Treta, Dwapar and Koli. The first one is Satya, where nothing but truth prevailed.

2. The place Kalikshetra was very popular in past and so a lot of hermitages were made by different great ascetices. Today the significance of the very sacred area has been synchronized only to the area named 'Kalighat'.

language means a landing place or crossing point of a river, canal or pond. The word 'Kalighat' therefore means 'ghat of Kali' i.e. goddess Kali's place near a water source.

It is popularly believed that the great magnificient city Calcutta has been named after Kali's abode over there. The first historical notice regarding Calcutta was found in the book 'Ain-i-Akbari' written by Abul Fazal in 1596. According to that 'Kalikata' was a place within Saptogram, an old port on the river Hooghly. Next record goes with Job Charnock, the East India Company's chief who selected a cluster of three villages in Bengal along the east bank of the river Hooghly (at the north 'Sutanuti' i.e. the area between present day Baghbazar and Burrabazar, at the south 'Govindapur' i.e. the area from Esplanade to Hastings and 'Dehi Kolkata' in between Burrabazar to Esplanade) for his trading centre. Till then the area was dampy, full of jungles and pestiferous ponds - a land of wild animals. Calcutta's position was improved when it became an independent settlement after being purchased as Zamindary in 1698, from the Sabarna Chowdhury's. Deed of purchase exists in British museum, London and the copy has been preserved in 'Victoria Memorial'[1], Calcutta. At that time Kalighat was a suberb area at the south of 'Govindapur' and under municipal act of 1888, that had been included within Calcutta. But it is also difficult to say when and why those three sister villages were recognized under one head 'Calcutta'.

According to devoted members of Haldar family Kalighat is of supreme importance among the different renowned *pitho-sthans*. It is called 'Maha-pith' because of two reasons:

(1) This *pith* is situated in combination of three important spots namely the 'Keoratala smasan' (cremation ground), 'Adi ganga' (the Ganges) and'Nakuleswar vaivav'(*saimbhu* Siva) in three directions.

(2) People exhibit their best regards by touching the feet of the revered. As the revered foot of Soti had fallen in Kalighat, the sacredness of this *pith* has been enhanced greatly.

Around the Kali temple, the plot of land measuring 595 *bighas*, 4 *cottahs* and 3 *chhataks* are found as devottar property. A lot of controversies are associated with the original source of land and the ownership right also.

---

1. It is a building made in 1910 in the memory of Queen Victoria. Many valuable documents of that period have been preserved here.

The background of Kali worship at Kalighat, so far as known, has been furnished briefly in the following lines. A very keen devotee named Brahmananda Giri was engaged in austere contemplation at a solitary corner of Nilgiri Hill, to achieve the blessings of the great goddess. After a long endeavour, he became weary and decided to commit suicide in despair. The goddess appeared at the pick of his excitement and granted a boon to ensure that she (the goddess) would never leave him, unless he wanted that.

A long period had passed after the incident and once another devotee named Atmaram came to meet Brahmananda. He told, he had been instructed by the goddess to convince Brahmananda and to take her in 'Kalikshetra' for giving publicity. At first Brahmananda did not believe but soon in meditation he became sure about the matter.

Incidentally under the spell of illusion by the goddess, an universal dissolution was created. The two devotees were instructed to hold a stone piece and to shut their eyes. Within a second they reached the said place (Kalikshetra). Thereafter, according to the direction of the goddess, they drew Kali image over that particualr piece of stone (18' long, 3' wide and 2'3" high) and installed that on 'Brahma bedi' to start worship. The legend behind the 'Brahma bedi' is that - Brahma, the creator of the world was prayed for blessings by all the gods, at the time of fighting against *Asurs*. The particualr spot is remarkable for his appearance.

After some days they discovered the self-originated Siva in the same area and also the Soti's relic from the nearby lagoon, Kalikunda (present day Kundupukur). In fact Soti's relic was first found by Padmavati, wife of Kamdev. Kamdev was the progenitor of Chowdhury-lineage of Barisha (District 24 - Parganas, south-west of Calcutta). Both the husband and wife were religious minded. They came at Kalighat for further concentration of mind, knowing the holiness of the area. Once Padmavati noticed an effulgence emanating from the eastern side of the lagoon. When she was trying to show her husband, Brahmananda and Atmaram were passing by the side. Following the talk, they became interested and finally took initiative to fetch the dazzling floating objecct (the stony glittering toes of Soti) from the water. Next day was *Snanjatra;* they bathed the relic ceremonially by uttering sacred spell, then worshipped and placed properly as the instruction from the goddess was obtained. Weight of the sacred relic was six and half seers. Now it is broken. A heavy conflict was heard to be happened among the *shebaits* regarding the right of possession and during the physical tussle, it dropped from the hand and broken into two pieces.[1]

However, Brahmananda and Atmaram both were living together peacefully sharing the same devotional flavour. But destiny was not very favourable. One day when Brahmananda was meditating before the image, a crazy girl came and started to disturb him. He became very angry and ordered the girl to leave the place. The girl vanished and an oracle was heard 'I am leaving as you no longer want me'. Brahmananda remembered the boon of the goddess at once. He realized the truth but became absolutely disappointed. Within a few days, he handed over the responsibility of worship to Atmaram solely and gave up his life. After sometime, Atmaram also gave up his life and one of his disciple named Ananda Giri took upon himself the charge of worship. In the mean time, *Kapaliks* from different areas (viz. Chhawal Giri, Trilochan Giri, Jungle Giri, Devidas Giri, Devnath Giri etc.) gathered at Kalighat to settle their hermitages. Also some people of low Castes like 'Bagdi', 'Pod' etc. settled in the same area, clearing the forest. Kalighat became a spot of nuisance for *Tantra* practice with all the attending virtues and vices.

Forty years after the death of Ananda Giri, a person named Bhubaneswar Giri became the *mohonto* to serve the goddess. *Gotra* - name of this Brahmin was 'Sandilya'. During his period, a widow lady came in Kalighat with a desire to pass few days in the sacred place. Bhubaneswar fell in love with her young daughter, Jogamaya. In course of time, Jogamaya gave birth to a female child, Uma. Jogamaya survived very little after the delivery and so Bhubaneswar had to face a lot of trouble to rear up Uma. However, when the daughter became grown up, once Bhubaneswar was instructed through an oracle to arrange her marriage and put the charge of worship on that son- in-law. The goddess expressed that she had become quite tired of the un-restrained *Kapaliks* and so wanted worship from the family - man (*grihi-lok*).

In the mean time another strange event happened. A Brahmin named Bhawanidas Chakraborty in search of his absconded father arrived at Kalighat. He was selling conch-shell bangles (*sakha*) to meet the travelling expense. Near the Kalikunda-lagoon, a small married girl came to him and wanted to wear a pair of conch- bangle. She wore and went to have a bath in the lagoon telling the merchant to wait for the price. Waiting a long time when Bhawanidas did not find the girl to come up from the

---

1 Ref: Kalighat Itibritya by Upendranath Mukherjee, p.78 and 79.

water, he became very anxious and so rushed to the adjacent temple to inform the matter. Bhubaneswar Giri, the authority of the temple, hearing the incident became equally anxious but wandered seeing a new pair of conch-bangle in the hands of the idol. He began to enquire in details and finally no doubt was left that the same pair (which was bought by the girl) was placed in the hands of the idol. Bhawanidas also became embarrassed by the grace of the goddess as the conch-bangles were taken from him. Later he entangled himself with Kalighat for ever, marrying Uma and taking the responsibility of worship.

Bhawanidas Chakraborty (his Title[1] was Chatterjee) of the *gotra* named 'Kashyap' opened a new *shebait*-lineage at Kalighat. He was originally a Vaisnava and so in the habit of keeping an idol of *Basudev* with him. It has been known that he used to worship *Basudev* till his last day of life and since then the idol is placed within the temple-room. It should not be out of context to mention here that, before coming to Kalighat Bhawanidas had one wife and two sons in his home-land 'Khannayan', a village of the District Jassore (present day Bangladesh).

Getting old, Bhawanidas became incapable to manage everything by his own hand. He had to bring his first two sons Jadabendra and Rajendra from the native land; Uma's son Raghabendra was too young for the purpose. Although Rajendra died soon after, Jadabendra could share the duty and responsibility of father to a great extent. Bhawanidas survived long, all of his sons predeceased him. Jadabendra left one son named Ramkrisna and Raghabendra's sons were named as Ramgopal, Ramgovinda, Ramnarayan and Ramsaran. Ram Krisna was the elest among those five grandsons. So in later days of life, Bhawanidas handed over all the charges of worship and management to him. The property was divided equally among the grandsons.

Bhawanidas died before 1741, the period of Maratha invasion.[2] The present title 'Haldar' was endowed by the plunderers *(borgi)*. There is a story that Ramkrisna was not satisfied with one-fifth share as gifted by his grand-father. He aspired for half of the share because his father was

1. There is a difference in Surname and Title. Surname is the common name given to a class of people who are supposed to be coming from the same origin while Title is endowed one, by the King, Zamindar, landlord and others. As the Title expresses some sort of prestige and status, people commonly write this after their name.

2. The Maratha plunders invaded Bengal in the middle of 18th Century during the rule of Ali Vardi Khan.

the son of Bhawanidas's first wife and the other son of that wife (i.e. his uncle) died unmarried. In the judgement of Ram Krisna, both the wife should inherit equal share of husband's property. But he did not dare to protest against grand-father's decision. Meanwhile the *borgis* invaded; they restrained from plundering at Kalighat knowing the divine majesty of the place. Moreover, they wrote a *panja* (decree) by which the right of the particular Mouja[1] named 'Haola' was gifted to Ram Krisna along with the honorary title 'Haoladar'. Ramkrisna got this right solely in his own name because he presented his introduction to the *borgis* as the only *shebait* of the spot. After a few days, Ramkrisna intended to deceive the other four brothers with the help of that *panja*. The brothers somehow came to know his intention; they formulated a plan to destroy the *panja*. Ramgopal's son-in-law, Harachandra Banerjee was employed to execute the plan. He developed a friendly relation with Ramkrisna and on an opportunate moment wanted to see the original *panja*. Ramkrisna was glad enough to show his authority. But clever Harachandra snatched that and chewed at once, as planned. Losing the *panja* Ramkrisna felt helpless but by the advice of other relatives he was compelled to live with the brothers in amity.

At this time all the brothers developed a consensus that they would keep the responsibility of management only, otherwise through dispute the regular worship activity of the goddess might be hampered. As per their joint decision a chief Priest was brought. Name of that Priest was Harekrisna Bhattacharjee. Two brothers named Sambhunath and Dulal were appointed as 'Misra' to look after the image. Again as initiation (*diksha*) was essential[2] for a worship in Tantric proceedings, a preceptor (*Guru*) was also selected. Name of the present *Guru* is Devaprasad Bhattacharjee who lives in 'Nepal Bhattacharjee Lane' at Kalighat. The road is named after the first person selected as *Guru*. Haldars gifted a plot of land to each of these three grades of employee. Present day Priests and *Misras* still live in their old settlements, 'Jadu Bhattacharjee Lane' and 'Govinda Ghosal Lane' respectively. As per the learned informant Amiya Kumar Haldar, in selection of the employees, special stress was laid on the *gotro* in order to avoid any fault or defect in worship that might arise because of difference in *gotro*.

---

1. A 'mouja'is regarded as an administrative unit. It may consist of either a single village or a cluster of villages.

2. It is said that the preceptor (Guru) is the root(Mul) of initiation (Diksha); initiation is root of hymn (Mantra); Hymn is the root of attaining god (Devata); God is the root of supreme spiritual attainment (Siddhi).

Informant Pulin Haldar, one of the renowned elderly devotee of Haldar family advocated a different view. He said that Bhawanidas gifted 100 *bighas* of land to each grandson. Rest portion of the land he divided among the Priest, *Misras, Guru, Kamar, Dhuli* and the Bagdi[1] keeping a small part in the name of the goddess herself. According to Pulin Haldar, Bhawanidas was wise enough as he realized that his wife Uma was an illegitimate child, therefore her descendants should not possess the right to touch and worship the goddess directly. He felt the necessity of appointing specialized persons from outside in order to maintain the sanctity. Thus, the management responsibility was only vested with the grandsons.

However, soon after the conflict with *panja*, Ram Krisna died leaving his only minor son Padmanav (ref: Genealogy.2). Ramgopal, being eldest uncle of Padmanav honestly decided that, though Padmanav's father tried to cheat them but they must not deprive their nephew. Padmanav should definitely inherit the full share of his father. From that time onwards, the system of 'pala ' (ref: Chapter III) was introduced. Although Padmanav was a descendant of the eldest son but as his uncles were all alive and he himself was a minor, his position stood only fifth in order of seniority and he was known as 'Naw-Haldar'. His eldest uncle Ramgopal became 'Baro-Haldar' and likewise others got the recognition as 'Mejo', 'Sejo' etc. in the following way.

Ramgopal	....	Baro-Haldar or Baro-ghar.
Ramgovinda	....	Mejo-Haldar or Mejo-ghar.
Ramnarayan	....	Sejo-Haldar or Sejo-ghar.
Ramsaran	....	Chhoto-Haldar or Chhoto-ghar.
Padmanav	....	Naw-Haldar or Naw-ghar.

(vide Genealogy. 2)

Descendant of each brother are still popular with their old terminological markings. At the beginning of the system named 'pala', each brother got six days in a month for worship management. But thereafter through 'give and take' process, the structure of the *pala*-share changed a little (vide Chapter III, p. 36).

---

1. Bhubaneswar Giri had an adopted daughter named Tara , whose son demanded the property-share afterwards. Considerate Bhubaneswar planned a source of income for them. He declared that whatever income would accrue from the goat's and buffalo's head, hide etc., would be recieved by Tara's inheritors. Present day *Bagdis* are descendants from that line.

In course of time, the growing popularity of the temple raised the income from penny to pound. On the other hand, multiplication of the number of *shebaits* brought about complications over share distribution and income disbursement. Functionaries also extended with the increased number of pilgrims. To keep a balanced equilibrium i.e. to maintian a neat management and to avoid unwanted litigations, a Committee (ref : Chapter III) was set up in collaboration between Government and the *shebaits*. This Kali temple at Kalighat as an age-old religious centre still attracts people from far and near.

CHAPTER 3

Present day Kalighat

A. The temple organization

B. The market and the professional group around the temple

In the context of present day Kalighat, two aspects are of prime importance which have been dealt within this chapter. Firstly, the detailed account of the functionaries associated with the temple activities, including the financial resources. Secondly, the existing market and professional groups centering the temple. Each of these aspects has been discussed separately, under an appropriate heading.

Part A : THE TEMPLE ORGANIZATION

With the regular elaborate service to the goddess by the *shebaits* and numerous public worships, the Kalighat Kali temple has taken a shape of complicated organization. An effective administrative framework has developed to maintain discipline. For understanding this total operative framework, a systematic analysis has been attempted depending on the primary data collected from different informants.

1. Owner or Shebait Group :

Old Haldar family of Calcutta claims that they are the actual owner of the temple and assoicated property. The Government has now declared the property as *devottar*. The Haldars of Kalighat have identified themselves as 'Shebait' for their services towards the goddess. By dint of their inheritance right they also enjoy a fair share of temple's income.

As the family is growing in size, the number of share- holders are increasing. Even some portions of the share have gone in the hands of the relatives like *dauhitra* or *bhagnedauhitra*. The daughters inherited their respective shares by the current law of inheritance and previously also where there were no male successor. However, each inheritor of this family is designated by the term 'Shebait'. *Shebaits* are supposed to be involved in worship and related activities by turn and this system is locally known as 'pala'

The term *pala* means the 'turn' and this system of *pala* is very significant in understanding the functions of the temple. *Pala* is determined on the basis of day and it rotates among the *shebaits* after accurate estimation of the proportion of the shares. Since *pala* is an immense source of income, it is treated as property among the *shebaits*. Those who get *pala*-days more frequently are considered as more fortunate. According to the nature of share, many a *pala* reappear after a long time e.g. thrity-five years, fifty-eight years and so on. Such shares are very very nominal. Major share holders may avail more than one *pala* in a month.

Pala owner of the day is recognized as *paladar*. In the temple, *palas* are often handled by the persons other than *shebaits*. Due to this, all *shebaits* may be *paladar* but all *paladars* are not *shebaits*.

Mainly for three reasons *palas* are transferred to others who have no blood relation with the *shebaits*. But essentially these persons should be the Brahmins. Firstly, some of the *shebaits* go out of the station, so they have to sell out their shares to somebody else who may or may not be *shebaits*. Secondly, *shebaits* who do not have any children, may gift their share of property to some beloved persons who are not always *shebaits*. Thirdly, liquid money collected from *pala* can be disorganized easily. Many *shebaits* due to want of reliable manpower or to avoid trouble on organizing or for some sudden personal inconvenience sell their *pala* temporarily. At these times outsiders penetrate; they perform the duties of *shebaits* with the motive of profit being called as *paladars*. Here the only precondition is, the persons should essentially be the Brahmins.

In fact there are some people who have been professional in *pala* manipulation. They buy *pala* from the original party at a low price and then deal personally to make large profit. Again, a *pala* can also be sold several times in a day from man to man in a low margin. Generally all such re-sales occur within the group. Professional persons of this type are plenty in number and most of them belong to *dauhitra* or *bhagne-dauhitra* group, whose original shares are too little. Each professional *paladar* possesses a set of utensils for regular use. Saila Mukherjee, Ram Banerjee etc. belong to this group.

Only the deep devout *shebaits* or those *shebaits* who have enough man-power to supervise, dare to deal the *pala* by themselves. Such self-controlled *pala* is called *Khaser pala.* In all *palas,* whether those are manipulated by the professionals or the *shebaits* themselves, appointment of some persons are necessary in different spots to collect the loose coins. Such appointed persons are known as *rojer lok.* Seven to eight *rojer loks* are required in a shift and two shifts are found in a day. For a person working in two shifts is really difficult, so persons differ in two shifts. Remuneration is negotiated and varies between Rs. 3/- to Rs. 5/-. These persons form another professional group. Shyama (Oriya), Ganesh (Oriya), Dilip (Brahmin) and others belong to this group. *Paladar* is free to pick up his required man-power either from this group or from outside.

Generally persons are appointed in the following spots :

Two persons are posted on two sides of the Kali image, locally called *ba-hate* and *dan-hate.*

On busy days, four persons are required-two persons on each side.

One person is placed near the *padopadma.*

Two persons are posted on two sides of the *tamrokundo.*

One person stands by the altar named *Tahobil* to supervise the sale of the heads (sacrificed sheep and goats) and to collect taxes against each immolation.

One person is employed at *Nakuleswar-tala.*

One person is posted at *Sosthi-tala / Monosha-tala.*

One person stands at the eastern door of the temple to keep an eye on all collected money within the temple-room. In the overcrowded days two persons are needed for this purpose. One person is needed to watch on the total affair, whether all collections are smoothly going on or not.

Besides, *paladar* may appoint more persons as per his liking. Usually *paladars* sell *Sosthi-tala / Monosha-tala, Nakuleswar-tala* and *Tahobil,* separately. Oriya Priests of *Nakuleswar-tala* buy *Nakuleswar-tala* along with *Sosthi-tala. Tahobil* is bought regularly by a person named Saila Mukherjee who belongs to the *bhagne dauhitra* group.

A status oriented conception prevails among the orthodox *shebaits.* That is,

(a) The male heirs of the original Haldar family are superior to others.

(b) In that order, next comes the *dauhitra* or *bhagne-dauhitra* group.

(c) Male members of the Haldar family who have married girls other than Brahmin, they themselves with their successors are considered inferior to the above categories.

(d) The most degraded group are those who can not trace any blood relation with the *shebaits* i.e. who have acquired property of the Haldar family through purchase or gift. Persons belonging to the last two categories have no right to serve the deity. If they wish to serve, that should be done by specialized Brahmins.

Since the days of the grandsons of Bhawanidas Chakraborty the system of *pala* came into existence. (vide Chapter II, p. 29-31). In a month, within thirty days, each grandson got six days' responsibility. Following that order, *pala*-year completes in three hundred and sixty days. For the same reason same *pala* does not come back on the same date in next calendar year. No breakage in the *pala*-rule has appeared so far; constant multiplication of the share-holders are minutely counted tracing the original five streams of the grandsons. This systematic calculation of *pala* inheritance in relation with each and every day is a very tough task. At present Amiya Kumar Haldar, a successor of 'Baro-Haldar' stream as the most efficient and competent person performs this crucial duty by the request of all *shebaits*. In each year *pala*-calendar is published in the form of a book-let in the month *Chaitra* (Mar-April). It announces the sequence of *pala* with the name of *paladars* for the whole year i.e. from the first day of month *Baisakh* (15 th April) upto the last day of *Chaitra* (14th April).

Amiya Kumar Haldar is bearing this critical responsibility of calculation for about twenty years. He follows his pioneers Prasanta Mukherjee (outsider person, not a *shebait*) and Narayan Chandra Mukherjee (a *dauhitra*). Narayan Chandra Mukherjee though was not highly educated, still he calculated a *pala-ponji* of twenty years (from Bengali year 1337 to 1357). Prasanta Mukherjee's[1] *pala-ponji* was for eighteen years (from Bengali year 1333 to 1351). Mr. Mukherjee's calculation was scientific as well as harmonious to Hindu scriptures, so it is considered as more perfect. He was inspired by many *shebaits* of that time like Surendranath Mukherjee and Aghornath Haldar of Bhawanipore, Abinash Haldar, Akhoy Kumar Haldar and Nanda Lal Haldar of Kalighat. He was able to manage a *pala*-list of few years from the records of late Kaliprasanna Banerjee of Rajabagan, Bhawanipore which he had preserved for himself.

---

1. A record book of *pala*-inheritors for some years together. This was very popular among the shebaits of Kalighat Kali temple.

Kashipati Haldar of Kalighat also helped Prasanta Mukherjee by letting him to compare the calculation with the part calculation of his deceased father Bireswar Haldar. Moreover, Radha Ballav Jyotistirtha, the lecturer of Astronomy in Sanskrit College and Bibhuti Bhusan Dutta, the lecturer of Calcutta University jointly helped him in achieving accuracy in month determination. So present day calculator Amiya Kumar Haldar follows his procedure mostly. As according to Hindu scripture the youngest brother gets the priority after the eldest, so in the *pala-cycle* Haldar has placed the youngest just after the eldest and rest one after another in the order of their seniority.

It has been evident that the number of *palas* in the part of 'Baro-Haldar', Ramgopal are more than the others and nature of all *palas* are not same. This is because of the fact that, at the time of distribution, the fourth grand-son ('Sejo- Haldar', Ramnarayan) gifted a *pala*-day (from his own six days) to elder brother ('Baro-Haldar',) for showing honour. The youngest grandson Ramsaran similarly presented one day but with a condition that the elder brother would receive all the *pacca* items (*i.e.* gold with other precious materials, cloths and cash money) of the *pala*- day and only the *Kacha* items (i.e. rice, sweets, fruits etc perishable items) would remain for his own. He also promised that the total expense of worship and *bhog* of the respective day would be borne by him. After such settlements, the initial *pala*-division was altered and stood as follows.

'Baro-Haldar' got 7 days per month i.e. 84 days per year.

'Chhoto-Haldar' got 6 days per month i.e. 72 days per year.

' Mejo-Haldar' got 6 days per month i.e. 72 days per year.

'Sejo-Haldar' got 5 days per month i.e. 60 days per year.

'Naw -Haldar' got 6 days per month i.e. 72 days per year.

Shebaits designate the varied nature of *pala* as described below.

(a) Nijaswa or Gharer pala

These are the primarily fixed shares for each of the five grandsons. Those who have gifted from their part, the number of their *gharer pala* has correspondingly reduced.

(b) Saja pala

These are not primarily fixed but gifted shares. Only 'Baro-Haldar' and 'Chhoto-Haldar' possess this sort of *pala*. Among the 84 days of 'Baro-Haldar', 12 days (one day in each month) and among 72 days of 'Chhoto-Haldar', 8 days are spotted as *saja pala*. The *saja palas* of 'Baro-Haldar' as the gift from 'sejo-Haldar' has been known but how the 8 *saja-palas* of 'Chhoto- Haldar' came into existence have no record. Possibly 'Baro-Haldar' regifted those *palas*. However, each share holder of this stream avails this *saja-pala* separately by turn.

(c) Hure-saja pala

Hure-saja pala is that share where the *kacha* and *pacca* items are divided among the 'Chhoto-Haldar' and 'Baro-Haldar' respectively. Each share-holder of this two streams avail it by turn. In each *pala*-year 4 days are found for *hure-saja pala*; after each 90 days one *hure-saja pala* is observed.

Income of the *pala* can be estimated roughly on the basis of days and occasions. In ordinary days (Mondays, Wednesdays and Fridays) the *pala*-price is usually about Rs. 1500/-. On Saturdays, Tuesdays and Sundays this price increase upto Rs. 2500/- or Rs. 3000/- because of more visitors. On special occasions like Bengali New Year's day, *Durga-puja* , *Kali-puja* etc price become Rs. 5000/- or Rs. 6000/-, if not more. On the specified dates for *Upanayan*, *Broto* etc the *pala*-price obvioulsy increase. In each month a meeting is conducted by the sub-Committee, where the *palas*' income are calculated date-wise in advance. *Paladar* is liable to deposit half of the income in the Committee. In case of strikes or natural calamities like flood, storm etc, the income gets unusually down; those situations are considered sympathetically by minimizing the amount of deposit. *Paladar* have to apply to the Committee immediately and highest consideration is to get half reduction.

Committee at the formative phase decided to pay *paladars* Rs. 80/- against the expense of *bhog-rag*. Now to keep parity with the inflation, that amount has been increased to Rs. 95/-. But according to Amiya Kumar Haldar this is still insufficient to *paladar's* actual cost, which is about Rs.300/-.

However, a *paladar* pays half of the estimated price of the *pala* (advance payment is made in the morning of the particular day) and receives Rs. 95/-. Committee has got a quota of rice, flour and sugar in the name of goddess Kali which are brought from the local ration shop, once in a week. *Paladar* procures his daily quota from the committee storage (the room adjacent to the Kitchen of Radha-Krisna temple, vide Map, 3) by paying the exact price. Twenty-eight (28) kg. rice is given on each day - twenty (20) kg. for feeding the beggars (vide Chapter IV, p. 75) and eight (8) kg. to prepare the *bhog* of the goddess Kali. Expenses of *naibidya*, milk and sweet of *sitol* (approximately of Rs 5/-) are borne by the Committee. The *payesh-bhog* of Nakuleswar and the beggars' meal (*Khichuri* and a sort of *chachchori*) are cooked in the Kitchen of goddess Kali (*bhog-ghar*) under the supervision of paladar, but separate utensils are used.

Where a *pala* is going to be sold permanently, there emphasis is put on it's rotation pattern i.e. how long it takes to reappear. Price is always settled through mutual bargaining. For instance, Sabitri Devi bought two *palas* permanently (about four years back) from one of her aunt (father's sister). Rs 28,000/- was claimed for those two *palas* together but as a close relative ultimately she received those in Rs 26000/-. Both the *palas* rotate once in every year.

Among the five streams of the main Haldar-lineage, 'Baro-Haldar's line gets more importance - they are superior in respect; their share-proportion is the greatest. Adjacent areas of the temple exhibit the houses of 'Baro-Haldar' heirs. In all important activities, aged persons of this stream come forward. Manik Lal Haldar is found to be present in the temple most of the time and it is known from the informants that as an eldest person (head) his presence is required in all special occasions - he acts as representative of the total Haldar family. Again in the performance of *Snan Jatra* (vide Chapter V,) only the successors of the Baro-Haldar' possess the right to perform *ango- snan*.

2. The Committee :

From the scheme framed by Supreme Court, New-Delhi, it has been understood that with the shares of the property (*pala*), dispute arose among the members of the family. Gradually that dispute arrived at the door of the Court. First case was filed up in 1937 in Trial Court. The judgement was declared in January 1949 by R.C. Mitter and Roxburg. Declaration was that, as the religious endowment of the goddess Kali was a public one, so either all *shebaits* should agree to frame a proper scheme for management in the interest of the deity, otherwise a scheme should be put through in a properly framed suit under the civil procedure because from the public point of view the matter seemed to be very urgent.

Following that in December 1949, five of the *shebaits* had filed a suit in the Court of District Judge at Alipore for framing a scheme for management. They also produced a draft scheme which was prepared in consultation with many a persons including lawyers too.

Time to time petitions with different suggestions about the scheme were filed by some defendants. There were also allegations and counter allegations regarding the properties of the deity. At the final hearing,

District Judge discussed various suggestions made by different parties and framed a scheme as a part of decree.

Against that judgement and decree of Lower Court (by District Judge J.C. Madjumdar of Zillah 24-Parganas at Alipore) three appeals were made on 3rd March, 1955. Those appeals were disposed from HIgh Court of Calcutta (R.P. Mukherjee and P.K.Sarkar were the two Judges) and a new scheme was settled - the decree passed at this time.

The managing Committee as proposed by the Lower Court should be consisted of *shebaits* only. It was not supported finally in the ground that in case of a public *devottar* property the management must not be confined to the existing *shebaits* only and that ought to include the representatives from the public to maintain the interest of the public of the different sections.

With that issue, ultimately two bodies were formed.

(a) 'Kalighat Temple Committee' (K.T.C.) was made for proper management. It was proposed to be represented by the majority of members from the *shebaits.*

(b) Council of 'shebaits' was made for proper control of endowment. It was proposed to be composed of only the *shebaits* who are intimately connected with the worship of the deities. Though functions and powers of the Council would be limited but for the final decision,'Kalighat Temple Committee' would have to depend on it.

It was also settled that a Trustee would act without any remuneration. Moreover, the entire income of the *devottar* estate (including all offerings and gifts to the deities) would belong to the deity solely. Only some portions of it would be set apart in order to meet worship expense and payments to the *shebaits* for ministering the deity.

Lastly, there was the provision that a person interested in amendment of the given scheme or in case of any doubt or disputes in decision made by the Committee of management could come up before the Judge.

Many appeals were submitted thereafter to the Supreme Court for modification and alteration of various clauses. Those were rejected for several times and lastly some clauses were amended. As a result, the structure of K.T.C. was completely changed. New K.T.C. scheme came into operation from Ist March, 1962 and the other amended rules of the scheme came into effect from 7th April, 1962. Present regulations are maintained after the last amendment though the internal disputes stand still. Yearly election of the 'Council of Shebaits' has remained postponed for an uncertain time.

All the *shebaits* and *paladars* for the time being constitute the Council. But minor or person of unsound mind should be represented by their guardians (natural or certified). Duties of the Council are as follows:

1. (a) This Council elects the representatives to the K.T.C. for the purpose of management.
   (b) Prepares draft budget estimates of the endowment for the consideration and sanction by the K.T.C.
   (c) Formulates the proposals to K.T.C. for the improvement of *seva-puja*, organizational framework of the temple and also for the utilization of income from *devottar* estate.
   (d) Elects an Executive Committee - a Chairman, a Vice- Chairman, a Secretary and others as determined at the General Meeting or under rules framed by the Council.
   (e) At the beginning of each Bengali year, the Council prepares a frame about the arrangement and sequence of *palas* for the next year and an up-to-date register of the total *shebaits*.

In framing the rule of procedure which governs the 'Council of Shebaits', it must not be inconsistent with the provisions in the scheme of the directions by the Court.

2. A General Meeting of the 'Council of Shebaits' is held at least twice a year in the Bengali month *Jaistha* (May-June) and *Falgun* (Feb-Mar).The Council may also be called to meet on other occasions if settled by the Executive Committee or on requisition. A month's notice is necessary specifying the day and hour of the meeting. Meeting of the month *Jaistha* is called 'Annual General Meeting' and all other meetings are termed as 'General Meeting'.

3. In the meeting held in *Falgun*, the Executive Committee is supposed to place proposals of the draft budget estimates for the ensuing year. Such proposals must be forwarded to the Secretary, K.T.C. not later than the end of *Falgun*.

4. Each *shebait* possesses one vote right irrespective of the number of *pala* which he holds. Guardians of minors have the right of casting one vote on that minor's behalf. One may exercise such a vote even being a *paladar*.

5. Any fifteen *shebaits* for some reason may request the Secretary (in writing) to call a meeting. All *shebaits* should get the notices ten days before, with the specification of particular nature of business. If no meeting is called by the Secretary within twenty-one days after receiving the requisition, the requisitionists may themselves call the

meeting giving seven days' notice to each of the *shebait* stating the place, date, hour and nature of the business. Such meetings will be held in the *Natmondir* or within the precincts of the temple area.

6. Twenty-five persons shall form a quorum for a meeting of the Council. If within half an hour of that appointed time a quorum if not present in the meeting, if called upon at the requisition of *shebaits*, shall be dissolved and in any other case it shall be adjourned to the same day in next week (same time and place). If at the adjourned meeting quorum is not present within half an hour, the members themselves shall be a quorum.

7. If neither the Chairman nor the Vice-Chairman is present at the meeting, then the 'Council of Shebaits' will have to choose one amongst them to be the Chairman for the meeting.

8. An Executive Committee will be elected at the Annual General Meeting of the 'Council of Shebaits'. Committee will consist of office bearers and fifteen other members of whom ten members shall be elected from the five streams of the *shebaits*, two from each branch. Remaining five will be elected by the Council (any one from any stream) but all of them should be at least matriculate or must have passed School-final or Sanskrit Title Examination, recognized by the State.

9. Members of Executive Committee and office bearers will hold office until the new members are elected at the next General Meeting.

10. Casual vacancies occurring between two Annual General Meetings shall be filled up by the Executive Committee till the next Annual Meeting.

11. All matters coming up before the Executive Committee or Council shall be decided by a majority of votes. In case of equality of votes, the Chairman shall have the right for casting a second vote. Voting may be done either by lifting hands or by ballots.

Name of the present Secretary of the 'Council of Shebaits' is Pradyut Kumar Haldar who resides in Kali Lane and the name of the present Chairman is Prasad Das Banerjee, who resides in Mahim Haldar Street.

An account of 'Kalighat Temple Committee' (K.T.C.) as obtained from the functioning scheme.

This Committee has been formed for management by the eleven members in two groups.

Group A :

Five persons to be elected by the 'Council of Shebaits' from amongst themselves, one from each stream of the five stream of *shebaits*. All elected members should be at least Matriculate or must have passed School-final or Sanskrit Title Examination, recognized by the state. This election shall be held by ballot.

Group B:

Six members other than the *shebaits* to be appointed, being nominated by each of the following :

1. The District Judge, 24-Paraganas, who will be the Chairman of the Managing Committee and have a casting vote right in addition to his original one. Name of the present person is not known as always change.
2. The Executive body of the Bharat Chamber of Commerce, Calcutta. Present person : R.R. Vianiwal
3. The Vice-Chancellor, Calcutta University. Present person : P.K.Mukherjee.
4. The Executive body of the 'Bharat Sevasram Sangha' of Rash Behari Avenue, Calcutta. Present person : Santosh Ganguli.
5. The Calcutta Corporation. Present person : Rathin Talukar.
6. One jointly nominated by the President of 'Bangiya Siksha Parisad; and Principal of 'Government Sanskrit College', Calcutta. Present person : Nityananda Smrititirtha.

If any of them fails to nominate a person within one month of being called upon by the Secretary, District Judge of 24-Parganas takes this duty.

Rules and Regulations :

1. K.T.C. shall continue to function despite of any casual vacancy due to death, retirement etc. of it's members. Any vacancy shall be filled up in accordance with the provision of the scheme (election or nomination as the case may be).
2. K.T.C. shall hold the charge of management and responsibility of all properties belonging to the endowment. A duplicate record of all properties as permanent record is kept to the District Judge of 24-Parganas. Time to time, the additions, alterations and modifications are informed.

3. The Committee functions for four years at a time. At the end of second year, three of the Committee members will retire. Such names are decided by lottery. But the retiring members will continue to function until the vacancies are filled up.

4. Retitrng persons will be eligible for re-election or re- nomination as the case may be. But in case of retirement by death, resignation, default etc, the places shall be filled up from the respective categories from which originally the members come.

5. Immediately after determination of retiring members, K.T.C. shall intimate the respective bodies or persons to send new nominees. If the vacancies are not filled within two months from the date of intimation by the Secretary, some of them as were to have retired shall be deemed to have been re- elected or re-nominated for a fresh term.

6. At the end of fourth year, among the old eight members (i.e. other than those who have become members at the end of second year), four will retire in the same manners and the vacancies will be similarly filled up. The retiring members will continue to function until the vacancies are filled up.

7. At the end of the sixth year, all other remaining old members (four) will retire.

8. Any member may resign his membership (in writing, addressing to the Secretary, K.T.C.) at any time and that resignation will be effective after the acceptance by the Committee.

9. Casual vacancies occurring by death, resignation etc. in K.T.C. will be filled within two months from the date of intimation by the appointing authority and such persons shall be subject to retirement on the ground that he had become member from the date of such appointment.

If the appointing authority does not forward the name of new member within the scheduled time, remaining members of K.T.C. will proceed to fill up the vacancies and retirement rule will be the same.

10. No act done by K.T.C. shall be invalid by reason merely of any vacancy in the Committee of any irregularity or illegality in the appointment or election of any member.

11. No person can be nominated or elected as a member of K.T.C. before attaining thirty-five years. Also a man of unsound mind, a member of salaried staff under K.T.C. or the 'Council of Shebaits', a man who has been convicted by any Criminal Court cannot be elected or any disabilities during the term of his office, shall cease to be a member of the Committee.

12. All matters coming up before a meeting of the Committee of Management shall be decided by majority of votes. In case of equality of votes, Chairman shall have the power of second or a casting vote. Voting will be by erecting hands unless the Committee decides by a majority on any particular occasion that the voting will be by ballot. The Chairman's decision as to the result of voting will be final. All other rules of procedure shall be drawn up by the Committee.

13. No member of K.T.C. shall as a member, be present at the meeting when any matter in which he is either directly or indirectly concerned or interested is being considered or voted upon it.

Five members - at least two from each group (A and B) will form the quorum for a meeting of the K.T.C.

14. K.T.C. shall meet at least once a month. Any five members by notice (in writing, duly signed) may produce requisition for a meeting to discuss about any particular matter. This requisition shall be placed before the President (in his absence before Vice- President) to direct the meeting. Notice of the meeting shall be issued by the Secretary, within fortnight of the receipt of the notice.

15. Ordinarily three clear days' notice will be given for a meeting of Committee. In emergency, President (or Vice-President) may convene a meeting by giving a shorter notice.

16. Secretary should record all the resolutions passed at the meeting and a short note of the proceedings of each meeting in a record-book should be maintained. In his absence, Assistant Secretary will do the needful. If both are absent, the Chairman of a meeting shall take necessary steps. Copies of the Minutes of proceedings of a meeting shall be sent to all the members within a fortnight of the date of the meeting and shall be laid before the next meeting for confirmation.

17. K.T.C. shall have the following office staff :

    (a) President, who is the member nominated by the District Judge, 24 - Paraganas,

    (b) A Vice - President,

    (c) A Treasurer,

    (d) A Secretary,

    (e) An Assistant Secretary.

The office bearers nominated in group (B) shall be elected at the first meeting of the Committee at the end of every three years.

Duty and responsibility of the President is to see whether the rules in the scheme are duly followed or not. In case of any deviation or non-observance, attention of the 'Council of Shebaits" and K.T.C. are drawn. At every meeting whenever any question of order arises his decision shall be final and binding.

The Treasurer shall be responsible for proper maintenance of accounts, collections and disbursements. He shall also keep an account of the assets and liabilities of the *devottar* estate and send at the end of each year a copy to the 'Council of Shebaits' for their records. All the books of accounts shall be kept at the *devottar* office within the precincts of the temple. Accounts shall be audited annually or at shorter intervals by an incorporated Accountant and Auditor appointed by the K.T.C. The audited accounts with the report shall be placed before the Committee and that shall be open to inspection by any member of K.T.C. on giving due notice of his intention to do so in accordance with rules made by the Committee. The Treasurer will also be responsible for the proper custody of the Title deeds and important documents of the *devottar* estate.

18. K.T.C. have the following powers :

(a) To appoint and dismiss the personnel of the temple establishment including Priest, *Misras, Kamar, Mali, Chowkidars,* Accountants, Clerks etc. and also to determine their salaries, allowances and conditions of service etc. and at the same time to make rules and regulations regarding same.

(b) To take steps for maintenance of proper discipline inside the temples and compound and also day to day management of different temples, management of festive occasions and daily supervision of all the collection of offerings of all kind and to make rule concerning the same.

(c) To make rules concerning *seva-puja* in due conformity with the usage and the established practice of the endowment.

(d) To make rules for the admisssion of pilgrims and visitors into the temple-room and *Jor bangla.*

(e) To sanction the budget estimates of the endowment in *Chaitra* (March-April) every year to come into effect from the year beginning i.e. from the month *Baisakh* (April-May). Proposal is made by 'Council of Shebaits' and sanctioned by K.T.C. as per rule framed for the purpose.

(f) To keep money of the *devottar* estate in 'State Bank of India' to be operated on the joint signature of the Secretary and the Treasurer or during their absence on the joint signature of the President or the Vice- President and the Treasurer or the Secretary.

(g) To invest the money of the temple in securities recognized by Trust-Act and in immovable properties.

(i) To make arrangements for the proper custody of all other properties of the deity and to make investigations as to various disputed ornaments or properties and the amount of money lying in 'State Bank of India;, Bhawanipore Branch, Calcutta, in the account of 'Kalighat Kali Mandir Shebait Sabha' (It has been amended as 'Kalighat Kalimandir' as per order of the Court dated 12th July, 1957) or in the hand of any *shebait*. Power should be exerted to give suitable directions and take such action in this behalf as may be deemed desirable and necessary and also to take such steps for the recovery of movable and immovable properties belonging to the estate now in the possession of persons, Court or elsewhere.

(j) To convert or sell all unserviceable ornaments or articles offered or belonging to the deity and to invest the proceeds there of and or utilize the same for the purposes of endowment.

(k) To buy necessary articles for the worship of the deity.

(l) To keep the main temple and the temples of all associated deities in a proper state of repair and to add to and improve the same.

(m) To institute and defend the suits and all proceedings relating to the *devottar* estate.

(n) To make rules for holding meeting of the Committee and sub-Committees, for budget and audit, for the implementation and functioning of the schemes etc.

(o) To take all steps necessary to give effect to this scheme and to manage and control the affairs of endowment.

Provided that (b), (c) and (d) rules are to be framed by the K.T.C. only after the 'Council of Shebaits' have been given an opportunity to express their views.

19. No immovable property or Goverment securities, stock and shares belonging to the *devottv* estate are to be sold or immovable property leased out for a period exceeding five years, except with the express permission of the Court of the District Judge, at Alipore previously obtained.

20. All money standing to the credit of the *devottar* estate in any Court of Law, Civil or Revenue shall be withdrawn on the joint application of the Treasurer and the Secretary pursuant to a resolution passed by the K.T.C.

21. Suits on behalf of the *devottar* estate are to be filed by the Secretary of any member of the Committee as may be decided by the Committee or management.

Present members of the Committee have been enlisted below :

President	:	Dr. Sudhanshu Mohan Banerjee M.A.,L.L.B.,Ph.D.,I.A.S. 23, Kabir Road, Flat -3 Calcutta - 700 026
Vice-President	:	Vacant.
Treasurer	:	Amiya Madhab Haldar 47, Gurupada Haldar Road, Calcutta - 700 026
Secretary	:	Ajit Kumar Mukherjee 7, Kali Lane, Calcutta - 700 026
Assistant Secretary	:	Vacant (Actually Ajit Kumar Mukherjee was in this post. In absence of Secretary he holds that post)

These persons have been appointed by election in 1978. It will be valid for six years. There are a few office staffs. From March 1978, these posts have been created. Before that only one post of Typist cum Office-clerk existed. Emoluments to the present staffs are poor.

Internal Audit Clerk (part-time post)	:	Amar Mukherjee 21/B, Iswar Ganguli Street, Calcutta - 700 026
Typist cum Office-clerk (regular)	:	Sambhu Haldar 13/A, Kali Lane, Calcutta - 700 026.
Office Assistant (regular)	:	Prabir Kumar Mukherjee 7, Kali Lane, Calcutta - 700 026.
Head Assistant	:	Now suspended.

As per the rules and regulations, these persons would function with the respective designations for six years, upto the next election.

3. The Temple Personnel :

Besides the owner group (*shebaits*) and the Committee members, all other people associated with the temple can be broadly designated as 'Temple Personnel'. Designations are according to their nature of services.

GURU

All the Haldar family members have a common preceptor who is regarded as *Guru* or *Kula Guru.*[1] Though the performance of *Guru* in relation to the regular activities of the temple is limited but he possesses the highest rank in order of prestige. Name of the present *Guru* is Devaprasad Bhattacharjee vide also Chapter II.

Daughters-in-law of the Haldar family before receiving *diksha* from the *Kula-Guru* can not be accepted as a true family member.

BHATTACHARJEE MASAI

Chief Priests of the main temple hold the second high rank and they are locally known as *Bhattacharjee masai*. At present four such Priests work in the temple by turn. Names are : Prafulla Bhattacharjee, Santipada Bhattacharjee, Muktipada Bhattacharjee and Aloknath Bhattacharjee (vide Genealogy.3)

Chief Priests are traditionally related with the temple. The same lineage is serving since the days of Harekrisna Bhattacharjee, the first appointed Priest by Haldars (ref : Chapter II, p.30). With the increase of persons in descending generations, hours of service have been divided. Even their *dauhitras* had been introduced. Aloknath Bhattacharjee is a *dauhitra* successor, whose *gotro* is 'Bharadwaj' instead of 'Kashyap'. But recently the number of Priests are retreating as most of the persons of present generation have been disinterested in this occupation. For higher income they are drifting towards different other jobs.

In the temple only three performances (*nitya-puja*, offering of *bhog* and *sondhyaroti*) require original Sanskritic hymn. So those performances can not be done without Chief Priest. Duty of the Priests rotate day-wise and naturally one has to come to the temple thrice a day. They decide about the turns amongst themselves and formally inform to the Committee

---

1. 'Kula' means lineage, Therefore 'Kula-Guru' means the preceptor of corresponding generations.

office. Committee never pays them any remuneration. Only on the day of *Ramnavomi*, each of them gets a *dhuti-chador* from the Committee as dress.

Chief Priest on duty receives in the morning five *poas* of unboiled rice, five types of fruit, *chhola* (pea), sweets and betel-rolls i.e. all those are offered in *naibidya*. At noon he gets one full dish *bhog* items (i.e. lunch for ten persons approximately) with entire quantity of curd, sweets and betel- rolls that are offered in the *bhog* during the noon. In the evening similarly one *poa* milk, *luchi*, *sandesh* offered in *sitol* are under his schedule. One has to maintain fasting on the date of his duty; offering of *bhog* without fasting is a great sin.

In case of *asauch*, a Priest can send his known person or Priest of his own house to officiate on his behalf. Besides the worship in the temple, they also serve in the Haldar houses and outside non-related houses for Siva worship, *Chondi-path*, *Santi-sasten* (ref : Chapter VI, p.116) and even for *'Dasakarma* and *Sraddha'* performances (ref : Chapter VI,).

A special rule exists for a few special occasions of the temple. On *Monosha-puja*, *Durga-puja* and *Sitola-puja*, special privileges are offered to them, which they have to share mutually. This privilege is nothing but getting the meat from the sarificed goat. A Priest who enjoy this privilege in *Durga-puja*, will be subjected to enjoy the same in other two occasions of that year but not in later years until all his fellows enjoy the chance.

MISRA OR MISRA BRAHMAN

In order of prestige, the third rank in the temple is ascribed to the *Misra* or *Misra-brahman* who are also called as *misri masai*. These Brahmins act as dresser cum decorator and are always present in the temple-room (while open) to look-after the image.

At present *Misras* are eight in number. Two persons work at a time - both helps each other. Three shifts are found in a day :

(a) From opening to 10 a.m.

(b) From 10 a.m. to 4 p.m.

(c) From 4 p.m. to closing.

Persons who work in the last shift of the day get a holiday on the next day. Persons working in the second shift should abstain from food as they have to carry the *bhog* from kitchen to the temple-room. Since the same persons do not work daily in same shift, so no trouble is created in this *respect*.

All of these eight *Misras* are not traditionally associated with the temple. Original Misra successors reside at 'Govinda Ghosal Lane', Bhawanipore as they were historically settled in that area (vide Chapter II, p.30). They bear the surname 'Chatterjee'. Due to the decrease of their number (present generation is unwilling to keep tie with this old profession), four new *Misras* have been recruited who live in 'Iswar Ganguli Lane'. Their surnames are 'Banerjee', 'Mukherjee' etc. Colloquially all Brahmins of this rank are called by the title 'Misra'. Hiren Misra (Chatterjee), Jiban Misra (Banerjee), Nabakumar Misra (Chatterjee) etc. are a few names.

The duty of the *Misras* as aforesaid is always inside the temple-room to deliver *charonamrito, prcsadiful* and *tappa* to the public, to carry *bhog* from kitchen to the temple-room over the bridge before the *bhog* offering performance, to beat the *Kanshor* at the time of *sondhyaroti.*

They receive no remuneration from the Committee. During duty-hours the gifted money from the public is their income. They also serve in *shebait* houses on different occasions by arranging everything before the arrival of the Chief Priest. They may serve in other non-*shebait* houses as Priest if they so desire. On *Ramnavomi, dhutis* are gifted from the Committee, one for each. They usually wear only *dhuti* because the temple-room is very hot.

A neat regulation in enjoying the privilege is found in cases of these Brahmins too. But here the sacrificial meat is divided between two Misras in each turn. Others wait for their joint turn in later years.

SATHI-BRAHMAN

A large number of Brahmins are found to loit here and there in Kalighat, who help the public in worship. They are locally known as *Sathi-brahman* or *dala-dhara-brahman* or *panda.* Different language speaking persons belong to this category e.g. Bengali speaking, Oriya speaking, Nepali speaking, Hindi speaking etc.

Possibly 700 to 800 such Brahmins are present in Kalighat but there is no correct record. All of them are local inhabitants but having no relation with Haldars. They act either for full-time or part-time.

In past Committee used to keep records of these Brahmins. There was system of renewing enrolled names against the payment of two rupees per month. But about ten years ago a Committee member named Thakurlal Gangopadhaya (*(bhagne-dauhitra)*) raised question regarding the efficiency of the *sathi-brahmins*. He proposed that all such Brahmins should sit for an examination to evaluate their ability. Gangopadhaya doubted that many of those Brahmins had not the minimum knowledge in this line. Santipada Bhattacharjee (Chief Priest) was called as an renowned expert to examine them. Announcement of the proposal paved the way of a rebellion among the *Sathi-brahmans;* they understood that there is every possibility to failure and a failure would block their source of earning for ever. Therefore, they stopped the monthly name-renewal but began to pursue in the profession as usual. As a result, on one hand earning of the temple had stopped and on the other hand many other unfamiliar Brahmins got their place in this occupation. Now it is not at all unlikely if some persons are found in the group of *Sathi-brahmans* who are not even Brahmins by Caste.

At Present *Sathi-brahmans* bear no identification. Formerly they used to submit three copies of passport size photograph- one for the Committee, one for the local police station and other for his own in the identity card. In that system no outsiders could dare to commit any nuisance in disguise of *Sathi-brahman.*

Income of the *Sathi-brahmans* is highly flexible and lucrative. More gathering in the temple indicates more income for them. They are fully independent and wear no uniform. Joydev Mukherjee, Binod Roy etc. are known *Sathi-brahman.*

CHHAR-BRAHMAN

A group of Brahmin in the name of *Chhar-brahman* are found in the temple. They are traditionary servicing Brahmins of the *shebaits*, in short termed as *chhar-babu*. They live and eat in the *shebait* houses in lieu of the work as order carrier. General pattern of their duties have been cited below.

(a) They attend all sorts of worship oriented errands in the respective *shebait* house.

(b) On pala dates they have to carry *bhog* from temple to the house (*Chowkidars* do not serve this; they are not allowed to handle cooked *bhog*) and thereafter distribute that *bhog* to different known houses.

(c) They have to take the *jajmans* of the *shebaits* inside the temple worship.

(d) They accompany the female *shebaits* of the family, when they go to the temple for any reason.

Eventually in all sorts of problems, they are sheltered by the respective *shebait* family. Position of these Brahmins is considered more respectable than the ordinary *Sathi-brahmans*.

The system of Brahmin recruitment by *shebaits* for personal purposes has lost its significance at present. Any Brahmin who look-after a shop run by a *shebait* is now loosely called as *chhar-brahman*. These persons are nothing but servants. Although they may live or eat in the respective *shebait* family, but the relationship between the two differ a lot from old days. Not only that, previously these Brahmins had to wear a brass disc in their arms as an identification mark of the rank which has now been totally extinct custom. For example, Pataki Chatterjee and Chitta Chakraborty are the two real *Chhar-brahmans* of the house of Chandi Haldar (24, Kali Lane) who are serving the particular family in traditional way but do not wear the identity symbol.

DASAKARME PARODORSHI BRAHMAN

Some genuine specialized Brahmins are found who introduce themselves as *Dasa-Karme parodorshi brahman*. They are quite at home in reciting sacred hymns and capable in all sorts of sacred performance. They prefer to act as Priest in outside houses because in Kalighat their abilities are not appreciated with proper remuneration. Still, they are fond of gathering in Kalighat to encash their idle times.

These Brahmins are independent. They sit on *Natmondir* or remain associated with the shops therewith. Authority does not object against their activity into the temple. They are better respected than the *Sathi-brahmans*. Some persons of this category are as follows : Kalidas Chakrabory who is found often on *Natmondir* in the mornings, Panchu Gopal Mukherjee in the shop of Devi Haldar, Nanda Lal Ghosal in the shop adjacent to the joint Siva temples.

DALAL

Some brokers are found around the temple who are locally known as *Dalal*. These persons are not Brahmin and cannot act as *Sathi-brahman*. They contact the parties from the way towards the temple and hand over those parties to *Sathi-brahmans* or shops. A per head commission is earned for the supply of the customers. Amount of commission depends on the quantity of sweets (*pera*) purchased by the party. More sweet purchase means more commission. Money which is spent on sweets follow some definite pattern like *soa panch anna* (thirty-five paisa), *solo anna* (one rupee), two rupees, five rupees etc. it may even go to hundred rupees or so.

Dalals are also independent and there is no record of their number. They run with the public to win over a customer. For example, Phani Lal Ghosh is found regularly along the 'Kali Temple Road'.

BHARI

There is an Oriya male Brahmin in the temple who supplies water from the tube-well (located at the south-east corner of the campus) to the temple-room and fills the reservoir of the kitchen. This person is locally called a Bhari. Usually he completes his duty before 10 a.m. If more water is required thereafter, he is called again.

The post of *Bhari* is non-traditional and he lives outside independently. Other source of his income is to supply water in different nearby shops and *Vienghar*. For the temple, he receives Rs. 2/- per day from the *paladar*.

THAKUR

There are some Brahmin who regularly cook in the kitchen of the goddess Kali. Not only they cook the prinicipal *bhog* for Kali but also prepare the *payesh-bhog* for Nakuleswar and lunch items for the beggars. These persons are known as *Thakur*.

None of the *Thakurs* works here traditionally. But few of them are working for generations together. Only one person is required for cooking. Same person does not get chance on consecutive days. One *Thakur* is employed for each day. The recruitment is done by the *paladar* on daily basis, item-wise. *paladar* may engage the cook of his own house. The only precaution is that the person must be a male Hindu Brahmin. Nilratan Chatterjee, Madhusudan Mukherjee, Sambhu Chatterjee (new) are cooking more or less regularly in the temple at present.

There is no hard and fast rule regarding the duty hours. A *Thakur* works usually from 9 a.m. to 5 p.m. They independently reside outside and no uniform is used by them. Remuneration varies from Rs. 20/- to Rs.30/- per day but with one full dish *bhog* (approximately ten persons' meal). Like the *Bhattacharjee masai* and *Misri masai* a cook have to undergo fasting till the *bhog* is offered.

Once a year (on the day of *Ramnavomi*) each of the cook get a *dhuti* from the Committee.

JOGARE

The assistant of the cook is usually appointed by the cook himself and is called *Jogare* in the local terms. Sometimes *paladar* appoints him separately paying less to *Thakur*. The matter is mutually settled between *Thakur* and *paladar*.

Jogare must be a male Brahmin. The recognized cooks may also act as *Jogare*. The system of assistant (*Jogare*) recruitment has been popular only recently. Assistants enjoy no privilege from the Committee.

PATKURONI

An old Brahmin lady named Parul Rani works daily for cleaning the kitchen, dressing and chopping the vegetables as well as fish, grinding of spices etc. She is designated as *Patkuroni*.

This is purely a non-traditional post and the person is not entitled to get any remuneration from the Committee. She is paid by the *paladar* at the rate of Rs. 3/- per day - one rupee for tiffin and two rupees for the labour. One plate *bhog* is also given for her lunch.

BASON MAJAR LOK

A person is required in the afternoon for washing the used utensils. The person is termed as *Bason majar lok*. Usually children from 'Bagdi' caste or beggars come to serve this function in lieu of Re. 1/- or Rs. 2/-. This person also receives one small plate *bhog* as an exra incentive. *Paladar* may bring a servant from his house for this purpose. In fact there is crisis for this service. *Chowkidars* regularly face trouble in searching out willing person in this job; it is their headache because they are supposed to reback all clean utensils in time to *paladar*'s house.

KAMAR

The immolator of the temple is locally known as *Kamar*. He belongs to the Caste 'Kamar' and traditionally associated with the temple. Name of the present immolator is Rabi Karmakar. He is actually a *dauhitra* of the original line.

All the immolations (*boli*) of the temple are supposed to be done by the *Kamar*. For the temporary absence, *Kamar* can commit the charge to any male member of 'Bagdi' caste. The particular falchion (*Khara*) used by the *Kamar* is said as traditional, donated by the Haldar family to the first immolator along with his residential plot of land.

In olden days immolator used to get a monthly remuneration from the Haldars but at present the system has changed. Now he gets one rupee and forty paisa (Rs. 1.40/-) from the public per immolation. Not only that, he receives all loose coins and money thrown over the spot and one head of the cattle per day from the *paladar*. Committee also presents him one *dhuti* in each year on *Ramnavomi.*

BAGDI

There are twenty-three persons of 'Bagdi' Caste at present, who possess traditional attachment with the temple vide Chapter II Their duty is to hold the animal at the time of immolation. Tremendous competition is observed among the *Bagdis* over the job. Of course they follow other non-traditional jobs too for better subsistence. For example, daily newspaper supply, milk supply etc. Originally duty of the *Bagdi* people was to wash and clean the utensils in the *shebait* houses and also the holding of animal at the time of immolation because in those days immolations did not occur frequently.

However, by holding the goat/sheep at the time of slaughter a *bagdi* gets fifty paisa from the party. The party also gives him either the skin of the animal or the equivalent price for the act of skinning. The price is determined according to the size and up-to-date market value of the animal. Usually it varies between Rs. 5/- to Rs. 10/-. Name of the few *Bagdis* are Khokan, Chhotka, Jagdish etc,

A few *Bagdi* women sit on the *Tahobil* (for details vide Chapter IV, p.71) to dress and sell the heads from the slaughtered animals. Which becomes the property of *paladar*. They get fifty paisa to one rupee per head basing on the size. As *paladar* always sells *Tahobil* to a professional person named Saila Mukherjee so payments to the *Bagdis* are made by that person. Accumulated money of the day are distributed among the workers equally. Number of women may be two or three or more as the case may be. None of the *Bagdis* can enjoy any extra facility from the Committee except at the time of Gajan ref : Chapter V.

DHULI

A Kayastha male named Bhombal Dey holds the post of Dhuli. His duty is to beat the drum at the time of immolation and *sondhyaroti.* In my observation, the duty is not followed strictly.

Monthly salary of *Dhuli* is Rs. 35/-. This is paid by the Committee. He has to wear a specific dress - a dust colour shirt, deplicated with K.T.C. monogram over a white *dhuti.* A new *dhuti* is presented by the Committee on each *Ramnavomi*. As 'Puja relief' he gets one month's salary on the day of *Kali-puja*. After two or three years when the old dress-shirt is torn, Committee also supplies him a new shirt. Beside these, *Dhuli* gets six paisa from *paladar* per each immolation.

The post of *Dhuli* is traditional in the temple and Haldars made settled the first appointed *Dhuli* with land. Although Bhombal Dey is associated with the temple for three generations, he does not belong to original *Dhuli*-lineage.

MALI

An Oriya Brahmin named Raghu Panda is at present in the designation of *Mali*. His duty continues throughout the day - from morning to night. He cleans the varandah of the main temple and its kitchen, the adjacent bridge, *Natmondir* etc. and keep all requirements (ghee, lamp, camphor, cotton, etc) ready for *aroti* performance. He is also responsible for the arrangement of *naibidya*.

Monthly salary (Rs. 60/-), 'Puja relief' (one month's salary) and a *dhuti* (on each *Ramnavomi*) are received from the Committee. Uniform is same as the *Dhuli*. Shirt is replaced by the Committee when that tears.

Duty of *Mali* has changed recently although the post is traditional in the temple. The original duty was to supply flowers in the temple. At present for that purpose few shops have been built within the campus (western side). Those shop-keepers are familier in the name of *Phool-mali*.

A short account of the *Phool-mali* :

Thirty -seven professional flower sellers from thirteen seats sell flowers. For the seats they pay monthly rent to the Committee. Of them, thirty-six parties share the twelve seats in three shifts - morning, noon and evening. Rest one seat is used by a party alone throughout the whole day. i.e. 1 + 12 x 3 = 37

These *Phool-malis* sell loose flowers as well as sticks and garlands. They procure flowers usually from their own gardens. In crisis, they have to buy. They maintain free supply of flower for the temple in every morning. A *Chowkidar* takes one clean leaf of 'Sal' tree and sprinkling Ganges- water over that he passes in front of the flower - shops. Each seller contributes some loose flowers willingly. Sometimes they gift garlands also. Further, the garlands are obtained from the outsider devotees. Usually *paladar* never buy flowers for morning decoration.

Name of some *Phool-malis* are Biswanath, Rabi etc.

SANAI-WALA

An instrumentalist team plays *sanai* in the temple. Name of the chief is Jhinku. The whole team is familier after his name and locally called as *Sanai-wala.*

The team comprises of four persons. Master (chief) regularly comes with assistants. He plays *sanai* and assistants play Dugdugi[1] and Harmonium. The persons come twice a day - once in the early morning, at the time of *nitya-puja* and once in the evening, at the time of *sondhyaroti.* They sit in a room on the first -floor by the side of the Committee office. The team is also called for special occasions with special remuneration.

Ordinarily the Committee pays Rs. 100- per month - the lion's share is taken by the chief and rest is divided among the assistants.

The team has no special uniform . Only the chief wears a black cap. Playing of *Sanai* is not at all a traditional convention; rather it is a recent addition (vide Chapter IV, p.).

CHOWKIDAR

There are eight persons in the temple who are known as *chowkidars.*

Name		*Home land*
Hiralal Ghosh	....	Bengal
Sunil Bose	....	Bengal
Bhubaneswar Tiwari (Bhuneswar)	....	Bihar
Jogindar Tiwari	....	Bihar
Surendar Tiwari	....	Bihar
Jahar Tiwari	....	Bihar
Lalmohan Ghosh	....	Bengal
Satadal Ghosh	....	Bengal

Although the post is traditional one but a vast difference in allotted

1. A small tabor played by moving it with one hand.

duties is marked between past and present. In past *Chowkidars* had to guard the temple at night because at that time the temple was devoid of a boundary wall. As a proof of sincere duty they used to ring a bell at times, throughout the night. They were the paid staffs of the *shebaits.*

Now duty has been multi-dimensional. Although primarily *Chowkidar* is a watchman but as the area is well protected now, they are not very keen on this basic duty. After set up of the Committee this drift in duty has been noticed. However, the new pattern of work is as follows :

(a) To carry the *Kacha* (un-cooked) food items from *shebait* houses to the temple and from the temple to the houses. They never serve those *paladars* who are not *shebait.*

(b) They are supposed to collect all the necessary articles for regular and special worships (i.e. *mete sindur, ator, noa, sakha, jabakushum* - brand oil etc) along with the oil and spices for cooking. A *Chowkidar* may bought these items from any shop but that should be the quality products. The earthen pots used in distribution of *bhog* are bought by them too.

(c) In special occasions some special duties have to be done. For example, i) At the time of cloth changing (which usually occurs twice in a year), they have to stain the new clothes to protect them against insects. ii) On *Durga-puja,* they bring the banana plant from a particualr place of 'Tollygunge' a per the convention.

(d) On crowded days they join with the *darwans* to control the rush.

(e) Rites and ceremonies of *shebaits* which are performed in the respective household require help of *chowkidar* for arrangement.

(f) During *sondhyaroti,* a *Chowkidar* must be present at *jor_bangla* for ringing the big bell over there with the rythm of waving of lamp.

(g) They clean the temple-room in the morning and collect the flower for *nitya-puja.*

(h) They bring all required utensils from *paladar*'s house in the morning and in the evening reback the same.

Duty is performed in four shifts. Those four shifts are shared by two groups. Each group is comprised of four persons. The mechanism is as follows :

(a) From 6 a.m. to 12 a.m. - First group
(b) From 12 a.m. to 6 p.m. - Second group
(c) From 6 p.m. to 12 p.m - First group
(d) From 12 p.m. to 6 a.m. - Second group

They make suitable adjustment amongst themselves in relation to the duty hours. Night duty stands as their period of relaxation (un-officially) and so enjoyed by all in turns.

Each person gets Rs. 1/- per day from the *shebaits*. Besides this, they receive loose coins of *Ghonta-tala* i.e. the money collected in the bowl placed under the big bell at *Jor- bangla*. Wearing of uniform is compulsory for *Chowkidars* while on duty. Committee provides this uniform. On *Kali-puja* they get a 'Puja relief' of minimum Rs. 50/-. On *Durga-puja*, they manage money and clothes from *shebaits* as a tip. Moreover, those who are Brahmin by Caste can make extra income following the profession of *Sathi-brahman* at times.

DARWAN

The day-guards of the temple are locally known as *Darwans*. At present they are ten in number.

Name		*Home land*
Rampujan Misir	....	Bihar
Rajendra Tiwari	....	Bihar
Rikhiram Sarman	....	Nepal
Kripal Dube	....	Bihar
Chandra Sekhar Jha	....	Bihar
Mangal Misir	....	Bihar
Brijkishore Jha	....	Bihar
Baijnath Misir	....	Bihar
Arjun Misir	....	Bihar
Harendra Tiwari	....	Bihar

The duty of *Darwan* is to control and direct the crowd from different spots. There are three convenient spots - east door of the temple -room, *Jor bangla* and main eastern gate of the temple boundary. Besides, two persons go on round visiting. Thus five persons are employed at a time. Duty is divided in two shifts and total four shifts run in a day. Two groups (comprising of five persons) alternately perform this shifting duty. Shifts are :

(a) From 6.30 a.m. to 10.30 a.m. - First group
(b) From 10.30 a.m. to 2.30 p.m. - Second group
(c) From 2.30 p.m. to 6.30 p.m. - First group
(d) From 6.30 p.m. to 10.30 p.m. - Second group

Income of a *Darwan* is highly flexible. They receive Rs. 69/- per month from the Committee. Public either in wish or in force give them money. The Brahmin *Darwans* also act as *Sathi- brahmans* in leisure to enhance the income. Wearing of uniform in duty hours is compulsory. That dress is provided by the Committee in time. They avail the 'Puja relief' like others.

The post is non-traditional. After the Committee establishment it has been created.

PEON

There are two persons in the post of *Peon,* namely Nalini Chakraborty and Sankar Banerjee. They work as messengers of the Committee - convey important informations to the house of *shebaits*, Priests, *Misras* etc. and bring essential signatures in need.

Each person is supposed to work in two shifts and accordingly four shifts for a day is the usual rule. But as Nalini Chakraborty is too old and lives very far, so Sankar Banerjee considers him. With the mutual understanding, at present Chakraborty works from 10 a.m. to 5 p.m. and Banerjee works in two shifts :

(a) From 7 a.m. to 10 a.m.

(b) From 5 p.m. to closing of the temple.

Post of *Peon* is also non-traditional. They use the Committee given uniform like others. Monthly salary is Rs. 69/- and 'Puja relief' is one month's salary. As they are Brahmin by Caste so at times (in leisure within the duty hours) they act as *Sathi-brahman* for extra income.

JHETEL

In the designation of *Jhetel,* two persons namely Basudev Kayal and Purnadas Parui are found. But the duty of both have changed recently.

Basudev was appointed as a cleaner of *Kundupukur*. But as that tank has been renovated and all responsibility has been taken up by affluent 'Birla' - family, now he brings the ration for the temple and carries out other errands. (Separate *Darwan* and *Jhetel* have been appointed for *Kundupukur*)

Purnadas's duty was to clean the temple campus from morning to night. Now he acts as an office-keeper. His present duty is to watch on the office in absence of office staffs.

Both of them get monthly salary (Rs. 35/-), 'Puja relief' (a month's salary) on *Kali-puja* and a *dhuti* on *Ramnavomi*. Like others they also have to use the uniform supplied by the Committee. Their post is purely non-traditional.

JHARUDAR

Two sweepers namely Laxman and Lachhman affliated to Calcutta Corporation work in the temple, being called as *Jhaṛudar*. They work jointly. In the morning they sweep the whole campus by broom-stick and in the evening after charitable feeding of poors (*doridro-narayan seva*) wash the campus. Firstly they amass all the rubbish in a spot at the northern side of the campus and therefrom dispose outside, in a separate garbage-car.

Their post is not traditional and they possess no uniform. But the Committee keeps their record and pays Rs. 35/- per month along with yearly 'puja relief'.

FINANCIAL RESOURCES

This aspect is a part and parcel of temple organization, so should be mentioned alongwith. In Kalighat, property and finance jointly signify the financial position.

(a) Property : Property can be divided into two types basing on their nature.

(i) 'Immovable property' means the property which cannot be moved. It includes *devottar* land of the goddess Kali which is free from tax. Area of *devottar* land has been gradually decreased (in comparison to the initial phase of early nineteenth Century) due to the transference of its parts into different names. On the occasion of *Ramnavomi*, a procession travels through the old areas of the *devottar* estate (vide Chapter V). At present the *devottar* land comprises only the temple and its boundary, *Kundupukur* and some stray plots around the temple.

(ii) 'Movable property' includes jewellaries, cash money and utensils. The image is always decorated with gold ornaments. All gold and silver belongings, all precious metal ornaments and articles like tongue, eye, *belpata* etc which are offered to the deity are considered as *devottar* property. *Paladar* cannot claim those. They only receive the light weight silver or gold plated articles i.e. those which do not exceed 10 *tolas*.[1] Similarly in case of brass or bell-metal

1. A measure of weight which is equal to 160 grains.

objects, they are entitled to receive those items which are worth of maximum twenty rupees. However, from the spare or unused articles, sometimes heavy ornaments are made and old ornaments those undergo natural wear and tear are also replaced. All spare ornaments and valuable objects remain deposited in the safety vault, in the name of goddess Kali.

The cash money of the goddess has been deposited in the State Bank of India, Bhawanipore Branch, Calcutta.

(b) Income : Sources of income are varied in the temple. 'Regular' sources are,

(i) Half of the total income (in cash) of daily *pala*, which is estimated in advance and varies from day to day according to the occasions.

No income is counted from *dakshina* separately. Because the *Sathi-Brahmans* who help the pilgrims in worship get this *dakshina*.

The gate-fee system has been eradicated, so no inome is obtained from this too. Before the set up of the Committee there was a system of gate-fee. One paisa per head was claimed for visiting the goddess from the door; twenty-five paisa was claimed for visiting the goddess from close distance *i.e.* entering into the *Garva griha*. Another twenty-five paisa used to be charged as worship fee.

(ii) The jewellaries, gold coins and ornaments, silver utensils and ornaments, other articles (gold or silver made) like *munda* (human head), *mundamala* (chain of severed heads), *Khara, Karna* (ear), tounge, teeth, arms etc which are daily offered in the temple by the public.

(iii) Rent collected from the shop-keepers and others for using the *devottar* land.

(iv) Money collected from the box placed in front of Radha-Krishna temple.

(v) Interest obtained from the deposited money.

'Irregular' or 'Occasional' sources are donations. Anyone can donate at any time, whatever amount he likes.

Besides, many solvent pious people after fulfilment of their desires, like to contribute to the temple by making certain addition or renovation. For instance, the northern gate of the temple-campus was made by the 'Birla', the renowned business family of Calcutta. In May '81, a Marwari gentleman painted the whole campus with all associated temples. The coloured decoration of the outer surface of the dome was made by the effort of a gentleman from Uttar Pradesh. Similarly the *Natmondir*, tube-well (within the campus), white marble mozaic of the main temple (worth of four lakhs), all are the contributions from the public. time to time.

Although this sort of contributions cannot directly be categorized under income or property, but no doubt they add to the capital value of the temple. Moreover, such patronageor, voluntary service often lessens the expenditure of management authority. The different facets of expenditure have been enlisted in this connection.

(i) *Paladar* of each day is paid Rs. 95/- for the arrangement of *bhog.*

(ii) Payments to the traditional employees of the temple along with the present office staffs of the Committee as remuneration.

(iii) Expense to maintain, preserve and improve the temple condition and the *devottar* estate.

(iv) Expense to institute and defend suits and all proceedings relating to the *devottar* estate.

(v) Expense for the budget and audit.

(vi) Expense to secure health, comfort, discipline, convenience and benefit of the pilgrims including the arrangements of light and sanitation. (The electric meter of the temple is separate from the shops therein but there is no arrangement for sanitation practically). On special occasions, expense of erecting bamboo posts, rendering police-service, arranging special *bhog* etc. are managed by the Committee.

(vii) Expense for the repairs, renewals and purchase of necessary equipments for the worship.

After deducting the total expense of the year from the income, the balance of each year is treated as *devottar* and that is deposited in the bank. There is a provision in the rule that the excess amount may be utilized through religious or charitable performances e.g. propagation of Hindu culture, development of Hindu religious education, sacred songs, religious discourses etc. But those are rarely followed.

According to the present treasurer Amiya Madhab Haldar, exact estimation of the fixed asset of the deity is impossible because before 1978 for thirteen years there were no systematic account record. For that missing link, they are not in a position to declare the actual amount.

Part B: MARKET AND PROFESSIONAL GROUPS AROUND THE TEMPLE

Kalighat was a pilgrim centre long before the origin of the city Calcutta. In remote past as said in Chapter II, the goddess Kali was worshipped by the ascetics in a wretched hut within the dense forest. Actually popularity of the spot had been increased particularly after establishment of the present temple *i.e.* the second time permanent erection in 1809 (ref : Chapter I,). Because at this time Calcutta was developing rapidly - the area became accessible and at the same time concentration of population increased. The market for the first time was formed during that very period. Pilgrims especially who used to come from a long distance were always in the habit of collecting some handy goods from the place as taken to perpetuate the sacred visit in the memory. Trading on that pious sentiment, some craft communities assembled for producing and selling their commodities. A full-fledged miscellaneous market was established. The existing market is the continuation of the same though some old features have been modified due to impact of various modern forces. Likewise, many new features have also developed.

The present market can be classified into two sections basing on the usage or utility of the commodities.

I. The 'General market' for the local inhabitants. As Kalighat is a centrally located, densely populated area in Calcutta proper, so to meet the day to day requirements of the local people this section of the market has devolved.

II. The other section of the market can be identified as 'Special market' for the pilgrims and visitors. This section typically exhibits a symbiotic relationship with the temple. However, the nature of the commodities have been cited below.

1. Sweet : A special kind of sweet made of posset and sugar (*pera*) is essential for the worship of the goddess Kali in Kalighat. Those are made locally by a group of specialized persons.

2. Flower : Different kind of flowers are sold e.g. marigold, tuberose, china-rose etc. but china-rose is of supreme importance being the essential flower for the worship of goddess Kali. Flowers are available both in loose or garland form.

3. Chief ritual articles : These include vermilion packet, iron bangle (*noa*), red bangle (*Kor*), lac-dye (*alta* and *alta-pata*), :etc. Coconut, parched rice (*khoi*) and other edible items as used in worship by some people so are also kept in the shops.

4. Necessary items for '*Dasakarma* and *sraddha*' performances along with some cheap price garments like *dhuti- chador, sari, choli* etc.

5. Enframed pictures of different gods and goddesses (Laxmi, Saraswati, Durga, Ganesh, Siva, etc.), popular and great people (Ramkrisna, Vivekananda, Rabindranath, Saibaba etc.).

6. Small idols of gods and goddesses

7. Books : Fresh account books (ledger) which are used by the businessmen in year-ending and different sorts of religious books and booklets.

8. Conch-shell articles : Conch-shell bangles (*sakha*) with a great variety of size and design are available. Colours are white and red. Conch-shell finger-rings (*sakher angti*) and plain conch-shell (*sankho/sakh*) for blowing are also very popular.

9. Metal articles : These include mainly utensils like dish, glass, bowl, pitcher etc. of daily use. Beside those, worship equipments like incense-stick holder (*dhupdani*), lampstand (*pilsuj*), water-pot with spout (*Kamandulu*), kosha-kushi[1] etc. are kept. Metals are bell-metal, brass, copper and stainless steel. Iron implements such as knife, big curved knife with a base for domestic use (*boti*), pincers (*sarashi*) etc. are also found. Even images made of metal are available.

10. Toys : Plastic, rubber and wooden dolls and different types of other toys are found.

---

1. A two piece equipment required in Hindu worship.

11. Stationery goods : Make up articles (oil, soap, powder, perfume etc.), imitation ornaments and other decorative materials for women (e.g. hair - pin, ribbon, nail-polish etc.).

With the permanent shops, there are also a good number of temporary shops and moving hawkers. Number of those temporary shops and peddlers increase on special days (i.e. recognized dates for different worships, *Broto* and *Dasakarma* performances). As per the demand of the situations, they try to supply the articles. One common feature is, accumulated pieces of various fruits are supplied at a very low rate (thirty paisa) in a small earthen bowl on special worship or *Broto* dates; special fruit if any is included timely.

The recent additions which have been noticed are :

(a) Tea-stalls.

(b) Permanent and semi-permanent food-stuff stalls or restaurants.

(c) Stalls for keeping shoes and umbrellas.

(d) Photo-studios.

(e) Arrangements for selling the lump of river- soil (*ganga-mati*) and empty bottles.

All these provide standing services to the pilgrims and at the same time nourish the livelihood for a set of people. Snaps taken in the studios are borne as memento for the distant pilgrims. Similarly, the immediate variegated food-shops are very convenient for the pilgrims after their long travel and tedious effort. Arrangement of depositing the foot-wears before entering into the temple is definitely a disciplinary and protecting measure to check the anxiety of the new-comers in lieu of a very nominal charge (ten paisa). Water and soil of the Ganges is considered very sacred to the Hindus, so are of great demand. Being conscious about that value concept, some people have been engaged in selling empty bottles for easy collection of water. Likewise, the collected river soil in lumps are sold at a low price.

However, sweet shops are the central figure in the temple oriented 'Special market'. Usually the proposed amount of worship is spent on special sweets-'Pera'. Worships are commonly designated as *soa panch anna* (thirty-three paisa), *solo anna* (hundred paisa) etc. The sweet shops within the temple campus are most ancient and the shop holders were originally of 'Tanti' caste (weaver),. At the beginning, sweet selling or shop opening was regarded as a degraded occupation to the authority (*shebaits*) so they permitted the local weaver group to open shops in their area for serving the pilgrims. But in later period many such shops have been introduced by the *shebaits* in adjacent area. Now they operate those shops by themselves. Their penetration into so-called degraded occupation have been possible due to great influx of pilgrims at one hand and on the other hand, for the change of mentality. The job seeking attitude of the *shebaits* is absolutely new (in past they were not hankering for other job)and it has developed to step with the high cost of living. Popularity of *pera* has not decreased at all in competition with the modern confectioneries because its price, quality, quantity, display all are proportionate to each other and above all not yet unsatisfactory for the very purpose.

If we spread our observation at the fringe areas of Kalighat, we find some interesting pockets where different craft communities were settled at the formative phase of the market to promote their business. But those age old communities had to face a critical situation under the spell of advanced technology. The production level lowered for the loss of consumption and they were compelled to move on other occupations leaving the traditional one. Gradually they reached almost at the point of extinction, in relation to their products. Three such craft communities were very rich with their cultural heritage in Kalighat.

1. THE CHITRAKAR OR PATUA COMMUNITY

In the north of the temple, a locality is still known as 'Potopara' where the inhabitants were the Chitrakars (*patua*) i.e. whose professions were to exhibit and explain to the audience the painted scrolls (*pot*). These scrolls or *pots* were the vehicle of religious propaganda and also a means of mass education in theological lore.

The *patuas* of Kalighat were neither the autochthones of Calcutta nor the very old settlers in Kalighat. Their settlement was directly related with growing popularity of the Kali temple. Although they identified themselves as Hindu, actually they were half Hindu and half Mohammedan in rural traditional tracts.

According to historical record, from 1825-26, *patuas* achieved a steady market in Kalighat. They came from different areas of rural Bengal (Midnapore, Sonarpur, Barisha, Diamondharbour). According to W.G.Archer, Kalighat *pot* tradition are not older than 1910.

Patuas of Kalighat in later period developed an unique tradition which continued upto 1925-26 full- fledgedly and after that became weak. Kalighat *pot* tradition can be classified into six folds basing on the nature of matter. Those are Mythological pictures; Historical pictures; Social pictures; Animal pictures; Parables in pictures and Insinuating pictures.

This *pot* tradition of Kalighat is undoubtedly an outcome of great cultural tradition of India. Even the modern art has been influencd by this tradition. For example, Jamini Roy's art.

Now-a-days that enriched Caste community has lost the original professional skill. Their technology has changed completely from *pot* (scroll) painting to idol making. Also a drift towards other vocations has been observed. Reason is economic insecurity due to loss of demand and defeat in competition with modern industries producing lithographs and synthetic dolls.

Only one scroll painter (Sri Sris Pal) is found at present in 'Potopara'. Rest are all idol makers. Altogether there are twenty-two families at present.

2. KANGSHA BANIK OR BELL-METAL WORKER COMMUNITY

Within the short range of the temple, in the same direction another locality is found known as 'Kashari para' where the inhabitants are Kangsha Baniks (*kashari*) i.e. bell-metal workers. The locality comprises of few roads, all of which are after the name of the Kangsha Baniks. Kundu, Dey, Pramanik, Nandan, Pal etc. are the common titles among them.

The inhabitants are originally of 'Saptogram', Hooghly. They came and settled in Kalighat when found it as a good business centre. Here they used to make and sell their commodities i.e. acted both as worker and trader of bell-metal. At present nobody can be said bell-metal worker- as now they work with gold, silver and brass. Many of them have been interested in other business or job. Urbanization and industrialization are probably the causes of their diversification. Metallurgic knowledge of advanced civilization has produced aluminium, porcelin, stainless steel etc which are more handy, cheap and easy to clean. Naturally those pulled down the market of bell-metal utensils. To qualify with the modern demand the workers shifted from their unique profession and ultimately the craft died in that particular area.

3. SANKHAKAR OR THE CONCH-SHELL CUTTERS

Close to 'Kashari para' another area is found which was named after Sankhakar (*sakhari*) or the conch-shell cutters - a particular Hindu Caste. Now they are an extinct community, with reference to the tradition.

The dealers of conch-shell were also a migrant in Kalighat. Their occupation was to cut and design the conch-shells in the form of bangle. Conch-shell bangles (*sakha*) are the traditional sign of marriage for every married Hindu women. Market at Kalighat appeared as a beautiful business centre to the Sankhakars because the Hindu married women who used to come to the temple were in the habit of buying those bangles not only for themselves but for other relatives and also for the great goddess Kali. They would think it (gifting of *sakha*) an act of virtue which would save them from widow-hood because there is a rule that a wife should break her *sakha* for ever at the death of her husband.

Due to the impact of modernization, the value system of the society has changed a lot. Though *sakha* is still considered as an important sacred sign of Hindu marriage but its regular use has decreased greatly. Only a small group of ladies have taken it as an indispensible part of married life. Therefore, the sell dwindled down. For strained livelihood, the particular caste community has compelled to give up the traditional occupation and forced to take up other occupations.

Most interesting and remarkable feature of present day Kalighat is that the transactions of both bell-metal articles and conch-shell bangles are still continuing whereas, the respective traditional practitioners have been totally extinct. Reason for this is, the businessmen have replaced the craftsmen. Businessmen are traders - they do not manufacture the articles; only procure and sell. Bell-metal articles are purchased from 'Burrabazar', Calcutta being manufactured in 'Baharampur' and 'Khagra' of the District Murshidabad, 'Simla' of north Calcutta mainly. The conch-shell bangles are similarly purchased from the nearby hat[1] of 'Chetla', where the makers come with their products. Raw materials (conch-shells) come mostly from Madras, a southern State of India. Makers i.e. *sakharis* of 'Barrackpore' and 'Bagbazar', Calcutta after purchasing the material give them proper shape and design; nextly sell. Some finished products are also imported from the famous market of Dacca (*sakhari bazar* of present day Bangladesh). Distant people specially the rurals and semi-rurals are the chief customers. They do not get these in own areas so they collect at the time of pilgrimage. However, this demand is not too high and met up easily by purchase from retailers. On the whole a new market with up-to-date necessities has gradually replaced the old one.

BEGGARS

Beggars are the black spots for all societies. They are considered as social outskirts due to the fact that, centering the profession of begging anti-social elements are assembled and different sort of crimes are committed.

---

1. 'Hat' is the weekly market of rural Bengal. Sellers assemble with different goods from distant places due to absence of a permanent market in their area. 'Hat' in the area Chetla is a continuation of that rural form. It assembles twice a week - Wednesday and Saturday. Wednesday is still full-fledged.

But it has been found that the existence of beggars at Kalighat is mainly out of a traditional cultural need associated with religious practice. In Hindu philosophy, 'charity to the poors' is an extremely religious affair. This virtuous deed on one hand, helps one to accumulate the spiritual merit (*punya*) and on the other hand, emancipates him from many sins(*pap*). People also think, alms (*viksha*) giving particularly in holy places and if simultaneously with religious performances becomes more effective. With such pious idiology, Hindu pilgrims in course of their visit in holy places make deliberate charity in the form of money, food, clothings etc.

A great lot of pilgrims visit Kalighat everyday; basing on their alms the profession of begging is nourished and continued in a full-fledged form. Many beggars live in Kalighat by generations. Begging is their chief means of living though some of them are interested in jobs also. For example, they serve as tea-stall workers, servants, maids etc. Only a few have been able to get out of their traditional begging practice and some others like to keep it as side profession. There is a considerable association of diseased and handicapped persons, but it is a matter of great disgrace when we find many of such persons are in disguise. The lazy people, to enjoy a secure livelihood gather here and the feeding programme for the poors conducted by the temple authority (ref : Chapter IV) is another advantage for them. Some beggars are entangled with various sorts of crime like robbery, theft, murder, smuggling etc. Females are mostly prostitutes and a separate quarter has been developed within a short range of the temple.

Inspite of the said malpractices, the beggars of Kalighat possess some positive qualities. They serve the local people (*shebaits*) in problems and at times they too make charity. For example, at the time of last war between India and Pakistan, they contributed money and supplied different usable articles (socks, blankets, mugs etc.) to the soldiers. Similarly, at the time of natural calamities e.g. flood, draught etc. like the rich people they try to help the sufferers from their small savings. Savings of the beggars are deposited in the local shops against interest. Thus, with the principal amount and interest the total savings increase.

The number of the beggars at Kalighat is not at all decreasing, rather increasing. Their profession will be continued as long as the temple will remain popular and so long as the Hindu philosophy in attaining spiritual enhancement will remain unchanged. Because the pious act of Hindus in the form of doling will foster the profession of begging. It can be concluded that the surrounding market and the beggars are tied in an intimate and inseparable relationship with the temple.

CHAPTER 4

Regular Routine in the Temple

If we pay attention on the day to day activities of the temple, we can easily discern a systematic order of services to the great goddess Kali. The daily routine is particular as well as regular and only in case of some special occasions a few alterations are visible.

In the early morning at about 4 a.m. the doors of the temple-room are opened by the *Misras* of the morning shift. (Keys are obtained from the *Misras* of last night's shift). At first before the closed doors they clap thrice and shout thrice with the word 'Jago', to make the goddess alert. 'Jago' is a Bengali word for calling a person from the sleep.

After entering into the temple-room, they recite a *stav*.[1] Then the image is released from stale decoration. Face, tounge etc. are wiped carefully with otto. The august feet (*Padopadma*) is washed with water. Water must be the Ganges-water. From the tube- well of the campus, this water is supplied by *Bhari*. It is considered that the Ganges is flowing underground connecting the *Kundupukur* , so the tube-well inside the campus is used for easy collection of Ganges-water. However, after cleansing, the image is embellished with garlands made of china-rose; vermilion is put on the hair-parting and sweets are given to the four hands and mouth. The expense whatsoever is met from the Committee accounts. Sweets may be supplied from any good local shop; there is no selective-ness in this respect.

An *aroti* performance known as *mongolaroti* by Kanai Haldar (vide Genealogy.2) is seen immediately after the adornment. This has been introduced by Kanai Haldar himself about thirty-five years ago. So long

1. a prayer to praise the deity.

he performs it regularly at his own expense. In his absence Manik Lal Haldar or Devi Haldar (vide Geneology. 2) take the charge of performance. These three persons are very punctual and usually all of them present themselves at the time of *mongolaroti*. Prescribed time of this *aroti* is *Brahmomuhurto*, a period of forty-eight minutes immediately proceeding sun rise. It is supposed that the gods and goddesses awake from sleep at this time. However, Camphor is burnt in an earthen pot and with that the performance is done.

This time *Sanai*, the musical instrument is played for about an hour. The system of playing *sanai* is not a family custom of Haldars, though now it is almost like a custom. Late Chuni Lal Haldar, a keen devotee of Haldar-lineage introduced the system about eighty-five years ago. At his own expense in each morning *sanai* used to be played. Gradually that system became universally accepted among the *shebaits* and after the establishment of Committee, expense was left under the budget of the Committee.

Next to *mongolaroti*, *nitya-puja* i.e. the daily worship of the goddess Kali is performed by the chief Priest. This is correspondent to sun-rise and continues for an hour.

A special account of Nitya-puja :

It is the compulsory daily worship of goddess Kali. Its contravention means a sin. From Santipada Bhattacharjee, the eminent Priest of the temple (vide Genealogy 3), it has been known that at Kalighat *nitya-puja* follows the *Tantra* named 'Torol'. India can be divided into three zones under the influence of *Tantra* namely Aswakranta Anchal, Rathakranta Anchal and Bisnukranta Anchal. Within these three zones, total sixty-four *Tantras* are distributed. 'Torol' is one of them. The whole West Bengal including present day Bangladesh comes under the influence of 'Torol' for Kali worship. He also said that each zone has its own speciality i.e. some additions or alterations are found on the particular *Tantra* - norms at the direction of *Guru*. This *Guru* is the spiritual guide of the Tantric Sect. Kalighat is not an exception from this sort of speciality.

However, for *nitya-puja* the Priest sits down on the floor in a seat (*ason*). *Naibidya* is prepared with half Kg. sunned rice grains, pieces of different fruits, milk and sweets. After the worship, Priest owns the entire offerings. Flowers are kept in a plate, called *pushpopatro*. In a silver dish, *Panchodevota* (deities namely Naryan in the form of *salgram sila*, *Baoneswar*[1] Siva, images of Ganesh, Durga and Jagodhatri) are brought.

---

1. some particular stone-pieces (white in colour) obtained from the bank of the rivers Godavari and Yamuna are ascribed as 'Baoneswar Siva'. It is believed that 'Baoneswar' never gets angry, not even by any fault in regular worship.

The silver dish is called 'Tat' and normally it is kept on a wall- shelf in the temple-room. After *nitya-puja* the dish containing the deities is taken back to its normal place.

Formerly public was not allowed to offer their homage before the completion of *nitya-puja*. But now most of the *paladars* are more prone to earning than serving the deity, so they allow public at the time of *nitya-puja* too.

After *nitya-puja*, in the morning there is no other performance within the temple-room. This is the high time for the common people to visit (*darshan*) or worship (*puja*). The temple remains so crowded that most of the time public have to follow a line. Although the worships are offered through *sathi-brahmans* but everyone is permitted to touch the image; no bar exists in this respect.

Worship of goddess Kali at Kalighat is closely associated with animal sacrifice which is locally known as *boli*.

The subject of sacrifice should receive the fullest view of the goddess as grace. Therefore *boli* may be performed at anytime except the time of *aroti* and *bhog* while the southern door of the temple-room remains block. There is no regulation regarding the number of animal sacrifice in the temple but at least one animal (a he-goat) must be sacrificed on each day; meat of that goat is cooked and offered with the principal *bhog* of the goddess at noon. This indicates, daily one *boli* is compulsory. People often make *Manosik* with *boli* (ref : Chapter VI, p.118) and prefer Tuesdays, Saturdays, Sundays and other holidays for such performance. On the occasion of *Durga-puja* and *Kali-puja*, huge number of animals are sacrificed. An average record has been shown below.

On Tuesdays and Saturdays	....	70 — 80 App.
On Sundays and Holidays	....	40 —50 "
On other weekdays	....	1 — 7 "
Durga-Puja		
On first day (Sosthi)	....	50 App.
On second day (Saptomi)	....	100 "
On third day (Astomi)	....	200 "
On fourth day (Navomi)	....	250 "
On *Kali-puja*	....	800 — 1000 & over.

As the meat of the first sacrificed goat is taken by the *paladar* for cooking in the *bhog*, many people do not want their *bolis* as the first one. They wait for the second turn. In those days, *paladar* finds no way other than to buy a goat from the market. From the second time bodies of the animal can be taken by the respective parties but heads (*mathi*) become *paladar's* property. He earns by selling the heads from an altar situated at the south-west corner of the temple-campus. This altar was set up by the favour of *Birla* family, a few years back. Local people call it as *Tahobil* or *Topil-er-jayga*. This spot is regularly bought by a person (Saila Mukherjee) from the *paladar* as already stated.

Traditional rule is to beat the Drum at the time of each immolation. But today that is not followed strictly. *Dhuli*, the responsible person for this work though found to be present in the temple for maximum time, still he does not act. Sometimes other persons do this.

A tax is charged from the party for immolation. Ordinary taxation for each sacrifice is two rupee and thirty paisa (Rs. 2.30/-) only. That amount is distributed among the following persons in the following way:

Paladar - Forty paisa is his quota. He has to pay five paisa from that to *Dhuli* as remuneration of drum- beating. Even without performing the duty, *Dhuli* gets this by rule.

Bagdi - For holding the animal at the time of immolation he acquires fifty paisa.

Kamar - Rest one rupee and forty paisa (Rs. 1.40/-) is owned by him as he decapitates the animal.

The ordinary taxation rises higher up during *Durga-puja*. It becomes three rupees and twenty-five paisa (Rs. 3.25 /-). Again, for a big goat as two persons are required for suitable grip, so there taxation increases upto five rupees (Rs. 5/-). In all cases, the amount is proportionately distributed among the claimants stated above. But when *paladar* has to buy a goat for first immolation, he raises the tax (one rupee more) for the day. Thus, he tries to cover the price paid by him for purchasing the goat.

Generally sheep and goat are sacrificed in Kalighat. Hindustanis prefer sheep sacrifice. The taxation remains same for both the animals. Buffalo sacrifice is a rare phenomenon. Generally, on third or fourth day of *Durga-puja* or on *Kali-puja* it is found but not regularly every year.

Last buffalo sacrifice occurred on 15th. November 1982, the day after the *Kali-puja*. Taxation of such immolation is twenty-one rupees (Rs. 21/-)

Kamar gets Rs. 5/-.

Bagdis (four persons) get Rs. 12/- i.e. Rs. 3/- per head.

The balance goes to *paladar*.

Dhuli does not get any share because drum-beat is forbidden in this case. Buffaloes cannot stand this sound and become restless. Sacrificed buffalo is neither demanded by the party nor by the *paladar*. Committee rings to the Alipore Zoological Garden, Calcutta. They send the car to take the decapited animal as eatage for the carnivores over there.

Lineage-norm of Haldars permits animal sacrifice only three times in a year. Those are termed as *nijaswa boli* by *shebaits*. In case of *nijaswa boli* nobody (*Kamar, Bagdi, Dhuli* or *paladar*) enjoys any cash payment. The prescribed occasions are :

Ṣitola-puja, Navomi-puja or *Durga-puja* and *Monosha-puja*. But at present in *Sitola-puja* no animal is slaughtered. Therefore, the special privilege as chalked for Priests and *Misras* (vide Chapter III, p. 47 +48) does not materialize. As an alternative, meat is bought from the *Bagdis* of the temple and with that Priests and *Misras* are fed. Practically arrangement is made for forty people because all associated persons of the temple desire for the *prosad*.[1]

The meat sold by the *Bagdis* are collected from the public at free of cost. They dress the body of the animal and after getting the usual remuneration they also demand for some meat. Generous people give that all at once but the quantity is usually poor. Again, all people are not generous and so they do not like such a gift. This has created a practice of pilfering among the *Bagdis*. They steal meat from every goat and sheep. People do not understand this because they beautifully display all the portions one by one like legs, ribs, neck etc. - the best meat from the hip area is kept out of sight for their own. This activity of the *Bagdis* is an open secret among the other temple personnel but as it does not hamper their interest by any means, so they never protest.

Two black goats are sacrificed in *Novomi-puja*. After completion of worship, this is done. Goats are taken to the temple-room for *sankalpo*.

---

1. After completion of any worship, the food items offered to the deity are called 'Prosad', to get part from that means acquiring god's grace.

Sacred vermilion is smeared on the forehead of *Kamar* and a flower wreath is put on his neck. Vermilion is also touched to his *Khara*. Then the *Kamar* takes the goats to the *Harkath-tala*. Two *Misras* hold a goat from two sides placing the neck suitably on the *Harikath*. *Kamar* immoltes both the goats one after another. The Committee bears the expense of buying goats. Generally before 9 a.m. the Navomi's worship including *boli* is completed. A little portion of meat with blood is kept in that spot in a cup made by banana leaf. Heads are taken near *padopadma*. Those are kept there until their immersion in the Ganges with the *Kalabous* on the next day. On the other hand, skinning of the body is done by the *Bagdis*. One body is equally divided between the two *Misras* who hold the goats at the time of immolation. Other full body is taken by the Priest. The same Priest or *Misras* cannot avail this privilege in each year as per the rotation rule.

In *Monosha-puja*, two black goats are required. Generally, the sacrifices take place in the morning at about 11 a.m. according to the particualr auspicious moment. *Sankalpo* is done in *Monosha-tala; Kamar* has to go there. Each and every procedure is like *Navomi's boli*. Only exception is that, in this case heads are not immersed. One is shared by the two *Misras* and other is taken by the Priest.

However, *boli* and homage offering by the public continue side by side upto noon and remain stop at the time of *bhog* offering. There is no restriction regarding age, sex, caste, class and sect. Except Muslim, all are allowed in the temple. Many Christians (travellers and non-travellers) come here; though they usually do not worship with offerings but by entering into the temple-room in bare feet they visit the great goddess.

Bhog is offered roughly at 3 O'clock in the noon. It is offered by the Chief Priest through prescribed hymn. At this time *paladar* (specially, if he is a *shebait*) is supposed to be present but most of them do not abide this norm. It is the duty of *Chowkidars* to clean the temple-room and its varandah prior to this important sacred performance. Next to that, *Misras* carry the *bhog*- items over the bridge very cautiously to keep the sanctity fully preserved. The Chief Priest, *Misras* and *Thakur* on duty abstain from food until the *bhog* is offered. The *bhog* comprises of many sumptuous dishes like.

Fried rice,

Pulse,

Fried vegetables (five types) e.g. potato, sweet potato, brinjal, *patol*, unripe banana, *uchhe*, etc.

A kind of *chachchori* or *sukto* (a curry with bitter gourd),

Fish curry (scale-less fish is forbidden),

Meat (only from goat and preparation should be without onion and garlic),

A condiment made of either *chalta*, (an acid fruit), tamarind or mango (tomato is tabooed),

Payesh (locally known as *annoprosad*),

Curd and sweets.

Besides these compulsory items, sometimes curries of other vegetables like pumpkin, green jack-fruit etc. are made as per the taste of *paladar*. Outsider devotees often wish to offer a particular item, in addition. They contact *paladar* and pay the cost.

Bhog is also offered to *Basudev* and *Panchodevota* at this time by the same Priest. As *Basudev* is vegetarian, so vegetable dishes (i.e. rice, pulse, *chachchori*, *sukto*, condiment, *payesh* etc.) are cooked first and kept separately. Those are taken in the temple-room first of all and offered to *Basudev*.

Offering of vegetarian as well as non-vegetarian dishes to the great goddess Kali is very elaborate procedure. During the performance, doors of temple-room are closed for an hour. It is symbolic, denoting the eating period of the goddess. At this time no one is allowed to be present inside, not even the Priest. Now-a-days, the closing period has been greatly reduced. Visitors and worshippers are the sources of income, so *paladars* like to keep the door open as long as possible. Of course there are some *shebaits* who try to follow every norm- to them serving is the prime motto, income is secondary. They think that the grace of goddess is the first thing to want; if she is not treated with proper respect and reverence, all efforts for income will be fruitless. Without her kind blessings, any attempt will stand merely futile.

However, after offering of *bhog* but before the closing of temple-doors, the *Misras* take the silver dish containing *Panchodevota* to the kitchen of the goddess Kali. There the remaining portion of cooked food (i.e. the food-stuff for *doridronarayan seva* which is not taken in the temple-room) is offered to the *Panchodevota*.

The Priest claps three times before opening the doors of the temple-room and then enters. Water is poured over the *padopadma* after an *aroti* performance with a conch. Here norm varies from family to family among the *shebaits*. For example, Amiya Kumar Haldar offers betel-roll, drinking water and sweets at this time. Some other families offer other items. But the performances like *aroti* (with camphor) and *pushpanjoli* (offering of flower) are found to be common for all. Whatever might be the individual norm of the *shebaits,* lastly the Priest rings a hand- bell to announce that the whole performance of *bhog* is over. Priest gets one full dish *bhog*-items (i.e. a meal for ten persons), entire quantity of sweet and betel-rolls offered in *bhog* by *paladar.*

When the temple-room remains closed during the *bhog* performance, *Sathi-brahmans* motivate the pilgrims waiting in the campus and often offer the homage from outside of the closed doors. This activity of *Sathi-brahmans* is a breach of the temple-rule.

Food distribution among the beggars is termed as *doridronarayan seva* or *kangali bhojan* or *prosad bitaran.* It starts after the closing of the temple- room. Anybody may receive this *prosad* though actually it is meant for the poors. Beggars enjoy this *prosad* as a full meal (once in a day) throughout the year, except in four days. Those days are *Saptomi, Astomi, Navomi,* and *Dasomi* of *Durga-puja.* On those busy days no arrangement can be made separately for the beggars. During that period they manage the meal from the *shebaits.*

Beggars sit in two rows (face to face) along the passage on the left side of the *Natmondir,* in front of the Kitchen of the goddess Kali. *Chowkidars* serve the food. Items are usually *khichuri* and a type of *chachchori.* Approximately one hundred and fifty local beggars get their daily lunch from the temple. After *doridronarayan seva,* in the afternoon, the campus is made clean by the *Jharudars.*

In the evening at about 6.30 p.m. an *aroti* performance starts which takes forty-five minutes to one hour to be finished. It is called *sondhyaroti.* A heavy silver lamp is used - one hundred and eight wicks, made by cotton and moistened with *ghee* are placed separately and camphor is put in the central bowl. During *sondhyaroti*, *Misras* beat *Kanshor,*[1] a *Chowkidar* rings the bell (*ghonta,* fixed overhead in *Jor bangla*), *Dhuli* beats the drum and the team of *Sanai-wala* plays *sanai* with other instruments. The campus becomes resounded. Public can be the onlookers but not the worshippers.

1. An instrument made of bell-metal

Just after the *sondhyaroti, sitol* is arranged i.e. afternoon snacks are offered to the great goddess. (Formerly this used to be termed as *baikali*). The *sitol* includes *luchi*, saltless fried potato, milk and sweets. Those come from the kitchen of Radha-Krisna (vide Map. 3) being prepared by the *Misras* of that temple. Duty of the Priest ends with the offering of this *sitol*. Now he gets twelve *luchis*, the entire milk and sweets of the *sitol*.

The sacred visits and worships again begin after *sondhyaroti*. At about 11 p.m. another performance named *besh/raj-besh* is found where the image is cleansed and wrapped with a new expensive sari. Garlands made of marigold and other flowers like *bel*, jesmine, tuberose etc are put around the neck. Sweets and betel -rolls are given to the four hads of the image and last *aroti* of the day is performed. All these are done by *Misras* of last shift. They utter the spell for sleeping (*sayaner mantra*) at last. They also put off the light of the temple-room (fan is put on during summer) and come out.

After locking the doors, *Misras* shout with the word 'Biswambhar'. 'Biswambhar' was the name of a sincere *Chowkidar* in past. This is a magico-religious belief to call the soul for protecting the temple. Due to long practice now this habit has turned to a superstition. However, after that *Misras* go round the temple and before returning home they deliver the keys to other *Misras*, who are to attend the next morning shift.

The temple remains open more than the usual hours on Tuesdays, Saturdays, holidays and other special occasions as public concentration becomes high. In winter day-time gets shorter; the temple opens comparatively later and closes earlier. But systematic routine of service is not at all altered, only the times vary to some extent.

CHAPTER 5

Special Occasion in the Temple

A. Of the Shebaits

B. Of the public

Worship of the goddess Kali by the *shebaits* as well as the assemblage of worshippers (*pujarthi*) and visitors (*darshonarthi*) project the routine events of the Kali temple at Kalighat. If we probe deeper, we are also able to discover a good number of special occasions, performed in the same spot. Some of them are celebrated by the shebaits and others by the public. For a few special occasions of the *shebaits*, financial expenditures are borne by the *shebaits* themselves. Others are borne by the Committee. But in both the cases, ritual procedures are chalked after the traditional norms of Haldar-lineage. Sometimes the normal routine of the temple is disturbed on account of these celebrations. (vide Chart. 6.)

All special occasions are going to be discussed elaborately in two different parts, A and B. Occasions celebrated by the *shebaits* are stated in Part A and B stands for the public celebrations at Kalighat. (vide Chart. 5)

PART A : OCCASIONS OF SHEBAIT

Occasions of *shebait* may be grouped under two headings. (1) Personal Occasions and (2) Official occasions. Personal occasions are those which are directly financed by the *shebaits*. They can again be classified into sub-sections :

(a) Regular performances i.e. the occasions which are found to be performed in a regular fashion. Only three occasions can be cited under this sub-section.

Chanchor

In the month *Chaitra* (March-April), on the eighth lunar day of light fortnight, *shebaits* perform this. Each *shebait* has to contribute personally for this performance. Though the occasion is mainly concerned with Radha-Krisna, but its relationship with the goddess Kali is evident through the performance.

However, in the evening of *astomi*, in front of Radha-Krisna temple 'Mayra' is burnt. Straw is wrapped at the tip of a bamboo pole to make the 'Mayra'. It is erected straight from a pit of the campus ground. At about 6.30 p.m. the Chief Priest (*Bhattacharjee masai*) arrives at the site. He utters certain hymn and sets fire to the straw. The performance recalls the story of 'Medhrasure badh'[1] of the old Hindu scripture 'Puran'. The word 'Medhrasure' being continuously misspelt has ultimately taken the form 'Mayra'. After the burning, the special worship of the day (*adhibash*) starts and ends within 8 p.m. to 8.30 p.m. (including the time for hom). Duration is generally three to three and half hours.

On the other hand, from the noon a motor lorry undergoes decoration which gets completed in the evening. At about 8 p.m. idols of Radha-Krisna are lifted in a cradle (that cradle is kept on a side of *Natmondir* throughout the year). Then the cradle is taken over the lorry and a procession is started with the affluence of light, band party and religious song (*sankirton*). They follow the straight track from the west gate of the temple along the 'Kalighat Road,' then turning right at 'Bhawanipore' by the side of 'Purna' cinema hall, ultimately return through 'S.P. Mukherjee Road'.

The male members of Haldar-lineage irrespective of age are supposed to wear the traditional dress, *dhuti* and *panjabi* and walk with the lorry. For women though there is no restriction but usually they do not accompany. In course of travel, from the lorry different perfumes, coloured powders (*abir*) etc. are sprinkled. In the afternoon *shebaits* exchange *abir* marks on the forehead among the known persons.

In my experience after personal observation, the procession did not appear as highly gorgeous as reported by informants. Participation was very poor and that comprised mostly of old persons. Finally no repercussion was found on the regular temple activities including the trading in the shops.

---

1. It is the story regarding the killing of an 'Asur' i.e. force of evil

When the lorry returns, idols of Radha-Krisna are brought near the lap of the goddess Kali in the main temple and an *aroti* performance is conducted. It takes place within 11p.m. to 11.30 p.m. On that night, the idols of Radha and Krisna are not removed from the main temple. After the closing of the temple, all lights of the campus are supposed to be put out and different sorts of specialized fire-works are to be burnt. For the last 8/9 years, this practice has been abandoned.

Ramnavomi

The next day of *Chanchor* is celebrated as *Ramnavomi.* It is also a communal festival where each *shebait* has to contribute personally.

At dawn (*brahmo-muhurto*), the idols of Radha-Krisna are shifted from the main temple to the *Dolmancho.* There they are placed in the cradle and the first worship of the day is performed (duration is one to one and half hours) by the Chief Priest of the main temple. It is called worship of *purbahnna* dol. After this, *shebaits* (both male and female) come here for a sacred visit with flower wreaths, sweets and *abir.* They touch the holy feet and rub the *abir* there. Outsider people i.e. people other than *shebaits* may also do this. *Misri masais* of Radha-Krisna temple remain present in *Dolmancho* as attendants. They deliver *abir* marks on the forehead of all devotees. At the same time *shebaits* play with *abir* amongst themselves. This continue upto noon till the Radha and Krisna idols are re-transferred to the main temple for a sacred bath. The act of moving the idols are done by the same *Misri masais.* Before this re-transference, another worship is performed in *Dolmancho* by the Chief Priest which is called worship of *madhyanna dol.* The particular auspicious time (*Kshan*) is followed and the worship takes one to one and half hours.

The sacred bath is termed as *abhisekh. Chowkidiars* make all pre-arrangements and the rite is performed by the Chief Priest openly in front of the goddess Kali. At first, turmeric and green coconut water are used to wash. Next to that, honey, milk and perfumes are applied one after another. Roughly one hour is required including the time of offering *jalpani. Jalpani* means the fruits, sweets and beverages. Those are sent by the *bhagne- dauhitras* mostly, who are initiated in Vaisnava idealism. Respective *Chhar - brahmans* carry those from the houses to *Natmondir.*

All *jalpanis* are displayed in *Natmondir.* Chief Priest worships Radha-Krisna after the bath and offers *jalpanis.* These performances end at best within 5 p.m. (on this day, *bhog* offering of mid-day is delayed because no other *bhog* can be offered after Kali's *bhog*). Thereafter, the

Radha-Krisna idols are taken to their own temple. Krisna idol is dressed in a cow-boy style and in that dress it is kept for three successive days.

However, in the morning of *Ramnavomi* (at about 10 a.m.) *dhutis*, *chadors*, sugar in earthen pots, sweets, *paitas* are distributed by the Committee (on behalf of the *shebaits*) to the Priests and Misras of the main temple in the *Natmondir*. Some other personnel of the main temple as said in Chapter III, also get one *dhuti* per head on this occasion. The Committee arranges for police posting to avoid indiscipline, nuisance and unpleasant situations.

Nishi-puja or Rahasya -puja

This is the special worship of every new -moon. On each new-moon night, many such worships are performed by individual effort and expense. A large number of outsider people prefer this worship, so for the interest of the clientele many Priests arrange this worship. Such worships take place in the *Natmondir* and Siva temples but never within the temple-room. *Hom* is the most important part of this worship.

Among the *shebaits*, only two families follow this worship in regular course by employing their traditional Priest. They are the family of Amiya Kumar Haldar and the family of Bibhuti Banerjee, a *bhagne-dauhitra*. Though originally it is the worship of *shebaits*, it appears to have lost its importance among them now-a-days.

The worship is to be performed at 'Mahanisha' i.e. the dead hours of the night-the hours between 11 p.m. to 3 a.m. The duration is about three hours. *Bhog* prepared with rice is offered. The Committee bears absolutely no responsibility for this worship.

(b) Flexible performances i.e. the lineage norms of *shebaits* which may or may not be followed regularly, basing on individual's own accord.

Lineage norms of *shebaits* are huge in number and chalked month-wise. Shebaits are also numerous in number. They are scattered all over Calcutta (Bhawanipore, Ballygunge, Behala, Tollygunge, Sealdah, Chetla, etc.) and even outside Calcutta, so for them to perform each and every norm is quite impossible. Again many a *shebaits* by selling their pala-share for ever, have severed the link with the original family. In fact there are only 14/15 families who endeavour to abide by these norms with exactitude. Recently they also feel inconvenience in performing the rites and norms because of soaring market-price.

'Official occasions' refer to those essential occasions which are performed through the initiative of Committee. Such occasions are as follows:

Rakshakali-puja

This is the most important worship of the temple - the annual Kali worship. Usually it is performed either on eighth or fourteenth lunar day of dark fortnight of the month *Baisakh*. But sometimes it goes to the month of *Jaistha*. Whatever may be, the day must be either Saturday or Tuesday.

On the preceding evening, *adhibash* is sent to the main temple from the *shebait* houses. Only those who are keenly devoted love to send this *adhibash*. A sacrificial fire is made for *adhibash* in the temple by the Priest.

The *Rakshakali* worship takes place at mid-night as per the particular auspicious moment. One Priest is sufficient for this worship. *Sankalpo* is made on the main *ghot* of the goddess Kali. Priest performs the worship on *Jor bangla*, facing the image. The hom also takes place there. A mark obtained from the oblation of fire called *hom- phota* is put on the forehead of the image and water is pured on *padopadma*.

Neither *bhog* is offered nor animal sacrifice is done. Only *jalpani* is offered. China-rose garland and lotus are essential for the worship. On this day *sondhyaroti* is not done - an *aroti* performance is done after the *Rakshakali* worship, before the performance named *besh*.

Snanjatra

Performance of *Snanjatra* is observed among all Sects *e.g.* Sakta, Saiva, Vaisnava etc. It is held on the day of full- moon of the month *Jaistha*.

This is the most crucial performance for the temple. The day is considered as more auspicious when it falls on Tuesday or Saturday. On the preceding evening, *adhibash* is performed.In that ritual, *mohi* (earth), *gandho* (perfume), *sila* (rock), *dhannya* (paddy), *durba* (grass), *phol* (fruit) and *doi* (curd) are touched to the image one by one and lastly hom is performed.. Not only that, from different *shebait* families different articles in trays (*dala*) are sent for *adhibash*.

At the dawn of the scheduled day, *Natmondir* is guarded with strong ropes. There, different articles namely perfumes, scented oil (Jabakushum' brand), Ganges-water etc., supplied by the *shebaits* are mixed up in big vessels. On the other hand, inside the temple-room, Chief Priest makes pre-arrangements for the performance and finally comes out. Only four of the *shebaits* (Manik Lal Haldar, Kanai Lal Haldar, Arup

Kumar Haldar and Pulin Haldar - vide Genealogy 2) enter, the doors are closed. Even the space between the door and floor is closed by using soft pudding made of wheat and water. Within that air tight room, everybody close their eyes with seven folds of cloth. It is highly undesirable to perceive the mutilated body fragment (*soti-ango*) by the eye. It is also believed that, great misfall comes upon the person who tries to see it. However, those four *shebaits* bathe the *soti-ango* and change the old cover (*ango-bastro*). The performance of bathing is known as *ango-snan* and the water after bath is called *snan-jol*. Only those four *shebaits* have the right to bathe *soti-ango*. Because traditionally it was the duty of 'Baro-Haldar'. Now the elders of five main streams of 'Baro- Haldar' perform this jointly. The fifth person named Chandi Haldar (vide Genealogy 2) plays another vital role. He keeps the keys of the locked temple-doors at the particular time, remaining outside. Actual duty of this person is to keep the Keys and to mutter the sacred names standing at the door, as long as the other four performers will remain inside. But now he does not stand at the door or mutter the sacred names; only keeps the keys with him. As the performance is a very secret affair, so it is entirely restricted to those five persons. It is said that once one *Misra* tried to see the incident, he became blind right at that moment. Prior to *ango-snan*, all sorts of management are done by the *Chowkidars*. After *ango-snan* and *ango-bastro* change, special songs and *stotro*[1] recitations are found on *Natmondir*. About four hours are consumed in the performance of *ango-snan* and *ango-bastro* replacement. The four *shebaits* come out of the temple-room in a half conscious state.

Snan-jol and *ango-bastro* are considered as very very sacred. So to possess tiny portions, a great rush is found thereafter in the temple. Police-force is kept ready by the Committee to check the chaos. Sale of small empty bottles and earthen cups (*Khuri*) to collect *snan-jol* is a special phenomenon.

On this day, regular routine of the temple is hampered; morning-cleansing of the image as well as *nitya-puja* take place in late morning. Expense is borne by the Committee.

Janmastomi

In the evening, *adhibas* is performed in Radha -Krisna temple. *Shebaits* send trays containing different worship items (*adhibash-dala*). The worship starts at night following the star Rohini.[2] The oblation of fire takes place in the vestibule of that temple. After the worship, the idol of Basudev

---

1. The verse for praising a deity.

2. It is the fourth of the twenty-seven stars of Hindu astronomy. The performance of Janmastomi starts when the earth enters into it's fold.

is brought down near the *padopadma* of the great goddess Kali, as a symbol of Krisna-birth. In this day, aroti performance of the evening is done at this time. The whole celebration, starting from worship in the Radha-Krisna temple to *aroti* in the main temple, requires atleast three hours.

The temple is not closed at night. Committee bears the whole expenditure and only one Priest is employed for this worship. Police in plain dress patrols.

Nandotsav

The day after *Jamastomi* is observed as *Nandotsav* in the Kali temple. At about 8 a.m. on the varandah of the main temple (opposite of the Kitchen of Goddess Kali), performance for *abhisekh* is held. Half an hour is required - *Basudev* is bathed with the articles like turmeric, *panchogabya, panchamrito,* fruit juices, perfumes etc. One Priest is involved in the performance. Public - worships in the main temple remain adjourned at this time.

After the ritual *abhisekh, Basudev* is placed back in its original place. *Bhagne-dauhitras* initiated in Vaisnava idealism offer snacks and sweets. Sweet balls made of palmyra fruit are essentially offered. *Nitya-puja* of this day is delayed, as performed after the completion of *adhibash.*

Monosha-puja

In the temple, this worship is performed only once in a year by the effort of the Committee. The specific date is the fifth lunar day of the light fortnight in the month of *Bhadra.*

Monosha ghot[1] is placed within the temple-room fifteen days before the scheduled date, on another *panchomi* after the performance named 'Jol dhala'. There is certain specific procedure. In the morning, maintaining the suspicious moment *(Kshan)*, *sankalpo* is made on the *monosha ghot* at *Monosha-tala.* Then the *ghot* is placed inside the temple-room. Starting from the day of placing the *ghot* and upto the final day of worship, on each day a *bhog* for the goddess Monosha (within a *hat khola*)[2] is offered along with the mid-day *bhog* of the goddess Kali. This is arranged by the *paladar, of the day.*

---

1. The pot used in Monosha-puja is called monosha ghot. Sankalpo is made on it for the purpose of worship.

2. This is an earthen rice plate with bowls for different curries.

Songs are sung praising the grace of the goddess Monosha throughout the whole night, before the day of *Monosha- puja*. This performance is called 'monosha jagano'. At dawn, *Chowkidars* enwrap a branch of cactus plant in a sari; keeping that within a cane basket (*dhama*) and blowing conch (*sakh*) they walk from door to door of the *shebaits* to collect money. This money is received by the persons who remain engage in whole night programme.

On the scheduled day of worship, the space before the *Monosha-tala* is barricated. *Sankalpo* is done by the Priest. Worship starts usually at about 11 a.m. as per the auspicious moment and continues for about one and half hours. The essential ingredients of *Monosha-puja* are milk, banana and turmeric. *Naibidyas* are offered from the *shebait* houses but no bhog prepared with rice is offered. *Dhuli* presents himself in that spot for beating the drum. *Chowkidars* and *Darwans* control the public rush. *Kamar* also remains present for certain proceedings prior to animal sacrifices. Two goats are sacrificed as stated in Chapter IV.

Durga-puja

It is the most elaborate and complicated occasion for the temple. It can be performed after seven different scriptural directions (*Kalpo*). In Kalighat, the *Kalpo* named 'Krisna navamydi kalpo' is followed . From the ninth day of dark fortnight, on each day morning at about 7 a.m. Priests (those who will be involved in worship) worship individually for an hour roughly, which is totally different from the regular course *nitya-puja*.

Therefore, *Durga-puja* in Kalighat lasts for fifteen days. In the evening of *Sosthi*, a performance named *bodhon* is performed at *Sosthi-tala*. This is the time from when all the Priests are involved in the worship in the following way : One Priest from Haldars' behalf, one from *Bhagne-dauhitras*' behalf, one from *Guru*'s behalf, one from local Banerjee family's behalf[1] and one from late Chunilal Haldar's behalf[2]. The Priest on behalf of Haldar-lineage is selected among the Chief Priests of the temple as per the rotation norm (ref : Chapter III, 47). Other Priests offer *puja* and receive the offered items from the respective behalf.

---

1. From the ancient time, this family residing at Kalighat performs their yearly Durga-puja in the temple with the shebaits, as permission was obtained from the shebaits. Their puja is termed as jora bari tarafer puja.

2. Chunilal Haldar was a great devoted shebait who introduced a separate Durga-puja from his part. Sabitri Devi at present represents this.

However, in the evening of Sosthi, i.e. the sixth day of light fortnight, *sankalpo* is done on *Durga* image. No worship from the public can be offered at this time in *Sosthi-tala. Shebait* have to be present there. Two banana plants with some other particular plants and branches are tied in the railing of Siva temple over there. Those banana plants are taken from a specific place at 'Tollygunge', Calcutta as per the traditional norm. In the main temple *sondhyaroti* gets late and with a minimum *besh* performance the temple is closed. No separate *bhog* is offered in *Sosthi*'s worship.

In *Durga-puja, Guru* and *Tantra-dharok*[1] are urgently called. Because *Durga-puja* cannot be started without the formal permisssion of Guru; guidance is similarly forwarded by *Tantra - dharok*. This tradition was introduced by Bhawanidas Chakraborty himself. Present *Tantra-dharok* is neither traditionally related with the temple nor he practices *Tantra* in actual sense. The old scripture record (*puthi*) followed by Bhawanidas has been torn but still that is kept at the *padopadma* of the goddess Kali during *Durga-puja.*

In the morning of *Mahasaptomi*, i.e. the seventh day of light fortnight, under a big silver umbrella, the two banana plants (one for Haldars' behalf and other for *Bhagne-dauhitras*' behalf) are taken to *mayer ghat* for bathing. A band-party accompanies. Nextly, the rite namely, baron is performed in the *Natmondir* and thereafter the banana plants (in the form of *Kalabou*) are tied at two sides of the image Kali with the railing. The saris for worship are wound covering the image of Kali and *Kalabous* together. Special earthen lamps (*Jag-prodip*) are kept within the temple-room. *Saptomi*'s worship takes two to three hours to be finished.

At the completion of this worship, *naibidyas* from the *shebait* houses are accumulated in the *Natmondir*. Being offered, those are returned for the respective *shebait*. At noon, bhogs are similarly offered one after another. Lastly the *bhog* for goddess Kali is offered by the paladar which contains only rice, meat and *payesh*. From *Saptomi* to *Dasomi* (four days), *doridronarayan* seva remains stopped. In those days, the kitchen of the goddess Kali is used by *shebaits* who live at distant places. *Paladar* prepares *bhog* in other place. Some distant living devoted *shebaits* are found to make contracts with the nearby *shebaits* for preparing *bhog*, in lieu of money.

---

1. A person who holds the book *Tantra* at the time of worship.

At night, in the same manner *bhogs* are found to be offered by the *shebaits* one after another. As a result evening *aroti* is delayed, with which *Saptomi*'s worship ends.

Public concentration in the temple increase from the day of *Saptomi*.. Besides, during the successive nine days from first. day to ninth. day of the fortnight, Hindustani and Marwari people form the crowd; they remain engage in *Chondi-path*. Though normally the temple-room is cleansed everyday, but from *Saptomi*, all *nirmalyas*[1] are dumped in a corner upto the immersion of the *Kalabous*.. *Besh* and *sayan* performances are similarly stopped. The gate is not closed at night. But *nitya-puja* is never skipped. It may be delayed, still definitely be done.

Worship procedure for *Astomi* (8th day) is more or less same with Saptomi, except the *jag-prodip* worship which is done only in *Saptomi*.

Speciality of *Durga-puja* lies in the *Sondhi-puja*. It may occur anytime in the morning or noon or night. It continues for forty-eight minutes, covering the last twenty-four minutes from *Astomi* and first twenty-four minutes from *Navomi*. At this time *sankalpo* is done with Chamunda image. Worship though takes place in *Garva griha*, one hundred and eight candles are lighted at a time on the *Natmondir*. *Naibidyas*, sent by different *shebaits* are also kept there. No separate *aroti* is required for *Sondhi- puja*.

General procedure of *Navomi*'s worship is same as *Saptomi* and *Astomi*. Distinguishing event is that, after the worship two goats are sacrificed. As the *shebaits* were originally Vaisnava, so they do not partake the sacrificial meat; it is given to Priests and *Misras*. Compound gates are closed at the time of sacrifices; public are not allowed inside the campus. Another rite namely *Kalyaner puja* is performed afterwards by the *shebaits*.

At about 4 p.m. *hom* for the performance named 'Dakshinanto' starts. 'Dakshinanto' refers to that performance where *shebaits* (male members) gather in *Natmondir* to distribute sweets among the Priests and *Misras*. Priests sprinkle holy water (*santi-jol*) and get *dakshina* from the *shebaits*.

No special performance is found in the morning of *Dasomi*. It is the non-cooking day for *shebaits*. They call this occasion as 'Arandhan'.

---

1. The sacred flower, leaves and other articles which are abandoned after worship.

Within 8 a.m. Radha-Krisna idols are brought to the *Natmondir* along with the throne. Last day cooked wet rice is offered by the *shebaits* at noon. Last of all *nijo- bhog* of the goddess Kali is offered.

The gates do not open after the completion of *sidur khela.* At this time *Kalabous* are taken to *Natmondir*. Keeping *Guru* in between the *Kalabous*, last greeting is performed. At this very time Manik Lal Haldar as representative of *shebait*-lineage has to go for collecting alms, at least from five local houses. This is a ceremonial begging and alms includes rice grains and uncooked vegetables. After that, *Darwans* hold a silver unbrella and Priests carry *kalabous* under that for immersing them in the Ganges. This procession is also accompanied with a band-party.

Before the Priests' return from the Ganges, cleansing of the temple-room should be finished. All stale flowers and leaves dumped from the day of *Saptomi* have to be cleared up at this time. Huge vermilion that are deposited here and there due to the performance of *sidur khela,* are also be washed by sprinkling sand and thereafter spraying water by hose-pipe. The convention is to visit the image in the main temple with usual make up (*adimurti*) at the return to the temple after immersion. Therefore, *besh* for the day is performed earlier within 9 p.m. From this day, *sayan* is arranged as usual.

Priests recite a prayer named 'Aparajita' and an *aroti* is followed. At this time different kinds of sweet and snack are sent to the *Natmondir* by the *shebaits*. The members are also united there to wish each other, forgetting all past disputes.

During Durga-puja police posting is compulsory. But Darwans' duty at the time of *bhog* is indispensible because police cannot identify *paladars* and *shebaits* from the general mass.

Sitola-puja

This worship takes place in *Natmondir* on eighth lunar day of dark fortnight, in the month of *Chaitra.* Many a Priests are required because it is an elaborate worship containing *hom*, reading of different sacred books, recitation of sacred verses etc.

In the morning, water is poured on the *padopadma* of the image Kali with a view to cool the goddess Sitola. Round about 12 O'clock the day the worship starts and continues atleast for three hours. At the beginning, *sankalpo* is done and each Priest partakes his selected responsibility. Worship requirements are *naibidya,* curd, green coconut, fruits, flower garland, cloth etc. *jalpani*, china-rose garland and lotus come from *shebait* houses. Special *bhog* with rice is prepared in the kitchen of goddess Kali. Formerly, a system of ainmal sacrifice was associated with this worship. The sacrificial meat was used to feed the Priests and *Misras* of the main temple. Now the system has been modified- no special animal sacrifice is practised; the required quantity of meat is bought from the *Bagdis* of the temple (vide Chapter IV,) to cook and serve among the Priests and *Misras*. This is known as *'Brahman bhojan'* and takes place in the *Dolmancho*.

Gajan

In the month of *Chaitra*, *Gajan* is celebrated at Kalighat. From the beginning of the month most of the male *Bagdis* in the temple follow *sanyash*. People other than Bagdi Caste may observe *sanyash*, but they do not have the right to undergo *jhap* performance which is an important event in *Gajan*. After *jhap*, *sanyashis* have to take bath in the Ganges and thus the period of asceticism becomes over.

The rite namely, *jhap* is found to be performed twice in Kalighat. The first one occurs one day before *Chaitra sankranti* (last day of Bengali year) and the place is adjacent to *mayer- ghat*. This is called *Kata-jhap*. The other one occurs on the particular day of *Chaitra sankranti*, in front of Nakuleswar's temple. This is called *boti-jhap*.

There is an old *Bagdi* named Upen Das who regularly follows *sanyash* and is called *mul-sanyashi* (leader). All other *sanyashis* obey him and carry out his instructions. Expense of *mul-sanyashi* is met by the Committee and *shebaits* also give him as per their likings. During the period of asceticism, *Bagdis* are respected as Brahmins. They undergo purification in food and act. Saffron colour dress is worn with holy thread (*paita*) and meal is eaten only once in a day. *Shebaits* have to pour water at the feet of the *sanyashis* when they come to house. Formerly, the *mul-sanyashi* used to get an expensive sari called 'Benaroshi' and gold ornaments from the Haldars but now that system has been abolished. Today the *mul-sanyashi* gets only a 'Benaroshi' Sari from the Committee when his mendicancy is over. A team of drum beater regularly comes from 'Joynagar' (a southern suburb of Calcutta) on this occasion.

However, prior to *jhap* performances another rite called *ful korano* is performed. *Sanyashis* take bath in the Ganges and wear only a white *dhuti* around the waist in short and tight form by a *gamchha*. Then they put flowers upon the head of the image Kali and go on dancing in the *Natmondir* in tune with drum-beats until the flowers fall down. An elderly representative from *shebait* lineage must be present there. Usually,

Manik lal Haldar (vide Genealogy I) attends this. If long time is consumed and the flowers do not fall, blame goes to that representative. For such cases, there is a system to punish him. It is believed that due to his fault flowers got late to fall.

After this *ful korano* performance, *sanyashis* uplift the leader at shoulder height and walk to *mayer ghat* where *kata-jhap* has to be performed. Drum beaters accompany them.

In front of *mayer ghat* two long bamboo posts are erected. A platform is made on a height joining the two posts. Just beneath that, thorns of date-palm tree are kept. At first climbing on the platform, each *sanyashi* throws fruits among the public. Fruits are green coconut with spike, banana, green mango, orange, apple, marmelos, myrobalan etc. Those are kept in a *gamchha* with copper coins and some sunned rice grains smeared in turmeric-paste. These are supplied mainly by the Committee. *Shebaits* may also gift those voluntarily. Local faith is that if one such thrown fruit is eaten by a barren woman, she must bear a child.

After the distribution of fruits, *jhap* i.e. jump of the *sanyashis* starts one after another from the higher scaffold over the thorns. They remain unhurt by the grace of lord Siva. Each *sanyashi* must distribute fruits before his jump. *Mul- sanyashi* performs it at first.

Until they come back to the temple after *jhap*, the temple-room remains closed. *Sanyashis* first offer homage after the reopening of the temple. *Chowkidars, Darwans, Misras* all stand alert centering this performance.

In *boti-jhap* the same *sanyashis* participate. Here the *ful korano* performance is done with the goddess Kali as well as Siva. Previous day's procedure is repeated in the Kali temple and after that *belpata* is placed over Nakuleswar. *Sanyashis* dance in the same fashion until the leaves fall. It is called *babar mathar ful korano.*

For *boti - jhap* bamboo posts are erected on the road before the Nakuleswar's temple. Platform on a height is made alike, from where the *sanyashis* are supposed to jump down. Here sharp blades attached with wooden batten are lain unlike the *kata-jhap*. Actually the batten with blades are kept over a sand bag, placed within a rope structure. The rope structure is lifted from the ground by a large number of persons.

The next rite after *boti-jhap* is known as *ban phora*[1] or *dasloki jwala*. It is the burning of incense by the *sanyashis* while walking. *Sanyashis* decorate themselves in flower ornaments and go round the Nakuleswar temple (seven times) and Kali temple (three times) with such act and finally dip into the Ganges to put out the fire.

The male members of *shebait* family are supposed to be present at the time of *jhap* and *ful korano* performance. But now they are reluctant to be present. Rather a great crowd of outsider people is found to be formed. A few years back, on this very day another performance named 'Charak' was celebrated where the *Bagdi* people associated with the temple used to clothe themselves in different dresses and go as they like. Subscription in this respect were collected from the *shebaits*. However, it has been stopped recently due to internal conflict.

It is notable that after each thirty-six years, such a year is obtained where the particualr auspicious moment (*Kshan*) for a worship falls short. Naturally in those cases, problem arises with the traditional lineage performances (*Kulachars*) which require some more time. The year 1977 (1383 B.S.) was such a year. A tremendous argument took place among the Chief Priests and *shebaits* regarding whether traditional conventions (*Kulachars*) should be followed or the auspicious moment (*Kshan*) should be regarded. To solve the critical dispute, many Sanskrit scholars were invited. After a long discussion all reached to a conclusion that in such cases priority should be given to *Kshan* and not to *Kulachar* because in any important event like birth or death, the *Kshan* can never be altered. The guiding almanac for this temple is 'Gupta Press Panjika' and here all worships begin with the terminal auspicious time.

PART B : OCCASIONS OF PUBLIC

Beside the worships of ordinary standard, for different other purposes public are found to come in the Kali temple at Kalighat and the temple becomes highly congested. We can classify those purposes in the following way:

---

1. Actual convention around this rite was to penetrate two iron trident on two sides of the belly. Tips of those two tridents were kept enwrapped in a cloth-piece moistened with ghee and set to fire. Incenses used to be added constantly to keep it ablaze. The practice was very popular in Bengal inspite of its tremendous painful sensation. In 1863, this convevntion has been banned with law by the Government.

BROTO (VOW) CELEBRATION

Broto is actually a kind of worship with the speciality that a story is to be heard after the worship. Different interesting stories are associated with each *broto*. These stories tell the usefulness of observing the respective *broto* and evil effects of neglecting them. To maintain fasting in performing *broto* is essential like any other worship.

Types of *broto* vary with the regional norms (*deshachar*) and lineage norms (*Kulachar*). In Kalighat, the popular *brotos* for West Bengal people are celebrated. This has been known from Kalidas Chakraborty, a well-known Priest (*Dasakarme parodorshi brahman*) of Kalighat. For some *brotos* there is no restriction of sex, although these performances are fundamentally meant for the women. In all *brotos*, the theme remains more or less same- 'if the almighty god can be called with deepest heart's sensation, wishes must be fulfilled'.

In Kalighat four to five persons form a group under one Brahmin, who acts as a Priest. The Priest offers homages separately in each name with the mention of *gotro* and finally tells the story for the particular *broto*, for everybody. In total, thirty to forty-five minutes are required for such group.

Public are mostly from nearby locality (within walking distance). For good transport facility many people from distant places (8 to 10 miles away) come here. People of all economic classes are found. Reasons are many.

(a) Some people are accustomed in performing *broto* in Kalighat, traditionally.

(b) Some prefer Kalighat because here two purposes (visiting of the goddess Kali and broto celebration) can be served at a time.

(c) Glory of the area (*pith-mahatma*) is highly emphasized by some persons.

(d) Some people simply imitate others (neighbours and relatives) without any personal reason.

(e) A portion of people for the reason of *Manosik* (ref : Chapter VI,) celebrate *broto* at Kalighat.

(f) Those who try to save time and energy for procuring necessary requirements, they prefer Kalighat because here on the particular dates a group of businessmen wait with all necessaties.

(g) Some come for low expense. As the requirements are supplied in a massive scale, so those are cheaper. For example, pieces of differen fruits are sold in thirty paisa only within a small earthen bowl. At the same time rate of *dakshina* remains low, because Priests treat few people together in each time.

(h) In Kalighat, all the *brotos* are performed in simplest way. Naturally, the elaborate procedure of rigid norms are not to be maintained; piety can be shown by little effort.

A great rush is visible in the temple on particular dates. The regular routine of services in the temple is not at all disrupted. Rather the income rises up on those days because people never go back without visiting or worshipping the great goddess Kali.

Broto types as observed in Kalighat has been noted month-wise, systematically. *Sathi-brahmans, Chhar-brahmans* and even other outsider Brahmins (specialized and non-specialized) act as Priests. Chief Priests or *Misras* of the main temple never involve themselves in this act.

Month Baisakh (April-May)

1. Siva- puja broto

This *broto* is directed to lord Siva. Little girls (unmarried) generally follow this. They come to the *Natmondir* on any convenient day, prepare small phallic emblem of Siva with the soil of Ganges and offer *belpata* and thorn apple's flower. At the end of worship, the emblem is floated in the Ganges.

In the morning such worships take place. One can perform this even more than one day. Termination should be done on fourth year. The aim is to get a husband as good as Siva.

2. Akkhoy-tritia broto

It is performed in the morning of the third lunar day of light fortnight. Both the male and female follow this to satisfy their deceased ancestors by offering hand-fan, new cloth, earthen pitcher (full of water) and fruits (either in full or pieces). Procedure is to worship Radha- Krisna with barley and then to gift the mentioned items to a Brahmin (Priest). Termination takes place after eight successive years. The aim of this *broto* is to pass this life with happiness and to achieve eternal peace after death.

Such *brotos* are performed in *Natmondir* or Siva temples or in *pera-shops* having space.

3. Harish mongol barer broto

It is performed on Tuesday mornings of this month. Married women usually follow this. It can be performed for more than one Tuesday or all Tuesdays by a person, but first Tuesday is compulsory for all performers. *Naibidya* is prepared with sunned rice grains, banana and sweets. Place may be *Natmondir*, *pera*-shops (having space) or road sides. Aim of this particular *broto* is to overcome all grieves of this world.

Month Jaistha (May- June)

1. Joy mongol barer broto

It is performed on Tuesday mornings of this month. Married, unmarried - all may perform this. Some follow for all days. Main gathering is formed by the married women as normally this *broto* is taken after marriage.

Requirements are very simple - fruits, sweets, vermilion, flower and a banana leaf-package containing sixteen rice grains, sixteen barley grains, sixteen paddy and a strand of *durba*. Some use arums (*Kochu*) leaf or jack-fruit leaf instead of banana leaf as per their traditional norm. For the beginners expenses are slight higher.

The *broto* is also performed by the Marwaris, Hindustanis and Biharis. The same Bengali Brahmins help them as Priest. Any suitable place like *Natmondir*, *pera*-shops, road sides is selected. Aim is to overcome all misfortunes of the world.

2. Jamai - sosthi broto or Aranya-sosthi broto

It is performed on the sixth day morning of the light fortnight. After offering homage in *Sosthi-tala*, some married women (specially having children) like to perform this *broto* with fruits, sweets, oil, curd, betel, betel-nut, turmeric etc in the *Natmondir*. Six threads are taken together are rubbed in the turmeric paste and called 'shat suta'. Those taken for the children to tie on their right hand. It is directed for the well being of the children.

3. Subitri chaturdossir broto

It is performed by the Hindu married women in the evening (about 8 p.m.) of the fourteenth lunar day of dark fortnight, usually at the *mayer ghat* and rarely on the *Natmondir*. Hom is an essential part of this *broto*. Sari (red or red bordered white), vermilion, iron bangle, sweet etc have to be offered. Women in cases of their inconveniences may send the offerings through husbands. Celebration of termination is observed on fourteenth year. Objective is to keep the husband alive.

Month Ashar (June - July)

1. Bipattarini broto

This is performed on two days - Tuesday and Saturday, which fall in between the third and nineth lunar day of light fortnight i.e. between 'Car festival' (*sojarath*) and 'Return car festival' (*ultorath*).

In the morning, women (married, unmarried, widow - all) come to Kalighat with thirteen types of fruit in pieces, thirteen betel leaves with thirteen betel-nuts (without catachu and lime), thirteen red threads together with thirteen knots etc. Men are also found to follow this *broto*. Aim is to prevent all dangers in the family.

Any one day of the prescribed two days is to be selected. At the end of the performance, the knotted thread called 'Bipattarini dori' is tied with arm. For the male right arm and for the female the left arm is appropriate. Next year the old *dori* is left in the Ganges and a new one is taken. For the beginners two basketful fruits are required (thirteen types in each). After the performance, one basketful fruits are given to the Priest with *paita* and *dakshina*; other basket is taken by one's own. Suitable places are *Natmondir* and its stairs, spacious *pera*-shops and other suitable places along the road.

Month Bhadra (August - September)

1. Janmastomi broto

It is performed on the eighth lunar day of dark fortnight - from evening to night. Male and female both are found to follow this *broto*. It is believed that this *broto* helps to efface all types of sin.

Worship is offered in Radha-Krisna temple with a *naibidya* made up of different fruits (palmyra is a compulsory item) and coming from the temple the story of the broto is to be heard from the Priest in any suitable place.

2. Ananto chaturdossir broto

This *broto* is celebrated on the fourteenth lunar day of light fortnight in *Natmondir* or any other suitable place. It helps to escape from all sorts of danger.

To Hindustani and Marwari people this *broto* is more popular and they engage Bengali Brahmins as Priest. One should observe *hobiswi*[1] on

1. To eat nothing but boiled sunned rice (cooked in own hand) with ghee only once during a day (during midday).

the proceeding day. If the *broto* is taken once, that should be continued for successive fourteen years. Rigorous rules and regulations are associated with this *broto* but in Kalighat it is performed in a simple form with banana, betel leaf and fruits

Month Kartik (October -November)

1. Itu-puja broto

It starts from the last day of the month Kartik but performed on Sunday mornings of the month *Agrahan* (November - December). It is meant for the women only (both married and unmarried).

On the first day, small *ghots* should be placed (number of *ghots* represent the number of female members in the family) by names in an earthen bowl. Within each *ghot*, plants of paddy, banana, arum and also the flower plants like *asok*, *aparajita* etc are planted. Worship is done by vermilion, *durba*, incense, fruits, sesame etc. Afterwards on each Sunday, water is poured into the *ghots* to keep the plants alive. The bowls are deposited in Siva temples, Radha-Krisna temple etc in lieu of money. Some like to worship in all dates. Story of the *broto* must be heard if worship is done. Finally, on the last day of the month *Agrahan*, the *ghots* are to be immersed into the Ganges. This *broto* signifies riches and happiness for the family. On *Natmondir*, *pera*-shops and in other suitable places these are found to be performed.

Month Agrahan (November - December)

1. Mulasosthi broto

It is rarely performed. The scheduled date is the sixth lunar day of light fortnight. Worship is to be done with radish and after the worship a winnowing fan is to be floated in the Ganges. It is believed that this *broto* helps to keep the children free from diseases. Place of performance is *Natmondir* and other suitable places.

2. Kului mongol barer broto

It is performed on Tuesday mornings and compulsory on every Tuesday for all performers. On *Natmondir* or in any other suitable places this *broto* can be performed simply with a *naibidya* and fruits (a pair of banana and a pair of hog-plum is essential). Merit of this *broto* is to keep all sorts of scandal away.

Month Falgun (Feb.-March)

1. Sivaratri broto

This *broto* is performed at the night of fourteenth day of the dark fortnight. Both men and women have the right to perform. No age, sex or marital status restriction is associated.

Sleeping is prohibited at night. Not only that, water has to be poured four times over the phallic emblem of Siva with milk, curd, ghee and honey respectively. In the morning, the officiating Brahmin (Priest) should be satisfied with sweets and *dakshina*. Thereafter, the performer can take food. The *broto* helps to attain four results at a time e.g. *Dharma* (proper attitude for life), *Artha* (money),*Kama*(passion) and *Moksha*(liberation).

Such *brotos* take place in different Siva temples in Kalighat and also in suitable street corners or vacant places where Brahmins are found carrying the phallic Siva.

Month Chaitra (March -April)

1. Nilsosthi broto

This is usually performed by the women having children, on the last day of the Bengali calender year. Evening is the most precious time. Performer should abstain from food and drink (even water) for the whole day and then pours coconut water over the phallic emblem of Siva.

In all Siva temples the celebration is found. This *broto* ensures the well-being of the children.

Any month.

1. Sankata broto

It is performed on Friday mornings of light fortnight, meant for the Bengali women. There is no bar regarding the marital status. But at present the popularity of this *broto* tends to decrease due to the spread of 'Santoshima broto'.

The performance usually takes place in *Natmondir*. Sour eating is forbidden for the day. Essential items for the worship are, chik-pea (*chhola*) and jaggery. If once this *broto* is started, sixteen times are compulsory. Some continue it until their wishes are fulfilled. At the time of termination, five *Brahmin* boys are to be fed. It is believed that this *broto* performance helps to overcome all anticipated dangers.

2. Santoshima broto

This is performed on Friday noon. All norms are same as that of *Sankata broto*. It has been popular after the name of the feature film where the grace of the goddess had been shown magnificiently.

Bengali, Hindustani, Gujrati, Marwari etc. - to all people, this *broto* had kept strong appeal. Usually the worship takes place in a separate temple known as 'Santoshima temple' situated near *Mayer ghat* and rarely on *Natmondir*. This *broto* aims to achieve riches, happiness and peace of this world.

SPECIAL VISIT OR WORSHIP TO THE GODDESS KALI

There are some specially important dates and occasions which are maintained not only by the Bengalis, but all other people like Hindustanis, Marwaris, South-Indians etc. Special desires (*Sankalpo*) always lie behind such visit and worship.

1. Saturday and Tuesday are considered as unique days for visiting and worshipping the goddess. A great rush of Bengalees is observed irrespective of class and caste.
2. Friday is considered as the most pure day among the South- Indians. They pour milk and coconut water on the feet of the goddess. One half of the coconut is given to the temple and the other half is taken by the devotee. They also offer *pera* as per the convention but usually they do not take the help of *Sathi- brahmans*. They feel more satisfaction by offering personally.
3. Hindustanis and Marwaris prefer Sunday and other holidays (specially mornings). They offer not only homages but also sacrifice goats and sheep.
4. To the Bengalis, it is very auspicious to visit the goddess in the month of *Bhadra*, *Pous* and *Chaitra*. Some people only visit, some offer homages also.
5. In the month of *Baisakh*, there is a system to offer twelve kinds of fruit (*phal*) to the goddess (once on any day of the month). Significance is to achieve good results (*bhalo phal*) in all matters.
6. In the month of *Bhadra* (any day), there is a system to offer palmyra *(tal)* to the goddess. Significance is to restore 'rythm' of the family *(sangsarer tal)* i.e. unhappiness, sorrow, danger etc. are supposed to be minimized.
7. In the month of *Agrahan* (any day), the goddess Kali is to be worshipped with newly grown rice grains. This signifies the 'food security' for the family.

8. In the month of *pous* (any day), the goddess is worshipped with radish and range. It is a symbol of 'economic security'.
9. During eclipse, touching the image and offering of *bhog* or *puja* is strictly prohibited. When the eclipse gets over, local pious people (mostly old men and women) take bath in the Ganges and offer homage to the great goddess Kali to get rid of pollution, created by the eclipse.
10. To have a bath in *Gangasagar*[1] on a specific day of the month *Pous* (*Pous-sankranti*) is considered as pious act. Therefore many local people as well as tourists (mainly non-Bangalis like Hindustani, Punjabi, Gujrati, South-Indian, Marwari etc.) in the way to and from *Gangasagar*, offer worship in the Kali temple. Again those who fail to go to the *Gangasagar* inspite of strong desire, take bath in the Ganges at Kalighat and offer homages to the main temple as an substitute of the said pious act.

On this day, some people are found to make rafts by banana-bark and offer those to the main temple with fruits. Finally, the rafts are floated in the Ganges.

11. At the end of the occasion *ambubachi*, Bengali widows from the neighbouring areas come to have a sacred dip in the Ganges of Kalighat. After that some of them offer homages in the main temple; some perform elaborate worships in the *Natmondir* by the help of specialized Brahmins. Again some widows offer milk with mango on the first and last days of *Ambubachi*
12. On the first day of the month of *Baisakh* (Bengali new-year's day) the temple remains overcrowded by the public from dawn to night. People have to stand in queue for entering into the temple-campus. Police force, appointed by the Committee regulates the rush. Batches are used by the *shebaits* and the personnel of the temple. The northern gate of the temple campus, known as 'Birla-gate' is kept open for this day. The strength of the crowd decreases in the evening, although the flow is found to be continued up to mid-night.

    Besides the sacred visit and worship, businessmen make a ceremonial renewal of their stock-book on this day. The performance is known as *Khata mohorat*. Brahmins of different category (even the *shebaits*) are involved in this performance. The convention is to draw an image of god *Ganesh* (a paste made up of ghee and vermilion is used for drawing) on the first page of the new

1. Confluence spot of the Ganges and Bay of Bengal.

ledger. Also the impression of *Asok stambha*[1] from one rupee coin or *mohor*[2] is depicted by immersing the particular surface of the said coin into the same paste and pressing against the page. On the top of the page the sentence Sri Sri Ganeshay Namoo' is written in Bengali. Finally the ledger is touched at the feet of the goddess.

13. *Akkhoy tritia* is an auspicious date. Those who fail to renew their stock-book on the first day of the month *Baisakh*, use this day. Some people prefer this day particularly to avoid the jostle of the crowd. However, morning is the best time for such performances.

    Gods namely *Ganesh* and *Satyanarayan* are worshipped by the public on this day. *Sathi- brahmans, Chhar-brahmans* and other specialized Brahmins act as Priests.

    Ancestor-worship is another practice of this day. Pitcher, hand-fan, sacred book like 'Gita' etc are offered to appease the deceased forefathers. Some like to sacrifice animals on this very day.

14. Phalaharini *Kali-puja* and *Ratonti Kali-puja* are two special Kali worship dates. Usually public do not follow this. Still sometimes some interested persons come. For example, those who traditionally perform this worship in home, in cases of inconvenience they come in Kalighat to keep the norm. Such performances take place in the late evening on *Natmondir*. Duration is generally three hours. The party may or may not bring their own Priest. Immolation depends on the respective lineage- norm. For the last few years no such worship is found.

15. Those who have the business of machinery but unable to perform a worship in the house, come in Kalighat on the day of *Biswakarma* worship with some handy tools and equipments. Such worships are performed in *Natmondir* by the specialized Brahmins. Some people buy idols of *Biswakarma* for keeping them in their workshops.

16. Fifteen days before *Mahalaya*, the crowd in the temple becomes scanty. This is because of '*Tarpan*' i.e. the performance that occur on the day of *Mahalaya* (ref : Chapter VI). Those who perform *Tarpan*, abide the last fifteen days as a period of pollution (*asauch*) and so do not come to the temple.

---

1. It refers to the stone pillars of King Ashok on which his edicts are inscribed. It is the official emblem of present day India.

2. An old day's gold coin of one rupee denomination.

17. In the month of *Aswin*, from 6th day to 10th day of light fortnight (*Durga-puja*) the temple remains highly crowded. Maximum concentration is seen on 8th day. The total gathering is shared by the Bengali, Hindusthani and Marwari people. Besides, from Ist day to 9th day (i.e. during *Navoratri*) a craze among the Hindustanis and Marwaris is observed. They engage Brahmins for worship, reading of sacred book 'chondi' (*chondi-path*) and *hom*. The temple remains open round the clock from 7th day to 9th day during *Durga -Puja.*

18. On the day of annual *Kali-puja* in the month of *Kartik*, public (mainly Bengali) concentration gets tremendous high in the evening. Eight hundred to thousand and even over animal sacrifices occur. Some perform their traditional *Kali-puja* in *Natmondir*. The temple remains open for the whole night.

19. No special gathering is marked in the Kali temple on the day of *Saraswati*'s worship.

20. On the occasion named *Ambaruni*, some people (Bengali) take bath in the Ganges and offer worship to the great goddess with mango.

21. During *Navoratri* i.e. Ist day to 9th day of the light fortnight of the month *Chaitra*, Hindustani and Marwari concentration becomes markedly high. Distant people too send their own Priests in Kalighat. They stay in rented rooms and perform worship, *Chondi-path, hom* etc alike the *Navoratri* of the month *Aswin. Chondi-path* cannot be done at night. *Hom* can be done both day and night.

22. On *Buddha-purnima*, a few people come in the temple for the ceremonial renewal of their stock-book because it is another auspicious date.

23. On the last day of the month of *Chaitra*, some people like to offer pitchers with water to please the dead ancestors.

SPECIAL PERFORMANCES IN OTHER SACRED SPOTS

There are various other sacred spots in Kalighat where public rush following special days or auspicious time for special performances. As they never forget to offer homage to the goddess Kali, so huge public penetration is noted in the main temple which is an encouraging factor for the *paladars*.

1. Monosha-puja

According to different regional norms *(deshachar)*, people (especially females) come to worship the goddess Monosha with milk and banana. These worships are performed at *Monosha tala*. People migrated from

East Bengal (Present 'Bangladesh') worship the goddess in the month of *Sraban* whereas the original residents of West Bengal follow the month of *Bhadra*.

2. Sosthi-puja

According to different regional and lineage norms worship of goddess Sosthi differ. People of West Bengal follow six such worships as mentioned below :

Sitol sosthi in the month of Magh,
Asok sosthi in the month of *Chaitra*,
Jamai sosthi or *Aranya sosthi* in the month of *Jaistha*,
Lunthon sosthi in the month of *Sraban*,
Chapeta sosthi or *Chapra sosthi* in the month of *Bhadra*,
Durga sosthi in the month of *Aswin*.

East Bengal people worship this goddess only once a year - that is the *Jamai sosthi*. Sosthi's worship is done by the married women especially who have children. Local people as well as people from distant areas, irrespective of their economic class come in Kalighat. There are also no restriction regarding *sadhoba* and *bidhoba*, no age bar, even no prohibition for barren or carrying women.

Although the edict is to bathe in the Ganges prior to worship offering, but very few women follow this. Most of them have their bath in home, then wearing a washed sari come to the *Sosthi-tala* with necessary requirement. The performance is for the well-being of the children, praying their long lives.

Some ladies try to offer worship strictly within the particular moment *(Kshan);* others maintain only the day. Again some, instead of items, offer only money kept for this purpose. The main concentration is observed during the morning. Priestess of *Sosthi-tala* officiates. Peddlers selling iron -bangles, vermilion, *alta-pata* etc. are found arund the spot.

3. Sitola-puja

Public worship the goddess Sitola at *Sosthi-tala* as this altar is also the abode of Sitola. At the recovery from diseases like Pox and Measels, people touch money to the head of the patient and in one convenient day offer worship with that money because it is believd that the presiding deity of those diseases is the goddess Sitola.

4. Dasohara and Ganga -puja

Both the occasions fall on the same day of the month of *Jaistha*. For *Dasohara*, people take sacred bath in the Ganges and offer ten types of fruit. *Sathi-brahmans* help them. For *Ganga-puja*, a few images of the goddess Ganga are brought by some Brahmins at the *mayer ghat*. Public offer their homages there by the help of those Brahmins. Worship requirements are coconut, sugar and sweets.

There is no restriction of sex for these worships. Though the worships continue upto the evening starting from the early morning, but the main concentration is observed in the morning.Usually each worship takes five to seven minutes to be completed. Mainly Bengalis are interested, some Hindustanis are also found to participate.

5. Chhat-puja

This occasion takes place in the month of *Kartik*. It is strictly restricted among the Hindustanis. Before sun-rise they worship at the bank of the Ganges with *chhatu*, jaggery and banana. Normally they bring their own Priests; otherwise appoint *Sathi-brahmans*. It is actually a worship of God Sun.

6. Janmastomi

In the month of *Bhadra*, centering the occasion *Janmastomi* the Radha-Krisna temple (within the campus) becomes overcrowded. Some perform the *broto* of *Janmastomi* (ref : p. 94) and some simply offer worship with butter and sugar-candy. From the evening of the particular day to next day dawn, those worships or *broto* celebrations continue. Bengalis, Hindustanis and Marwaris are the participants.

7. Barer-puja

Worships for the god Soni take place on Saturday evenings and such worships are commonly designated as *barer-puja*. The place of performance is neither *Natmondir* nor any other places within the temple boundary because it is believed by the people that the *Dakshinakali* (i.e. the Kali of Kalighat) is the preceptor of the god Soni. Therefore the worships take place in the Soni temple near the *Mayer ghat*. Also a lot of Brahmins sit with enframed pictures of god Soni in different places around the Kali temple to perform Soni worship on behalf of the public. Mainly Bengali, Hindustani and Marwari people come to Kalighat (regularly and occasionally) for this worship. They always worship the goddess Kali at first.

8. Satyanarayan-puja

This worship may be done in the evening of any full- moon. Radha-Krisna temples, Siva temples etc. are the places for such worships. After the worship, a story *(broto-katha)* has to be heard like that of the *broto* celebrations.

Hindustani people also perform this like Bengalis but they follow no specific date. On any day they are found to offer worship towards the god Satyanarayan. Another peculiarity is that they do not prepare *Sinni*[1]; instead they use a dry substance like *chhatu*.

9. Mahalaya

From the dawn, people (males are greater in number) come to the Ganges for the performance named *Tarpan*. Some of them maintain the auspicious moment strictly; others do not. Brahmins from different places throng at Kalighat to meet the great demand of the day. A Brahmin handles four to six persons together in performing *Tarpan*. Fifty paisa to two rupees per head is claimed by the Brahmins as *dakshina*.

People have their baths in the Ganges before or after the Tarpan as they like. Some only touch the Ganges-water and sprinkle that over the head; some wait for the tide to get fresh water.

System of *Tarpan* also exists among the Punjabis, Gujratis and South-Indians. But in Kalighat the crowd comprises only of Bengalis and Hindusthanis. Local people as well as the people from adjacent areas irrespective of Caste and class come here. A large number of people put emphasis on the glory of the particular area.

10. On Tuesdays and Saturdays, reading of Sacred 'chondi' by Brahmins are frequently observed. Not only in *Natmondir*, but also in rented room and other suitable space such performances are found. Time is morning or noon. Bengali, Hindustani and Marwari people are generally fond of this performance. A Brahmin is appointed by each devotee on behalf of his family.

---

1. It is a mixture (paste like) made of milk, wheat, banana, jaggery, coconut etc., essentially used for the worship of the god Satyanarayan.

CHAPTER 6

Role of the Kali Temple in Dasakarma, Sraddha and other Rites

Among the Hindus, the life span of an individual (male[1]) is marked by certain rites of passage which are ten in number and known as *Dasa Karma.* They are performed for 'this worldly benefit' and one extra rite namely *Sraddha* is performed for 'other worldly benefit'. *Dasa Karma* practice is the formal prescription of ·e Hindu society. The Brahmins and the upper Castes 'must follow these but for the lower Castes all are not 'must'. Practically the Brahmins and upper Caste too do not perform each of these and the lower Castes perform only a few of them. However, the *Dasa Karma* as 'ideal forms' are as follows :

1. Vivaha : Marriage.

2. Garvadhan : After marriage, at the time of first monthly course (within sixteen days) on an 'even number' date the newly married couple have to perform this rite. At night, uttering Sanskrit spells the husband touches the vagina of wife spreading his right hand over the shoulder of wife from her back. In conclusion she drinks a sacred mixture, *pancho-gabya.* This performance before the first sexual intercourse is to achieve a good male child.

3. Punsaban : On the third month of the first pregnancy on the due date according to almanac the husband has to perform *Briddhi-Sraddha.* At the end of the rite husband keeps

1. As our society is patriarchial, so males are mainly emphasized for the rites of passage.

a few drops of juice out of the buds of banyan leaves below wife's nose, while she smells it. This is done for the good health, good fate and long life of the coming child who is expected to be a male issue.

4. Simantayan: (In short called Simantan) — On the fourth or sixth or eighth month of the first pregnancy, this rite is done. The pregnant woman takes her bath on the date as per the almanac and wears a silk cloth. *Yajna* is performed and the husband ties two *Yajna dumur* (a kind of fig) along with neem, mustard seed, *bhela*-fruit and bach i.e. dried roots of betel plant in a silk thread and making a garland of those, places that garland at the neck of his wife. Later on he takes a porcupine needle and touches it thrice on the forehead of the spouse. It is done for the same purpose as in *Punsaban*.

5. Panchamrita 'o'Sadhbha-kshan : — *Panchamrita* and *Sadbhakshan* are supposed to be done on the fifth and the ninth month of the pregnancy respectively. But usually both are done together at the same date guided by the almanac. *Dahi* (curd), *dudh*(milk), *ghee* (butter oil), *chini*(sugar) and *madhu*(honey) - these five articles are mixed togehter to make *Panchamrita.* In the morning the pregnant woman has to wear a new sari given by her husband or father -in-law and to sit on a flat wooden seat *(piri)* and to drink a few drops of *Panchamrita.* At noon along with three or five married women *(ayo)* of the same caste she takes her meal with fish and *payesh* together. One male child of husband's lineage feed some *payesh* to the pregnant woman first, then the meal is taken. A lamp is lit before and a conch is blown. This is done to purify the child inside the womb. A long life of the male issue is expected.

6. Niskraman : — After birth of the male issue, on the third day *(tritia)* of the third light fortnight *(suklo paksha)* the baby is bathed in the morning and in the evening the mother along with the son stands at the right side of her husband and looks at moon ritually. By this performance the future of the son is made clean like the light of the moon.

7. Namkaran : One year after the birth of the son, this rite is performed for the name selection.

8. Annaprasan: During the sixth or eighth month the first rice eating of the son takes place through a ceremony as per an auspicious date of almanac. This ceremony is elaborate and composed of many rites. At first the *Briddhi-Sraddha* is performed by the father in the morning. Then the other rites are followed.

9. Churakaran : This is the shaving of the head-hair of the male issue which is performed ritually at the first or third year after birth as per the auspicious date in the almanac. On this occasion also, in the morning *Briddhi-Sraddha* is performed by the father. Mother sits on a mat of *Kush*-grass keeping the son on her lap at the left side of her husband. The barber shaves the head- hair and leaves that either in a bamboo groove or in a pit.

10. Upanayan : On the seventh, ninth, thirteenth and fifteenth years, the ceremony of sacred thread taking is performed. The last limit is fifteen years and three months. The ceremony is meant for the Brahmin and Kshtriya castes. For the Brahmins this is considered as the second birth, which is spiritual. The *Briddhi-Sraddha* is performed in the morning and almost all the rites performed in the marriage (for the groom) are observed here. The head is shaved and the ear- lobes are pierced - these are in addition, of course. The dress is at first the saffron coloured *dhuti* and *chador* dyed by the dust of a earth called *gerua mati* dissolved in water. Thus dying is supposed to be done at home. Nextly, silk made *dhuti* and *chador* are worn which is called *rajbesh*. The ceremony ends in a feast. The new Brahmin has to be confined in a room for three successive days and during this period he is not permitted to look at the sun, at the face of woman (except mother) and not even at men of other castes. On the third day before sun-rise parents take him to the nearest river for a sacred dip and there his dress is left in water and he is dressed in *rajbesh*. After coming back to home he resumes to his normal life.

The 'other worldly rite' is known as the *Sraddha*, where the water and rice (in case of Brahmin, cooked rice) is offered to the dead ancestors. The *Sraddha* rite is of four types.

(a) Adya-Sraddha : It is the first *Sraddha* rite which is performed a few days after the death of a person.

(b) Batsarik or Sapindakaran: This *Sraddha* rite takes place at the completion of one year. It includes twelve offerings for each of the twelve months in a year in addition to one half yearly special and one yearly special. The *Sraddha* for each month may be done separately being called as *Masik-ekadrista*.

(c) Parba-Sraddha : It is the offering for the deceased ancestors in every year on the day of *Mahalaya*. This rite is locally known as *Tarpan*.

(d) Briddhi-Sraddha : It is the offering for the deceased ancestors before the rites named *Annaprasan*, *Upanayan* and *Vivaha*, aiming at procreation (*briddhi*) of family members. Beside these four types of Sraddha rites, there is another brief *Sraddha* rite which is meant for the married daughters. Married daughters are supposed to perform that on the fourth day of death. This rite is known as *Choturthi*.

As a matter of fact, each rite of *Dasa Karma* and *Sraddha* requires heavy expense as different facets of expenditure (i.e. to employ the Priest, to collect necessary articles, to invite the relatives and neighbours, to organize a feast etc) are involved. The rites are also overwhelmed with various strict rules and regulations (*bidhi-nisedh*). It is quite impossible for a person to omit these conventional rites because they basically act as the processes of social sanction, without which immense criticism and bad reputation are created in the society. The associated strict rules and regulations get simplified and expense is reduced if the rites are performed at Kalighat. At the same time people restrain from criticism. Thus, it is strange to notice that in a highly organized social-cultural pattern, many exceptions and deviations are permitted after the glory of the goddess Kali in the specially significant holy place (sanctum sanctorium). The most important role of Kalighat has been observed in relaxing the rigidity of Hindu rites, in the perspective of present day situation.

In Kalighat, *Dasa Karma, Sraddha* and all other rites are performed by the local Brahmins. Most of such Brahmins are non-specialized *Sathi-brahmans* with inadequate knowledge. They themselves are well-aware about their shortcomings, still dare to pursue in the profession as it is believed that all errors and ommissions are minimized in a *pith* by the majesty of the sacred place. Further, as they serve at a very low rate so public prefer them. The truely qualified Brahmins (*Dasakarme parodor-shi brahman)* criticize them as degraded and taunt with the term bhatbaun.

The specialized Brahmins are all Bengalis, linguistically.Non-specialized Brahmins belong to various linguistic groups. Public generally seek Brahmins of own group but low cost performances of Kalighat rarely follow any preference rule.

An agency system is found to be present. Agents have to find out parties and supply them to the Brahmins to avail commissions. They may belong to any Caste and community and there is no specific rate regarding their commission. The matter is mutually negotiated between the Brahmin and agent.

Usually the Brahmins who remain in this line as regular full-timers, keep a set of cheap-rate unperishable items i.e. the articles commonly used in different rites. They receive money placing those items before the parties. Such a practice is locally known as *mullo dhorey neoa.*[1] Again the part-timer Brahmins often borrow those in lieu of money.

Majority of the people contact a Brahmin of Kalighat and put all responsibilities upon him. Charge of the Priest varies according to the nature of the rites as well as the span of time. Less money means less rituals and rapid performance. Priests are in the habit of cutting short the rituals in case of small payments. Sometimes they also contact with two or more parties simultaneously and perform the rite in one sitting with smaller contribution from each party. The involved parties too are benefitted, economically. However, the rates are highly flexible and involves considerable bargaining.

---

1. In each Hindu rite, many articles after being offered become Priest's property. So to avoid a fresh purchase, the Priest places the articles from his stock taking a nominal charge. In this system, on one hand performer's money is saved to some extent and on the other hand, Priest receives cash payment; but the custom is fully obeyed. Thus, the practice has been very popular.

Some auspicious dates are noted in the almanac for different rites and the rites are supposed to be performed within some prescribed hours. Therefore, the performances which occur other than such fixed dates and hours, can expect a little more time from the Brahmins. There are some people who come to Kalighat for rites, but to them expense is not at all a factor; they hire rented rooms and many of them employ their known specialized Priest with higher remuneration.

The fixed clientele (*jajmans*) when come to the *shebaits* for the performance of rites, they hand-down the responsibility to their respective *Chhar-brahmans*. *Shebaits* become personally involved only in three situations.

(a) When the party is very kith and kin.

(b) When the party is going to spend a very large amount.

(c) When the party is very renowned or influential.

There are some specific places for specific performances. The rites differ from each other in nature and features, details of which have been furnished hereafter in a systematic way.

PART A : DASA KARMA

Vivaha

Though *Vivaha* i.e. marriage is the first important rite among all other rites of Hindu, it has been forbidden at Kalighat. The temple authority does not acknowledge any marriage performed at Kalighat because most of them are not social; there is a good admixture of fraud and illegal cases. Some cases are fugitive. To the authority, registered marriages are of higher merit for those who want low cost legal marriage; nobody should come in Kalighat for the performance of this particular rite. But in fact a large number of marriage rites are noticed in Kalighat (they never occur on *Natmondir* like the past days) which get sanction thereafter socially and sacramentally. Undermentioned three types of marriages have been identified here.

(1) Marriages with financial difficulties

This sort of marriages follow the exact date and time (*Kshan*) as chalked in the almanac. In a rented room, in the presence of relatives such marriages take place. The Brahmin (Priest)performs the essential rituals in miniature form. He by himself arranges for all necessary articles and equipments. His charge stands between Rs. 50/- and Rs.100/-. No barber is called.

Those who want to perform this rite in a little better way hire a room or rooms for a few more hours. They try to contact a sincere Brahmin by paying a bit more. As the Priest spends more time, his claim varies from Rs. 200/- to Rs. 250/-. Besides, there are other expenses e.g. cost of dress, decoration, house-rent (in terms of hour), feast etc.

Local house owners let out their spare rooms. Some enterprises have come forward with illumination and cookery. Poor people of adjoining locality come for availing such services, at low cost.

(2) Marriages without financial difficulties

These are locally called as *golmaler biye*. Reasons are as follows :

(a) When consent is not available from the guardians of both the parties simultaneously or where one or more influential person of the family objects.

(b) When there lies social stigma. For example, in case of marriage of a pregnant girl or where marriage of a girl is going to be resisted by the local rowdy boys due to some reasons or other.

Economically weaker and middle class people are usually involved in such type of marriage. Candidates try to maintain the prescribed date and time of almanac, sometimes that may not be possible.

(3) Clandestine marriages

These are locally known as *palano biye*, as the couple flee from their residences. This type is considered to be the most degraded type because no proper date or time is followed; no ritual is maintained. Within a short while, uttering a few mystic words by the help of *Sathi-brahman*, the couple inter-change their flower garlands and thereafter husband puts vermilion on the hair -part of the wife. Ten to fifteen minutes are required and expense varies within Rs. 10/-.to Rs.25/-. This sort of marriage is practised mostly by the uneducated poor people.

Low cost and easy social sanction are the special attractions for marriages at Kalighat. Here inter-Caste, intra- family, inter-province and even inter-ethnic marriages are practised.

Kalighat is also popular to the people other than Bengali. For instance, Hindustani people often marry in Kalighat. They generally pick up Brahmins (Priest) of their own group to avoid the difference in sacred formula (*vivaha-mantra*). Nepali and Gujrati people also come but very rarely. Many Rajasthani people (they possess a sword) after marriage come here for a sacred visit. Beside these, many local Bengali Hindu (irrespective of caste and class)take their newly married daughters-in-law in the temple to visit the goddess Kali before entering in the house. They circumambulate the temple once or thrice or seven times as per respective likings.

Panchamrita, Simantayan and Sadhbhakshan :

These are not found to be performed at Kalighat. A few local families take their pregnant daughters-in-law to the temple for sacred visit on specific auspicious dates. Some of them before the performance *Sadhbhakshan* in home, offer worship to the goddess Kali and go round the temple.

For Haldar-lineage, there is a custom to take the mother and the new-born baby in *Sosthi-tala* to offer worship to the goddess Sosthi. At present as most of the mothers are unwilling to go to that spot, so gradually the system is going to be abolished.

Annaprasan

Some favourable dates are chalked in the almanac for this rite. On those days *paladar* sells some portion of *payesh* (which is served regularly to the goddess Kali and *Vairav* Nakuleswar) specially, as 'Annoprosad'. This *annoprosadl*[1] is very important because it is pushed into the mouth of the baby and that fulfils the rite without any elaboration and heavy expense.

People under four categories use this *annoprosad* as an alternative of *Annaprasan* rite.

(i) The poor people of the locality and neighbourhood who cannot afford the expense of the rite.

(ii) The people who are afraid to follow the rite having received certain hindrances in past.

(iii) Who have practised to use *annoprosad* for a few generations. This may be accompanied with *Annaprasan* rite in the home.

(iv) Who have no system of *Annaprasan* rite in the family but interested to follow this rite like others.

---

1. It is different from that of *prosad* i.e. the *bhog* which is found to be sold in all days and contained not only the *payesh* but every item those are offered to the goddess Kali . Although the *bhog* is considered as very sacred, but that can not serve the pupose of 'Annoprosad'

In Kalighat, performance of *Annaprasan* rite at low cost is not found. That is why to the poor people *annoprosad* is more convenient. Again those who by tradition perform the rite in sacred places, they follow it elaborately with proper proceeding. Naturally cost gets high.

For elaborate performance of *Annaprasan* at least three hours are needed as it includes many a rituals like *Briddhi- Sraddha, Kusundika* (in case of caste 'Brahmin') etc. Expenses remains within Rs. 300/- to Rs.400/-. In the morning, roughly between 7 a.m. and 12 p.m. *Annaprasan* rites have to be performed either in *Natmondir* or in rented rooms. People who cannot rely upon the Brahmins of Kalighat, bring their own family-Priest or any well-known efficient Brahmin. Such people usually buy each and every required item with special attention.

Churakaran :

The first time head-hair removal of a child follows an auspicious scheduled date as per the almanac. So on such dates, a large number of people are found to perform this rite. Those who miss the specific day, try to come on Saturday or Tuesday. Some families abide their own traditional norms for this rite. Accordingly, they come at the completion of thirteen days, one month, six months or one year after the birth of the child.

The *Churakaran* rites performed at Kalighat are the manifestations of either family custom or *Manosik* celebration. Conception of special sanctity (*pith-mahatma*) acts behind such performance.

However, the rite is very simple-the cost is not at all high. At first a *Sathi-brahman* is selected. After his performance (spell utterance for about five minutes), a local barber removes the hair. Those who over-emphasize the sanctity of the place, but cannot keep faith over *Sathi-brahmans*, they engage their own competent Priest. No preference regarding the barber has been noticed. After the removal, some carry a little portion of hair (sanctified by incantation) and put that to *Monosha-tala* by paying one rupee and twenty-five paisa.

The barbers earn Re. 1/-to Rs.3/- forcing the party. Rate of the Priests (*Sathi-brahmans*) are also not fixed. They receive Rs.3/- to Rs.5/- as per their ability to haggle. *Churakaran* rite never takes place on *Natmondir* proper. Although the ideal place of performance is the yard of *Monosha-tala*, but performances are often seen at the road sides or at the bank of the Ganges.

The rite is more popular among the Hindi speaking population (i.e. Bihari, Marwari etc.) than the Bengalis. They call the performance as 'Muran'. Saturdays and Tuesdays are preferred. South-Indians too like such removal at Kalighat. People from lower economic category are greater in number. After the rite, parties offer homage to the great goddess Kali.

Upanayan :

Specific auspicious dates identified by the almanac are strictly followed. The common places performance are *Natmondir*, other suitable places inside the temple campus, rented rooms, bank of the Ganges, even the narrow space aside any shop. Morning is the best time but due to shortage of favourable dates, those are continued upto early afternoon.

At present candidates are of older age-group. Men of 30/40 years are not uncommon. Even there are instances of performing the rite on the day before the marriage. People from all economic classes are found; of course there is difference in spending.

First ritual of *Upanayan* is to remove the head hair and pierce the ear-lobe by a barber. Then to have a bath in the Ganges. Nextly, a saffron coloured *dhuti-chador* is to be put on and the Priest ties *durba* with yellow thread in the right wrist of the candidate. Shoulders remain covered with a napkin (*gamchha*) over the neck. *Kush*-grass plaited *paita* is worn over the chest and back diagonally. *Briddhi-Sraddha, Kusundika* etc. are the other rituals. A guardian (father, elder brother or uncle) has to be present there to worship the deceased ancestors. It is locally called as *jal dan*. The main white holy thread is worn with the help of the Priest and the face of the candidate is covered by a *chador*. A bag for begging (*jhuli*) and a holy stick (*dondi*) is given to him. He is then supposed to go to the Ganges to float the stick (*dondi*). Mother or a motherly woman accompanies him at this time.

Thus, the sacrament of wearing the holy thread is over. The candidate gets the permission to remove the eye-cover and he is believed to be sanctified. This is the time to wear new white *dhuti*, *panjabi*, flower garland and *topor*.

At a time 2 to 3, even 4 to 5 candidates (who may or may not be related persons) sit for the rite, to a Priest. Because on one hand candidates demand for the low cost and on the other hand, by any means this rite can not be performed within short time. Priests and the parties both are equally benefitted through such a system.

More than one hour is required for this rite. The minimum remuneration of Priest stands at Rs. 100/-. So if four candidates come together,

Rs.25/- per head is possible. In fact per candidate Rs. 20/- to Rs. 30/- is claimed and the total time remains one hour. Brokers (*dalals*) for bringing the cases to the Brahmin get a commission (per head).

Those who perform the rite in a better manner, contact reliable Priests before the scheduled date. Requirements are collected by their own effort generally. As the Priests get more money, so they allot more time. Such performances follow the actual procedure, therefore need about four hours. Such high-rate *Upanayan* rites take place on *Natmondir* or in rented rooms. Few instances are as follows : Manik Lal Haldar (an old renowned *shebait*, vide Genealogy.2) on 4.6.81 acted as Priest for six candidates together in Rs. 450/-. Nanda Lal Ghosal (a *dasakarme parodorshi brahman*) on the same date was performing *Upanayan* in Rs. 250/- for two brothers.

Different factors work behind the coming.

(a) Lower income group prefer Kalighat for low expense. Such candidates follow the proper age. Deviation if observed is for economic crisis.

(b) Solvent people come for the underwritten reasons :

(i) Kalighat possesses certain advantages e.g. instead of head hair removal, money can be offered. One has not to pass three successive days in a closed room. At a older age the performance stands as a matter of shame. So unobservedly such candidates may come in Kalighat to perform the rite.

(ii) To many up-to-date westernized boys, *Upanayan* rite is a matter of hampering status and prestige. But by the compulsion of tradition bound guardians they undergo the performance with minimum exposure. To many guardians even, this traditional norm is unnecessary and unjustified but for prejudices and superstitions they do not dare to violate the norm. They like Kalighat to make it simplified.

(iii) Some busy guardians want to avoid the embarrassment of collecting different necessary articles. Kalighat saves their valuable time and energy.

(iv) Middle class income group of the city often faces acute problem of searching a separate room to confine the candidate for three days. Such space problem can be solved by performing the rite at Kalighat.

(v) Some people put extra emphasis on the special glory of the place. So they prefer to perform the rite at Kalighat. Some undergo *Manosik* for it and for others it is the family custom.

Performing the rite at Kalighat, people may arrange for a feast in the house. There was a system of taxation chalked by the Committee for *Upanayan* being locally called as *masul* which is no longer insisted upon. The rite seems to have lost its actual significance. Now it is just to maintain the norm - a compromise between the old and new value system. Purification of body and mind is no longer the main inspiration.

PART B : SRADDHA

In *Sraddha* rite there are different gradations of offering. For example, *Tin-dan* where three items namely land, water and cloth are offered. This is the simpliest form of offering. *Chhoy- dan* where six items namely land, mat (*ason*), water, cloth, rice grains (*anno*), lamp (*dip*) are offered. Poor people follow either of these two types. Priest arranges for all requirements and receive money in lieu i.e. *mullo dhorey neoa* system is followed.

Besides these two gradations, there are many expensive offerings e.g. *Solo-dan* (offering of sixteen items), *Til Kanchan* (offering of sesame and gold), *Brisotsarga* (offering of a studbull), *Dansagar* (a lot of offerings) and so on. Affluent people follow these expensive forms which are no doubt elaborate in procedure. They have to perform such rite in Kalighat either for their traditional family custom or due to unfavourable cultural atmosphere of the house. Some are also afraid of making arrangements by their own.

Priests have no fixed rate for any form. The expense for simple *Tin-dan* varies from Rs.10/- to Rs.50/-, whereas the expense of elaborate forms vary within Rs.200/- to Rs.500/-. The expensive performances are less frequent.

Sraddha rite can be performed at any day as per the respective lineage norms e.g. on tenth day or thirteenth day or after one month from the date of death. If due to certain reason,the party misses the particular day, the situation is called *potit*. Those *potit* cases have to be performed either on eleventh lunar day of dark fortnight (*Krisna ekadosi*) or on the day of new-moon (*amabasya*). Same prescription is followed in cases of *potit Batsarik* or *potit Choturthi.*

According to 'Purohit darpan'[1], *Sraddha* rites should be started from 8.26 a.m. So after that time, any time the rite can be started and can be

1. The manual which the Priests follow on all India basis.

continued upto 1 p.m. or 2 p.m. *Pindo-dan* is an essential feature of the *Sraddha rite. Pindo* is a small round ball made by rice-grains, ghee and banana. It is offered for the soul of the dead person. Next performance is *ekadasha* without which the whole rite becomes meaningless. Bed, cloth, *gamchha* are offered either in single or tripple in the name of Kali, Ganges and Nakuleswar.

Eldest son of the deceased person possesses the right to perform the *Sraddha* rite. Otherwise as Manu's[1] son Bhabadev has simplified the rules and regulations, so anybody can perform this funeral rite, even the married daughters.

Specialized Priests usually do not agree to undertake the low cost performances. They are interested in high-cost performances as those involve monetary benefit as well as professional satisfaction. Non-specialized Priests (*Sathi- brahmans* and other Oriya Brahmins) serve the people within short time in low expense. People from nearby areas say within 8 to 10 miles come for this purpose.

Adya-Sraddha if performed in proper way, takes roughly three to four hours. A short cut performance requires twenty minutes to one hour approximately. *Batsarik-Sraddha* needs at least one hour more as it includes fourteen separate *Sraddha* rites. Expense is obviously higher. Many people to avoid the heavy expense at a time, perform *Masik ekadrista* on each month. Thus expense is reduced to a great extent at the time of *Batsarik*, which is supposed to be performed on 11th day of dark fortnight or new-moon. For *Masik ekadrista* no fixed date is stipulated, although they have to be performed on 11th day of dark fortnight or new-moon. About one hour is spent against Rs.25/- if this monthly rite is to be done in proper way. Its brief form requires about 10 to 15 minutes with Rs 5/-.

On *Mahalaya*, people (both male and female) offer sesame and water to please the deceased ancestors at the bank of Ganges. This *Parba-Sraddha* or *Tarpan* starts from early morning and continues upto noon. Standing in knee-deep water *Sathi-brahmans* help the public in their performances. To have a bath before and after the rite is the norm. But all

1. The famous law giver of Hindus who lived probably in first Century B.C. 'Manu Smriti' tells about the laws of inheritance, marriage etc. of the ancient Hindus.

people do not go to the Ganges even-they perform the rite in dry places e.g. sweet shops, street corners etc. The orthodox persons try to follow the particular auspicious hours. They prepare a dough kneading rice- grains, banana, sesame, ghee and honey together. Hindustani people use flour or wheat instead of rice. About five to six minutes are consumed and one to three rupees are spent. The Brahmins usually take 3 or 4 candidates in a batch and recite sacred formula in Sanskrit, invoking the deceased ancestors to accept the offerings.

Shebaits are Brahmins by themselves, still they take the help of the professional persons who may or not be their house-Priest. A few of them are the exceptions. They themselves perform the rite reading from the sacred scriptures.

As the Ganges near the Kali temple has shrunken greatly and the water remains dirty for most of the time, so some people do not like the place. Still many people prefer the area for its extra holiness. However, the crowd forms only by Bengali and Hindustani people.

PART C : OTHER RITES

Besides the 'rites of passage' i.e. *Dasa Karma* and *Sraddha*, some other rites are found to be performed in Kalighat which have been discussed below.

Bidyarambha

It is the sacrement of initiation into one's studies. The best time is after the age of five years and three months but within seven years. Hindu almanac points out some auspicious dates for this purpose. The particular day of *Saraswati-puja* is one of them. But in fact this rite is performed very rarely at Kalighat.

The procedure is nothing but to bring a slate and a chalk where the Brahmin (Priest) after uttering hymn writes three letters and over that the pencil holded hand of the child is moved ceremonially. Finally, Priest touches that slate and chalk to the forehead of the child and the child have to offer a handful of flower. All these need about ten to fifteen minutes. The performance takes place in *Natmondir*. Some offer homage of *soa panch anna* (thirty three paisa) or more, some offer sweets and fruits. Thus the expense varies. Priest claims about Rs.5/- for his service.

Local people (usually the lower or middle income group) bring their child in the temple for this purpose.

Sastayan

It is a common notion that at the time of death people may be affected by certain evils. Intensity of those evils are measured as ***ekpad dos, dipad dos, tripad dos, charpoa dos, puskara*** etc. directed by the almanac. All such evils can be minimized by performing certain rites which are coloqually known as *Sastayan* or *Sasten.* It is believed that without the rite evil effected soul cannot be free from the attractions of 'this world' and so suffer. At the same time they create dangers for the family members living in this world.

Sastayan rite is of different types. Ordinary *Sastayan* is meant for *ekpad dos* or *dipad dos*. More powerful evils like *tripad, charpoa, puskara* etc. cannot be eradicated by ordinary *Sastayan* and for those elaborate *Sastayan* rites are needed. Evils also appear on Saturdays and Tuesdays, so people who die on those days require *Sastayan* performances essentially.

Usual places of such performance are either the bank of the Ganges or the Siva temples. But as most of the time the bank remain dirty, the performances are made in Siva temples and in rented rooms. A great sanctity is maintained with proper precept by the specialized Priest on specific date and time mentioned in the almanac.

In the morning the performance starts. Five to six hours are needed. Expense is naturally high, about Rs. 500/-. People prefer to do it at Kalighat because expenses are twice as much, if performed at home.

Five specialized Priests are appointed. The party if contacts one local specialized Brahmin, other Brahmins are available through his reference. Because in Kalighat all sorts of qualified Brahmins like 'Vedanta-tirtha', 'Smriti-tirtha', 'Byakaran-tirtha' etc. are found. However, those five Priests take the responsibility of five functions e.g. worship of Siva, sacred reading, yajna, offering of basil leaves to lord Narayan, worship of other gods and goddesses. Procedure of *Panchanga sastayan* is more elaborate and involved muttering of sacred names also. Sacred names like 'Siva','Chondi', 'Madhusudan' etc. are uttered either 108 or 1008 times. Therefore, more time and money is spent.

Bastujag

If constant detriments like death, accidents etc. are observed in a family or if somehow existence of evil spirit is felt in the house, the performance of *Bastujag* is essential to get rid of that ominus influence. The rite is not usually practised at Kalighat because Brahmins recommend to perform this in the home itself.

Groho-santi

It is supposed that the astronomical bodies i.e. the planets can create misfortunes in the family or can upset the physique of an individual. In such situations people strive for cooling down the planet by performing specific rites which are locally known as *Groho-santi.*

Along with these different rites, another form of performance is frequently found at Kalighat which is known as 'Manosik'. *Manosik* is actually a promise of the candidate which involves certain special worship or particualr sacrifice to the goddess when the prayer or wish is fulfilled. *Manosiks* do not follow any particular pattern - their nature totally depends on devotee's mental make up. Usual forms of *Manosik* at Kalighat are as follows :

Some common reasons for which Manosik are offered

(i) For the cure of any disease or for the improvement of health.

(ii) For getting a job or getting promotion to a higher rank or to make higher profit in the business etc.

(iii) To pass in the examination or to secure a high position.

(iv) For suitable marriage alliances of daughters, especially for the aged spinsters.

(v) To win a law suit in the court.

(vi) For the want of a child, specially male child or to save the child from an anticipated danger.

(vii) To bring peace and harmony in the family.

(viii) For the recovery of a person, lost or absconded.

(ix) To get rid of an anticipated danger or loss.

(x) For safe journey.

Some common offerings made on the fulfilment of Manosik

(i) Ordinary worship offerings like *soa panch anna, solo anna* to Rs.5/-, Rs.10/-, Rs.25/- or more.

(ii) Ornaments made of gold and silver like nose ring, ear ring, gold or silver plated iron bangles etc.

(iii) Parts of the body e.g. eye tongue, etc. made up of gold or silver.

(iv) Gold made *belpata* or *tip*[1] etc.

(v) Blood from the chest by splitting the chest.

(vi) Sugar or sugar ball, equivalent to the weight of a person.

(vii) Sacrifice of goat - single or double.

(viii) Some take bath in the Ganges and pass the whole way from the Ganges to the temple through a typical strainous practice locally called *dondi kata*[2].

(ix) Some babies are born dumb or cannot talk even when they grow up. In those cases a vegetable named *ol* is offered to the goddess Kali in order to bring the voice of the child. The performance is called 'ol diye bol photano' in local language.

(x) Sometimes favourite food items are sacrificed to the goddess which can never be taken afterwards in life

It has seen that the more uncertain or impossible is the desire, the more precious is the offer. *Manosik* i.e. contractual prayer has been so keen with human life that in every phase of new venture people recall the great goddess. For example, in Kalighat a singer was found to sing before the goddess prior to her first radio programme. This is no doubt a mode of *Manosik* to become successful for the final performance. Similarly, an open-air opera party, in the beginning of a new drama, acted before the goddess for their best representation at the stage. Again photographs of the goddess are often kept in vehicles and offering of worship is very popular at the time of registration of the vehicle or licence renewal. Such behaviours aim at the blessings from the great power for protected journey, therefore, it can be concluded that as uncertainities engulf the daily life, mankind strives to reduce mental pressure through the device named 'Manosik'

---

1. Small round marks which the girls use to decorate their foreheads, between, the two eyebrow ridge.

2. One has to lie on the ground and stretch the hands horizontally. There he puts a mark. Again standing on that mark he lies and put another mark at the end of his stretched hand. This process is repeated until the person reaches to the destination.

CONCLUSION

OBSERVATION AND CONCLUSION

What we commonly designate as 'Kalighat Kali temple' is actually a cluster of sacred spots centering the seat of main deity, the goddess Kali. Important feature of anysacredspot for worshipping the 'Sakti' is that it is always accompanied by a male consort (*Vairav*). In Kalighat this male consort is named as Nakulesh or Nakuleswar and so his temple is popular as Nakuleswar temple 'Nakuleswar-tala'. Among other remarkable spots there is an altar for the goddesses like 'Sosthi,''Monosha', 'Sitola' etc (Sosthi- tala or Monosha-tala), Siva temples, Radha-Krisna temple, altar for sacrificial fire (*Hom2-bedi*) and the river Ganges. Also there are other temples with other deities around the Kali temple.

Sacrificial spot (*Harkath-tala*) is essentially an important feature in Kalighat as animal sacrifice (*boli*) is a part and parcel of Kali worship. In earlier times human immolation is said to have been widely practised here. Now western educated people have stopped that practice. But animals like goats, sheep and even buffaloes are still sacrificed.

The Ganges passing nearby has shrunken to a great extent. Therefore, its distance from the temple has increased and due to silting of the river, the water has become very dirty. As the Ganges-water is considered as extreme sacred to the Hindus, that dirty water is used in all sacred performances without any irreverence. The nearby pool named 'Kundupukur', the bed of which has been cemented recently has lost its old significance. In ancient time it was a lagoon, believed to have water sources connected with the Ganges. So its water used to be considered as equally sacred as the Ganges-water.

Historical enquiry about the place takes us back to the time when geologically Bengal was formed (stated in Chapter II). Who first started Kali worship in that delta is in obscure. On scrutiny of the old records it has become evident that the most ancient worshippers were the Kapaliks, a sect of Saktas who practise human sacrifices. Gradually with the growth of habitation in the surrounding areas, the particular place began to be explored by the outsiders. Earliest reference of this sacred place came from the ancient Hindu scripture 'Puran'. But in fact for Kalighat no direct relation can be traced with the story depicted in 'Puran' for the absence of any direct evidence. A large number of myths, legends and hearsays are associated with the background.

However, the authority to worship shifted from the hands of human sacrificers (*Kapalik*) to the ascetics (*mohonto*) and lastly that was bestowed on 'Haldar' -family. Although the early history of Kalighat is not clearly known, we can safely identify the modern history of Kalighat which started with Bhawanidas Chakraborty, the progenitor of Haldar family at the end of the sixteenth century. The origin of Haldar family is clear-cut and can easily be traceable through genealogy. At present five major streams in the same lineage are discernible viz. eldest descent (*baro-ghar*),second descent (*mejo-ghar*), third descent (*sejo-ghar*), fourth descent(*naw-ghar*) and youngest descent (*chhoto-ghar*). Daughters' successors who inherited the share of the property in later period have been designated as *dauhitra* or *bhagne-dauhitra*. But all the heirs of this family designate themselves by the common term *'shebait'*.

Shebaits are liable to provide service towards the goddess. This responsibility is shared among the *shebaits*. As the income from the temple is immense, so in exchange of the service rendered, the *shebaits* receive the income. In a systematic mutual understanding a typical system of rotation for the service towards the goddess known as 'Pala' has been adopted. Each *shebait* handles this *pala* as per the proportion of respective individual inheritance. Hence, *pala* may be regarded as an equivalent to property - a source of earning.

Pala is sanctioned day-wise. Half of the day's total income is received by the owner of the pala. The other half has to be depostited to the Committee, which is an office of elected candidates for management and various disbursements. Committee was formed in 1960's, in collaboration with the government (representatives) and the *shebaits*. Government intervened in the affairs of the temple to safeguard the interests of the public, because the place is a public *devottar* land. A scheme with different rules and regulations is operated in the temple. The Committee functions in two separate bodies : 'Kalighat Temple Committee' and 'Council of the Shebaits'

Among the personnel of the temple, some are appointed by the Committee office and others are traditional employees. Nature of job has changed or modified in few cases. On the whole there are varied ranks, duties and obligations which can ever be cited through a mere surface study. Although there are variations in remunerations of the employees, those are very nominal. The employees pursue in job because there is ample scope for extra or side income.

Finance of the temple does not solely rest on half of the *pala*'s income. It is nourished with the receipt of different donations - regular and occasional. Rents are also received per month for using the shops and altars, situated on the *devottar* land. Area of this *devottar* land has now become very limited due to constant devolution with time. Moreover, the huge ornaments and jewelleries stand as fixed assets of the temple. Such assets increase day by day because *shebaits* have restrictions, (as stated in Chapter III) in receiving those.

Religious spots always give rise to markets, nature of which depend on the prevailing demand of the area. Likewise, Kalighat Kali temple and adjacent market have been keenly associated in a symbiotic relationship. Special worship sweet *(pera)*, flowers, ritual articles, commercial handy goods (for social as well as religious purposes) made of wood, rubber, plastic, metal, conch-shell along with religious booklets are prominant in the market.

At the formative stage of this market, three renowned craft communities of Bengal found it as a highly commercial spot. So they settled here forming three compact pockets. Being old inhabitants of Calcutta, the particular areas were named after them. Those communities were scroll-painters' (*Patua* or *Chitrakar*) community, the Bell-metal workers' (*Kashari* or *Kangshakar*) community and conch-shell workers' (Sakhari or Sankhakar) community. People of those communities were not only the makers but sellers too. But as the society became more and more industrialized, the products came into competition ; old material with old technology could not win over those of modern. Naturally, the practitioners were compelled to give up their traditional occupation gradually to maintain smooth livelihood. As a result, though the communities are still living in the area but bear no special significance in relation to market.

Community of beggars is a notable feature in Kalighat. They subsist on public charity - money, food and clothings. There is a good admixture of different categories such as crippled and uncrippled, genuine and ingenuine, whole-timer and part-timer. Hindu views like sin-virtue *(pap-punya)*, pity-charity *(daya- dakshinya)* foster those beggars.

So far as the activity in the temple is concerned, it is found that the goddess Kali is served through a systematized way. It starts from the dawn when the doors of the temple are opened and the goddess is made awaken from sleep. After morning-cleaning and decoration, invocation is done by waving a lamp (*mongolaroti*). Next to that daily worship (*nitya-puja*) continues for an hour. Sacrifice of one he-goat is essential for every morning which is cooked and offered with the principal meal (*bhog*) of the goddess during the noon. The special charity to the beggars on behalf of the temple itself (*doridronarayan seva*) starts immediately after completion of noon-meal offerings, when the temple remains closed for half an hour approximately signifying the period for taking rest for the goddess. Evening food and drink offering (*sitol*) is followed by a second time greeting of goddess through waving of lamp (*sondhyaroti*). At night before the closing of the temple the image is decorated again, the third or last greeting of the day is done by waving the lamp and finally a sleeping atmosphere is created by putting out the lights and uttering a specific spell. Thus comes an end to the series of activities which starts in the early morning.

There are many special occasions found to be celebrated in the temple. Those are followed by the norms of the Haldar family and are conducted chiefly by the Committee. Many minor conventions are found, performances of which depend on individual accord. People rush to the temple for vow (*broto*) celebrations, for special worships to the goddess Kali and for offerings/sacred performances in other sacred spots in and around the temple premises. Soaring market price, different sorts of personal inconveniences in this present day competitive society are the factors responsible for the decrease of sacred performacnes. Moreover, the performances that are done by the public at Kalighat are very simple in procedure. They save time, money and effort of the performer.

People also come to Kalighat for performing some rites of passage. Hindu rites of passage are altogether eleven. Few of them are popular in the society and those are found to be practised in Kalighat. People from all cross-section of the Hindu society are thronged to this spot irrespective of caste, sect, economic group, linguistic group etc. It has been found that the sacrament of wearing holy thread (*Upanayan*) which is restricted among the Brahmins, is a most familiar rite observed in Kalighat. A great crowd is observed on the particular auspicious dates which are very few in a year. Performance connected with first rice-eating rite (*Annaprasan*) appears seldom. On auspicious dates people usually collect special sweet dish, called 'Annoprosad' offered to the goddess Kali and feed it to the baby as a substitute for the performance of the rite. First hair removing rite (*Churakaran*) is practised frequently. Date restriction is not pronounced for this rite and it is more popular among the folk people of U.P, Bihar and Rajasthan. The wedding rite (*Vivaha*), though not encouraged at Kalighat by the authority nevertheless is found to be performed very frequently. Some follow the particualr auspicious dates but some do not bother for that. It is believed that at Kalighat temple there is no date bar by the grace of the goddess Kali. Post-death rites in different forms are practised. These are observed on the particular dates counted from the day of death. Visually such performances are done at the bank of the Ganges and never inside the temple campus.

All these essential rites can be performed at low expense, within short time and with minimum effort. Even many deviations of norm are permitted and get social approval due to predominating divine concept of the place (*pith-mahatma*). The universal notion of the Hindus is that, any ritual, done in a divine place, although in a simpler or cheaper way, becomes socially well recognized and gets an unique status. This value is associated with the Hindu ethics and ultimately operates in restoring social euphoria. Thus, Kalighat being one of the divine places stands very important from social-cultural, anthropological point of view. Its potency for bestowing extra value over the existing normal social relationships is highly emphasized. Therefore, it offers some comparatively easier solution to some complex problem (social and economical) of the modern society.

At the end of this twentieth century all of us know that the spread of education has developed sufficient consciousness among the people. Now people are more prone to scientific explanation in all matters. Their rationality acts against each behaviour and phenomenon. In such a situation this becomes a matter of great astonishment when we find the educated people without seeking logical explanation, being rather guided by simple emotion pursue their visit with worship in Kalighat. Another point is that, commonly people under calamities or uncertainities seek for mental strength by clutching at religion. Early men and even the primitive men of today are the examples, who being ignorant about the diverse natural phenomena have shown the expression of awe and reverence and therefore, to get rid of the threatening circumstances have invented religious activities. The idea of God and the policy of appeasement provided them inner support to combat against varied crises. It can be argued that the fundamental problem of food security still persists among the poor section of the people, so they are prone to religious practices. With this issue one becomes amazed when he finds that not only the poor or uneducated but also the rich and well-educated people equally visit

Kalighat for religious purposes. Answer to this queer question seems to be clear when we analyze the expectations and desires of those people as revealed from the pattern of 'Manosik', 'Sankalpo' and 'Broto'. Life is full of uncertainities. The people who have nothing, he desires to get something; who have something, he desires to get more and more. Further, present industry based urban civilization has created a new type of uncertainity and insecurity in day to day life. So on one hand, hope and insecurity (in any form) and on the other hand, an universal power conception pull the people towards the door of religion where riches, education, technological development and urbanization have nothing to do. Therefore, Kalighat is still retaining its traditional functions amidst the Calcutta city. People try to unload their acute mental pressure under the banner of 'Religion'. Credibility of religion is perennial as it provides mental support and stamina to struggle for existence.

Hinduism is a higher form of religion. It is very wide and philosophical in nature. Here everyone is bound by a common search for truth. Purity of life and conduct is highly stressed in pragmatic life. The theory of rebirth and doctrine of Karma have been associated. To escape the cycle of birth and death man must go through sacrifice and rituals. Worship is the most simpliest mode - an act of crediting religious merit (punya) as well as a way to escape from sin (pap). To every Hindu, whatever Sect (Saiva, Sakta, Vaisnava, Ganapatya etc.) they may belong, the mythologically glorious religious spots are very dear. They place their highest merit of awe, faith and reverence in the sanctity of the places. This feeling is so deep-rooted that a surrendering attitude grows unconsciously towards the great power and the holy places. The places are so designated as 'Tirtha' and Hindus urge to visit all of them for more spiritual upliftment. A sense of commonness or unity plays in this respect among all Hindus inspite of varigated geographical disposition, dilectical differentiation, asymetrical physical features and wide range of regional cultural practices.

The Aryan and non-Aryan fusion which harmonized to give birth of Hindu civilization, there the superiority of Arya people was acknowledged for their vast literary work. The Hindus of the present day still regard Vedas as the source of all knowledge and authority for religion, philosophy and ethics. In the history, the period which has been chalked as Later Vedic period, from that period actually the Aryan society began to loose its purity i.e. changes became pronounced in socio-religious sphere. Rites, rituals, temples came into existence. Nature worship gave place to idol worship. Caste system became rigid and Brahmans established their supremacy over other castes. Brahmans announced that their presence would essentially be required in all sacred rites and ceremonies of the common people because of their special technical knowledge and skill.

Puran, the work of later Vedic period was purposively created to propagate good conduct and morals among the mass. It highlighted power of god to generate in the minds of the people devotion to god and fear of his wrath if turned away from the moral path. It also traced the genealogy of gods and goddesses with various other old dynasties to make the impression more realistic. However, Puran somehow picked and placed 'Kali' into the god family as an important goddess. Thus, the worship of goddess Kali originally being a non-Aryan cultural trait accepted into Hindu civilization. Not only this, worship of Kali acquired the status of great tradition under Brahmanic dominance and survived. This transformation of little tradition to great tradition seems to be typical in Indian situation. So far as the centre is concerned, Kalighat as a seat of Kali worship is still able to transmit its traditional influences among the contemporary people in sustaining the continuity of Hindu civilization.

APPENDIX

REGISTER OF THE NAMES

FOR GENEALOGIES

GENEALOGY. I :

1. Sudarshan Panda.
2. Bauri Panda.
3. Bhuban Mohan Panda.
4. Jagabandhu Panda.
5. Ganesh Panda.
6. Janmejoy Panda.
7. Ghanashyam Panda.
8. Janardan Panda.
9. Ganesh Panda. (Age - 56 Years)
10. Baidyanath Panda.
11. Nityananda Panda.
12. Daitari Panda.
13. Gayadhar Panda.
14. Mayadhar Panda. (Age - 56 Years)
15. Panchanan Panda.
16. Sukdev Panda.
17. Akkhoy Kumar Panda. (Age - 60 Years)
18. Pitambar Panda. (Age - 56 Years)
19. Santosh Panda.
20. Kantoni Panda.
21. Nidhiram Panda. (Age - 62 Years)
22. Madhusudan Panda. (Age - 53 Years)
23. Dukhishyam Panda. (Age - 48 Years)
    (Adopted son.)
24. Dibakar Panda.
25. Rabinarayan Panda.
26. Umakanta Panda.
27. Shesdev Panda. (Ego, Age - 41 Years)
28. Brajakishore Panda.
29. Bijan Behari Panda.
30. Ban Behari Panda.
31. Biman Behari Panda.

GENEALOGY. II :

1. Bhawanidas Chakraborty.
2. Jadabendra Chakraborty.
3. Rajendra Chakraborty.
4. Raghabendra Chakraborty.
5. Ramkrisna Chakraborty..
6. Ramgopal Chakraborty (Haldar).
7. Ramgovinda Chakraborty (Haldar).
8. Ramnarayan Chakraborty (Haldar).
9. Ramsaran Chakraborty (Haldar).
10. Padmanav Chakraborty (Haldar).
11. Ramballav Haldar.
12. Hariballav Haldar.
13. Kashiswar Haldar.
14. Bisweswar Haldar.
15. Siddheswar Haldar.
16. Bhubaneswar Haldar.
17. Durgaram Haldar.
18. Kalicharan Haldar.
19. Udayram Haldar.
20. Harananda Haldar.
21. Joydev Haldar.
22. Chandrasekhar Haldar.
23. Raghunath Haldar.
24. Ramnath Haldar.
25. Biswanath Haldar.
26. Ratneswar Haldar.
27. Rameswar Haldar.
28. Kenaram Haldar.
29. Ramdulal Haldar.
30. Sriram Haldar.
31. Raj Kishore Haldar.
32. Baidyanath Haldar.
33. Krisnadev Haldar.
34. Shyam Sundar Haldar..
35. Nanda Kishore Haldar.
36. Balaram Haldar.
37. Krisna Charan Haldar.

38. Saturam Haldar.
39. Gokul Chandra Haldar.
40. Ramkanta Haldar.
41. Ramkanta Haldar.
42. Gokul Haldar.
43. Ram Sankar Haldar.
44. Joyram Haldar.
45. Radha Madhab Haldar.
46. Kunj Behari Haldar.
47. Gurupada Haldar.
48. Haladhar Haldar.
49. Madhusudan Haldar.
50. Dwariknath Haldar.
51. Jagmohan Haldar.
52. Guru Prasad Haldar.
53. Madan Haldar.
54. Fakir Haldar.
55. Sambhu Haldar.
56. Digambar Haldar.
57. Gouri Kanta Haldar.
58. Ananda Haldar.
59. Nimai Haldar.
60. Ramlochan Haldar.
61. Rammohan Haldar.
62. Baidyanath Haldar.
63. Pran Krisna Haldar.
64. Parbati Haldar.
65. Baidyanath Haldar.
66. Radha Mohan Haldar.
67. Panchanan Haldar.
68. Krisna Prasad Haldar.
69. Ram Jiban Haldar.
70. Jadav Haldar.
71. Prankrisna Haldar.
72. Vairab Haldar.
73. Mahesh Haldar.
74. Jajgeswar Haldar.
75. Bhupal Haldar.

76. Nepal Haldar.
77. Natobar Haldar.
78. Raj Kishore Haldar.
79. Abhoy Haldar.
80. Nilmani Haldar.
81. Naba Kumar Haldar.
82. Ananda Haldar.
83. Dev Narayan Haldar.
84. Haralal Haldar.
85. Raj Krisna Haldar.
86. Kali Krisna Haldar.
87. Jadu Krisna Haldar.
88. Bhikari Haldar.
89. Brajo Mohan Haldar.
90. Hara Chandra Haldar.
91. Hari Chandra Haldar.
92. Shib Chandra Haldar.
93. Ganga Narayan Haldar.
94. Tituram Haldar.
95. Loknath Haldar.
96. Kamala Kanta Haldar.
97. Bhagabati Haldar.
98 Nepal Haldar.
99. Iswar Chandra Haldar.
100. Kali Chandra Haldar.
101. Kali Prasad Haldar.
102. Ishan Haldar.
103. Uma Chandra Haldar.
104. Sambhu Chandra Haldar.
105. Iswar Chandra Haldar.
106. Madhusudan Haldar.
107. Mahesh Haldar.
108. Ishan Haldar.
109. Laxmi Narayan Haldar.
110. Ramgopal Haldar.
111. Pashupati Haldar.
112. Tarak Haldar.
113. Nanda Haldar.

114. Pitambar Haldar.
115. Paran Haldar.
116. Kedar Haldar.
117. Laxmi Haldar.
118. Jadav Haldar.
119. Akkhoy Haldar.
120. Mahim Nath Haldar.
121. Khetra Mohan Haldar.
122. Paresh Haldar.
123. Sarat Haldar.
124. Harimohan Haldar.
125. Ananda Haldar.
126. Kinuram Haldar.
127. Durga Kumar Haldar.
128. Prankrisna Haldar.
129. Jogendra Haldar.
130. Nagendra Haldar.
131. Mahim Haldar.
132. Kalipada Haldar.
133. Rajkumar Haldar.
134. Krisna Kumar Haldar.
135. Chuni Haldar.
136. Nilkanta Haldar.
137. Jogindra Haldar.
138. Shib Chandra Haldar.
139. Rama Charan Haldar.
140. Bama Charan Haldar.
141. Dinanath Haldar.
142. Dwarik Haldar.
143. Aghor Haldar.
144. Atul Haldar.
145. Hari Haldar.
146. Paresh Haldar.
147. Gagan Haldar.
148. Bibhuti Haldar.
149. Charu Lal Haldar.
150. Mohan Lal Haldar.
151. Balai Lal Haldar.

152. Krisna Lal Haldar.
153. Sukhalal Haldar.
154. Shyam Charan Haldar.
155. Harimohan Haldar.
156. Nibaran Haldar.
157. Ramchandra Haldar.
158. Gopal Haldar.
159. Bireswar Haldar.
160. Khetu Haldar.
161. Bisweswar Haldar.
162. Tara Prasanna Haldar.
163. Khirod Haldar.
164. Suren Haldar.
165. Krisna Haldar.
166. Lalit Haldar.
167. Santosh Haldar.
168. Rajendra Haldar.
169. Surendra Haldar.
170. Sailendra Haldar.
171. Sadhan Haldar.
172. Bhajan Haldar.
173. Sanat Haldar. (Age - 70 Years)
174. Jitendra Haldar.
175. Sudhir Haldar.
176. Rajkumar Haldar.
177. Amrita Lal Haldar.
178. Jogendra Haldar.
179. Kali Krisna Haldar.
180. Ramchandra Haldar.
181. Gurupada Haldar.
182. Bireswar Haldar.
183. Sukhamoy Haldar.
184. Satya Charan Haldar.
185. Sushil Haldar.
186. Dasarathi Haldar.
187. Jitendra Haldar.
188. Dwijendra Haldar.
189. Anukul Haldar.

190. Atul Haldar.
191. Gurupada Haldar.
192. Krisna Pada Haldar.
193. Siva Prasad Haldar. (Age - 70 Years)
194. Shankar Prasad Haldar. (Age - 65 Years)
195. Nrisingha Haldar.
196. Purna Chandra Haldar.
197. Keshab Haldar.
198. Brajanath Haldar.
199. Devendra Haldar.
200. Mahendra Haldar.
201. Baikuntha Haldar.
202. Behari Haldar.
203. Khetra Nath Haldar.
204. Ranjit Haldar. (Age - 50 Years)
205. Manik Lal Haldar. (Age - 50 Years)
206. Manoj Lal Haldar.
207. Hari Lal Haldar. (Age - 36 Years)
208. Hara Lal Haldar. (Age - 34 Years)
209. Hira Lal Haldar. (Age - 30 Years)
210. Ajoy Haldar. (Age - 37 Years)
211. Nirmal Haldar.
212. Trailakya Haldar.
213. Abinash Haldar.
214. Priya Nath Haldar.
215. Aghor Haldar.
216. Haridas Haldar.
217. Chandra Kumar Haldar.
218. Kali Kumar Haldar.
219. Amulya Kumar Haldar.
220. Hara Kumar Haldar.
221. Binod Haldar.
222. Narendra Haldar.
223. Sarat Haldar.
224. Not known.
225. Not known.
226. Not known.
227. Sukumar Haldar.

228. Biswanath Haldar.
229. Devabrata Haldar.
230. Subrata Haldar.
231. Satyabrata Haldar. (Age - 67 Years)
232. Prakash Haldar.
233. Bhujendra Haldar.
234. Nidhiraj Haldar.
235. Bijoy Chand Haldar.
236. Haradhan Haldar. (Age - 65 Years)
237. Bimal Haldar. (Age - 58 Years)
238. Gopal Haldar. (Age - 62 Years)
239. Pranab Haldar.
240. Not known. (Age - 49 Years)
241. Krisna Chandra Haldar. (Age - 45 Years)
242. Ashok Haldar. (Age - 43 Years)
243. Tapan Haldar. (Age - 41 Years)
244. Swapan Haldar. (Age - 39 Years)
245. Biswanath Haldar.
246. Becharam Haldar.
247. Kenaram Haldar. (Age - 66 Years)
248. Pravat Haldar. (Age - 60 Years)
249. Gopal Haldar. (Age - 50 Years)
250. Debdas Haldar. (Age - 42 Years)
251. Piyari Lal Haldar.
252. Jahar Lal Haldar.
253. Krisna Lal Haldar.
254. Narayan Haldar.
255. Tarapada Haldar.
256. Anukul Haldar.
257. Balai Haldar.
258. Ajit Haldar. (Age - 76 Years)
259. Bharati Haldar. (Age - 74 Years)
260. Kashipati Haldar.
261. Rabi Haldar.
262. Kali Haldar.
263. Tara Haldar.
264. Kanai Haldar. (Age - 74 Years)
265. Ajit Haldar. (Age - 70 Years)

266. Chandi Haldar. (Age - 72 Years)
267. Bhawani Haldar. (Age - 66 Years)
268. Devi Haldar. (Age - 60 Years)
269. Rabi Haldar.
270. Durga Haldar. (Age - 70 Years)
271. Amal Haldar. (Age - 65 Years)
272. Gouri Haldar. (Age - 60 Years)
273. Kamal Haldar. (Age - 52 Years)
274. Amiya Kumar Haldar. (Ego, Age - 68 Years)
275. Biman Haldar. (Age - 48 Years)
276. Saroj Haldar. (Age - 46 Years)
277. Bijan Haldar. (Age - 42 Years)
278. Rabindra Haldar.
279. Ganga Prasad Haldar. (Age - 67 Years)
280. Biswanath Haldar.
281. Amarnath Haldar. (Age - 50 Years)
282. Nakul Haldar.
283. Gopal Haldar.
284. Chitta Ranjan Haldar. (Age - 54 Years)
285. Anu Haldar. (Age - 51 Years)
286. Badal Haldar. (Age - 50 Years)
287. Dilip Haldar. (Age - 48 Years)
288. Indradev Haldar. (Age - 50 Years)
289. Somnath Haldar. (Age - 45 Years)
290. Ajit Haldar. (Age - 42 Years)
291. Kanti Haldar. (Age - 43 Years)
292. Kalyan Haldar. (Age - 41 Years)
293. Manimohan Haldar. (Age - 50 Years)
294. Pankaj Haldar. (Age - 44 Years)
295. Paritosh Haldar. (Age - 42 Years)
296. Kalidas Haldar.
297. Nagendra Haldar.
298. Narendra Haldar.
299. Surendra Haldar.
300. Anku Haldar.
301. Jot Kumar Haldar.
302. Kalidas Haldar. (Age - 57 Years)
303. Haridas Haldar. (Age - 56 Years)

304. Haripada Haldar. (Age - 51 Years)
305. Khagendra Nath Haldar. (Age - 48 Years)
306. Janaki Nath Haldar. (Age - 46 Years)
307. Sadhu Haldar.
308. Sanyashi Haldar.
309. Moni Haldar.
310. Moti Haldar.
311. Mohit Haldar.
312. Harendra Haldar.
313. Satish Haldar.
314. Prafulla Haldar.
315. Binoy Haldar.
316. Ghanasyam Haldar. (Age - 84 Years)
317. Narendra Haldar.
318. Umanath Haldar.
319. Jiban Haldar. (Age - 51 Years)
320. Bijoy Haldar. (Age - 47 Years)
321. Ajoy Haldar. (Age - 46 Years)
322. Durga Charan Haldar.
323. Pulin Haldar.
324. Beni Haldar. (Age - 75 Years)
325. Sudha Haldar.
326. Kamal Haldar. (Age - 58 Years)
327. Indu Haldar.
328. Not known.
329. Sisir Haldar. (Age - 55 Years)
330. Not known (Age - 50 Years)
331. Not known (Age - 48 Years)
332. Avik Haldar. (Age - 48 Years)
333. Souvik Haldar. (Age - 42 Years)
334. Not known. (Age - 45 Years)
335. Arabinda Haldar. (Age - 42 Years)
336. Amitabha Haldar. (Age - 40 Years)
337. Manik Lal Haldar. (Age - 70 Years)
338. Panna Lal Haldar. (Age - 66 Years)
339. Chuni Lal Haldar. (Age - 65 Years)
340. Prafulla Haldar.
341. Praddut Haldar.

342. Ranajit Haldar.
343. Pulin Haldar. (Age - 66 Years)
344. Sambhu Haldar.
345. Badal Haldar.
346. Amiya Madhab Haldar. (Age - 65 Years)
347. Biddut Haldar. (Age - 60 Years)
348. Rabindra Haldar. (Age - 40 Years)
349. Arup Haldar. (Age - 44 Years)
350. Not known. (Age - 42 Years)
351. Biswanath Haldar.
352. Jagannath Haldar.
353. Amarnath Haldar. (Age - 66 Years)
354. Kedarnath Haldar.
355. Kajal Haldar. (Age - 45 Years)
356. Goutam Haldar. (Age - 38 Years)
357. Soumendra Haldar. (Age - 35 Years)
358. Anshu Haldar. (Age - 30 Years)
359. Ankan Haldar. (Age - 28 Years)
360. Arun Haldar. (Age - 18 Years)
361. Barun Haldar. (Age - 16 Years)
362. Biddut Haldar. (Age - 32 Years)
363. Devdut Haldar. (Age - 28 Years)
364. Praddut Haldar. (Age - 14 Years)
365. Jamini Mohan Haldar. (Age - 35 Years)
366. Arup Kumar Haldar. (Age - 26 Years)
367. Govinda Haldar. (Age - 42 Years)
368. Ashok Haldar. (Age - 36 Years)
369. Asit Haldar. (Age - 34 Years)
370. Ajit Haldar. (Age - 28 Years)
371. Nisith Haldar. (Age - 30 Years)
372. Biddut Haldar. (Age - 28 Years)
373. Praddut Haldar. (Age - 26 Years)
374. Not known. (Age - 24 Years)
375. Bomkesh Haldar.
376. Bhawani Haldar.
377. Amarnath Haldar.
378. Paramesh Haldar. (Age - 66 Years)
379. Jagdish Haldar. (Age - 64 Years)

380. Suniti Kumar Haldar.
381. Ramesh Haldar. (Age - 55 Years)
382. Paramash Haldar. (Age - 53 Years)
383. Umesh Haldar. (Age - 51 Years)
384. Jogesh Haldar.
385. Anup Haldar. (Age - 48 Years)
386. Paritosh Haldar.
387. Prabir Haldar. (Age - 45 Years)
388. Samarendra Haldar.
389. Sourendra Haldar. (Age - 68 Years)
390. Sailendra Haldar. (Age - 66 Years)
391. Abani Haldar.
392. Anil Haldar.
393. Amiya Haldar. (Age - 52 Years)
394. Ajit Haldar. (Age - 60 Years)
395. Asit Haldar. (Age - 60 Years)
396. Provash Haldar. (Age - 55 Years)
397. Rabindra Haldar. (Age - 50 Years)
398. Samir Haldar. (Age - 50 Years)
399. Not known (Age - 47 Years)
400. Amar Nath Haldar.
401. Kedar Nath Haldar. (Age - 60 Years)
402. Satyendra Nath Haldar. (Age - 55 Years)
403. Debendra Haldar. (Age - 68 Years)
404. Dwarik Haldar. (Age - 60 Years)
405. Sambhu Haldar. (Age - 50 Years)
406. Not known (Age - 48 Years)
407. Not known (Age - 43 Years)
408. Not known. (Age - 48 Years)
409. Prabhat Haldar. (Age - 68 Years)
410. Amit Haldar. (Age - 30 Years)
411. Not known (Age - 21 Years)
412. Kali Prasad Haldar. (Age - 35 Years)
413. Viswa Haldar. (Age - 40 Years)
414. Partha Haldar. (Age - 33 Years)
415. Pinaki Haldar. (Age - 34 Years)
416. Haradhan Haldar. (Age - 45 Years)
417. Bhola Haldar. (Age - 40 Years)

418. Biswanath Haldar. (Age - 34 Years)
419. Sasthi Charan Haldar. (Age - 30 Years)
420. Baidyanath Haldar. (Age - 25 Years)
421. Gopinath Haldar. (Age - 20 Years)
422. Dhruba Haldar. (Age - 50 Years)
423. Sankar Haldar.
424. Somnath Haldar. (Age - 35 Years)
425. Arun Haldar. (Age - 50 Years)
426. Asit Haldar. (Age - 40 Years)
427. Dilip Haldar. (Age - 38 Years)
428. Anil Haldar.
429. Basudev Haldar. (Age - 45 Years)
430. Praddut Haldar. (Age - 40 Years)
431. Sunil Haldar. (Age - 32 Years)
432. Sekhar Haldar. (Age - 35 Years)
433. Swarup Haldar. (Age - 38 Years)
434. Ranjit Haldar. (Age - 50 Years)
435. Not known. (Age - 48 Years)
436. Not known. (Age - 42 Years)

GENEALOGY. III :

1. Harekrisna Bhattacharjee.
2. Chandra Sekhar Bhattacharjee.
3. Girish Chandra Bhattacharjee.
4. Manikya Chandra Bhattacharjee.
5. Jadunath Bhattacharjee.
6. Priyanath Bhattacharjee.
7. Bhusan Chandra Bhattacharjee.
8. Sripada Bhattacharjee.
9. Kalipada Bhattacharjee.
10. Panchkari Bhattacharjee.
11. Bholanath Bhattacharjee.
12. Not known.
13. Benimadhab Bhattacharjee.
14. Kalipada Bhattacharjee.
15. Durgapada Bhattacharjee.
16. Devipada Bhattacharjee.
17. Chandipada Bhattacharjee.
18. Nirapada Bhattacharjee.
19. Amulya Bhattacharjee.
20. Prafulla Bhattacharjee. (Age - 70 Years)
21. Dhanapati Bhattacharjee.
22. Amrita Bhattacharjee.
23. Biswanath Bhattacharjee.
24. Manindranath Bhattacharjee.
25. Radhanath Bhattacharjee.
26. Bibhutinath Bhattacharjee.
27. Anadinath Bhattacharjee.
28. Amalnath Bhattacharjee.
29. Aloknath Bhattacharjee. (Age - 45 Years)
30. Arun Bhattacharjee.
31. Prakash Bhattacharjee.
32. Amit Bhattacharjee.
33. Babu Bhattacharjee.
34. Bablu Bhattacharjee.
35. Santipada Bhattacharjee. (Ego, Age - 60 Years)
36. Muktipada Bhattacharjee. (Age - 52 Years)
37. Siddhipada Bhattacharjee.
38. Brahmapada Bhattacharjee.

REFERENCES

Anderson, N.	1964	*Our Industrial Urban Civilization,* India, Asia Publishing House
Archer, W. G.	1953	*Bazar Paintings of Calcutta,* London.
Basham, A. L (ed)	1975	*(A) Cultural History of India,* Oxford, Clarendon Press.
Basu, Nagendranath	1317 (B.S.)	*Biswakosh* (an encyclopedia in Bengali), Calcutta.
Bhattacharya, J.N.	1968	*Hindu Castes and Sects,* Calcutta, Editons Indian.
Bhattacharya, H.	1980	*Hinduder Devdevi : Udvav O Kramavikash* (in Bengali), Calcutta, Farma. K.L.M. (Pvt) Ltd.
Bhattacharya, N.	1368 (B.S.)	*Kalighater Oitihashik Katha* (in Bengali), Calcutta.
Bhowmick, Haripada	1978	'Kalighater Bigraha ki Kalimurti?' (in Bengali) In *Purasree,* Publication division Directorate of Information & Publication of Calcutta, Vol.1, No. 6.
Bhowmick, P.K.	1960	'Four temples in Midnapur' in *Man in India,* Vol.40, No.2, pp. 81–108.
Bhowmick, P.K.	1980	*Aspects of Indian Anthropology,* Calcutta, Subarnarekha.
Bose, B.C.	1875	*Hindu Customs in Bengal,* Calcutta, The Book Company Ltd.
Bose, N.K.	1953	*Cultural Anthropology and Other Essays,* Calcutta, Indian Associated Publishing Co.
Bose, N.K.	1961	*Cultural Anthropology,* Bombay, Asia Publishing House.
Calhaun, D.W.	1978	*Social Change in an age of Change,* Second edition, New-York, Harper & Row Publishers.
Chakraborty, P. and Malhotra, K.C.	1978	'Social structure of a pilgrim town, Tarakeswar (W.B.)', Indian Statistical Institute. This paper was presented at Xth International Congress of Anthropological and Ethnological Sciences to be held at Delhi, 1978

Chakraborty, P., Malhotra, K.C. and Pal I. 1980 'Puri Pilgrim Study - Area of origin and socio-economic characteristic of the pilgrims' in *Bulletin of the Cultural Research Institute,* Vol. XIV No. 3, pp.73-79

Chattopadhay, S. 1356 (B.S.) *Chabbish pargana O Kalikata* (in Bengali), Calcutta, The City Book Company.

Chattopadhay, S.K. 1891 *Kalikshetra Dipika* or *Kalighater Puratatwa,* Calcutta.

Chowdhury, B. 1981 *The Bakreswar Temple,* Delhi, Inter-India Publications.

Cohn, Werner. 1967 'Religion in non-western cultures' in *American Anthropologist,* Vol. 69, No. 1.

(A) Committee of the Royal Anthropological Institute of Great Britain & Ireland. 1951 *Notes and Querrie on Anthropology,* Sixth edition, London, Routledge & Kegan Paul Ltd.

Dasgupta, S. 1367 (B.S.) *Bharater Sakti Sadhana O Sakta Sahitya* (in Bengali), Calcutta, Sahitya Sansad.

Dasgupta, S. 1384 (B.S.) *Bharatiya Sadhanar Oikya,* Calcutta, Biswabharati.

Deb, Raja Binoy Krisna, edited by S. Roy Chowdhuri. 1977 *The Early History and Growth of Calcutta,* India, Radhi.

Datta, Prankrisna 1981 *Kalikatar Itibritya,* Calcutta, Pustak Bipani.

Duverger, M. 1964 *Introduction to the Social Sciences,* London, George Allen & Unwin Ltd.

Epstein, A.L. (ed) 1967 *The Craft of Social Anthropology,* London, Associated Book Publishers Ltd.

Foster, G.M. 1973 *Traditional Societies and Technological Change,* Second edition, India, Allied Publishers Pvt. Ltd.

Gannep, Arnold Van 1960 *The Rites of Passage,* London, Routledge and Kegan Paul Ltd.

Ghosh, Binoy 1978 *Paschimbanger Sanskriti* (in Bengali), Calcutta, Prakash Bhawan.

Ghosh, M., Dutta, A.K. and Ray, B 1972 *Calcutta : A study in Urban Dynamics,* India.

Government of India 1953 *Census 1951 W.B.*, Land and Revenue Department, The Tribes and Castes in West Bengal, W.B. Government Press, Alipore, W.B.

Government of India 1961 *Census 1961*, Vol. II, Calcutta, West Bengal District Census Hand-book.

Haldar, Dhanapati. *Mahatirtha Kalighat* (in Bengali), Calcutta, Raju Publications.

Majumdar, R.C. 1977 *Hindu Sabhyata O Sanskritir Kramavikash* (in Bengali), Calcutta, Calcutta University Press.

Mc Cutchion, J.D. 1972 *Late mediaeval Temples of Bengal*, Calcutta, The Asiatic Society.

Mukherjee, Meera 1978 *Metal Craftsmen of India*, Calcutta, Anthropological Survey of India.

Mukherjee, Upendra. 1332 (B.S.) *Kalighat Itibritya* (in Bengali), Calcutta.

Nigurananda 1386 (B.S.) *Mahatirtha Ekanna Pither Sandhane*, (in Bengali), Second edition, Calcutta, Sarat Publishing House.

Ostor, Akos. 1978 'Puja in Society' in *Eastern Anthropologist*, Vol. 31, No. 2, pp. 119–175.

Paribrajak 1978 'Kalighater Kalimurti Aviskar' (in Bengali), in *Purasree*, Publication Division Directorate of Information & Publications of Calcutta, Vol, 1, No. 5.

Pelto, Pertti. J. and Pelto, G.H. 1978 *Anthropological Research*, Second edition, Cambridge, Cambridge University Press.

Plog, Fred and Bates, D.G. 1976 *Cultural Anthropology*, New-York.

Prasad, R., Hallen G.C. and Pathak, K. (ed) 1971 *Conspectus of Indian Society*, Agra, Satish Book Enterprise.

Rao, M.S.A. (ed) 1974 *Urban Sociology in India*, New-Delhi, Orient Longman Ltd.

Radhakrishnan, S. 1979 *The Hindu view of Life*, Bombay, Blackie & Sons (India) Ltd.

Ray, Alok (ed) 1978 *Calcutta Keepsake*, Calcutta.

Redfield, R. 1955 'Societies and Cultures as natural systems' in *J.R.A.I.*, Vol. 55. (The Huxley memorial lecture).

Redfield, R. 1969 *The Little Community* and *Peasant Society and Culture*, London, The University of Chicago, Press.

Risley, H.H. 1892 *Tribes and Castes of Bengal*, Vol. I, Calcutta, Bengal Secretariat Press.

Sen, Kshitimohan 1371 (B.S.) *Banglar Sadhana* (in Bengali), Calcutta, Biswabharati.

Sen, Kshitimohan 1384 (B.S.) *Bharater Sanskriti* (in Bengali), Calcutta, Biswabharati.

Singer, Milton. 1972 *When a great tradition Modernizes : an anthropological approach to Civilization*, India, Vikash Publishing House.

Singer, M. and Cohn. B.S. (ed) 1968 *Structure and Change in Indian Society*, Chicago, Aldine Publishing Co.

Sinha, Surajit 1966 'Religion in an affluent society' in *Current Anthropology*, Vol. 7, No. 3, pp. 189 - 195.

Sinha, Surajit 1972 'Kali temple at Kalighat and the city of Calcutta' in *Cultural Profile of Calcutta*, edited by Surajit Sinha, pp. 61 - 72, Calcutta, The Indian Anthropological Society.

Sinha, S. and Saraswati, B. 1978 *Ascetics of Kashi - an anthropological exploration*, Varanashi, N.K.Bose Memorial Foundation.

Srinivas, M.N. 1960 *Methods in Social Anthropology*, Bombay, Asia Publishing House.

Sur, Atul 1388 (B.S.) *Hindu Sabhyatar Nritatwik Vasya* (in Bengali), Calcutta, Sahityalok.

Vidyarthi, L.P. 1961 *The Sacred Complex in Hindu Gaya*. Bombay, Asia Publishing House.

Vidyarthi, L.P. 1962 *Aspects of Religion in Indian Society*, Meerat, Kedarnath Ramnath.

Vidyarthi, L.P. 1979 *The Sacred Complex of Kashi (a microcosm of Indian Civilization)*, India, Concept Publishing House.

Young, P.V. 1956 *Scientific Social Surveys and Research*, Third edition, United States, Prentice-Hall.

LOCAL TERMS - MEANING AND SIGNIFICANCE TRANSLATED IN ENGLISH

ADHIBASH	The ceremonial performance on the eve of any solemn worship.
AGRAHAN	The eighth month of Bengali Year corresponding to the period from middle of November to middle of December.
AKKHOY TRITIA	The third lunar day of the light fortnight of the month Baisakh (April-May). It is considered as very auspicious date to the Hindus.
AMBUBACHI	It is the three consecutive days in the first week of the month Ashar (June-July) for Hindu widows to keep fast in.
ANNA	Equivalent to six paisa.
AROTI	The act of greeting a deity by waving a lamp.
ASAUCH	Personal impurity caused by birth or death of a relative.
ASHAR	The third month of the Bengali year corresponding to the period from mid june to mid July.
ASON	A square small carpet to accommodate one person in sitting position.
ASTOMI	The eighth lunar day both in light and dark fortnight .
ASUR	Forces of evil.
ASWIN	The sixth month of the Bengali year, corresponding to the period between mid September to mid October.
BAISAKH	The first month of the Bengali year corresponding the period from the middle of April to Middle of May.
BASUDEV	An epithet of lord Krisna.
BELPATA	Three leaves (in a stalk) of a marmelos tree, essentially used in Hindu worships.
BENAROSHI	Expensive silk sari with zari works on that. The name is after the place where those are produced.
BESH /RAJBESH	The dressing and decoration of the goddess Kali at Kalighat,which is done at eleventh hour of the day i.e. before the closing of the temple.
BHADRA	The fifth month of Bengali year corresponding to the period from mid August to mid September.

BHAGNE-DAUHITRA	Sister's grand-sons.
BHELA	A kind of wild fruit (non-edible).
BHOG/BHOG-RAG	The principal food offered for the deity. Specially it indicates noon rice meal.
BHOG-GHAR	The kitchen of a deity.
BIDHOBA	A widow lady.
BIGHA	A measure of flat area. One 'Bigha' is equal to 6400 Sq. cubits or 1/3rd. acre approximately.
BISWAKARMA	A god, who is an architect. It is the common notion that he made the world.
BODHON	Invocation of a deity. The word is frequently used in relation to 'Durga-puja', on the eve of the worship.
BOLI	Immolation.
BORGI	The Marhatta plunderer.
BRIDDHI	It is a type of 'Sraddha', for getting the blessings from deceased ancestors. (For details vide Chapter VI).
BROHMA	The first person of Hindu Trinity, entrusted with the task of creation.
BROHMOCHARI	The worshipper, who is not supposed to be married.
BROTO	Vow i.e. a self-inflicted austerity praying certain benefit from supernature.
CHACHCHORI	A more or less dry dish prepared with vegetables and spices which may or may not include fish-bones.
CHAITRA	This is the last month of Bengali year corresponding to the period from mid March to mid April.
CHAMUNDA	A manifestation of mother goddess (Durga).
CHARONAMRITA	It is the liquid substance delivered by the Priest to the devotee as the grace of the god. It is made up of milk, Ganges-water, honey, ghee etc.
CHATURDOSSI	The fourteenth lunar day both in the light and dark fortnight.
CHHATAK	A measure of land area. One 'Chhatak' means five hands long and four hands wide i.e. twenty square hands (one hand indicates eighteen inches).
CHHATU	A flour made of barley or maize or gram etc., eaten mainly by the Hindusthani people.

CHONDI	A manifestation of mother goddess (Durga).
CHONDI-PATH	Reading of ancient sacred literature 'Chondi'. Purpose is to grow sacredness in the soul and total atmosphere.
CHOTURTHI	The fourth day of both light and dark fortnight.
COTTAH	A measure of land. One 'Cottah' means 320 Sq. cubits.
DAKSHINA	The fee or gift that is given to the Priest by the proprietor for his helping in the sacred act.
DASOHARA	The tenth lunar day of light fortnight of the month Jaistha (May-June) - the date of descent of the Ganges upon the earth.
DASOMI	The tenth lunar day of both dark and light fortnight.
DAUHITRA	Daughters' sons.
DESHACHAR	Regional norms.
DEVOTTAR	A property belonging to a deity.
DHARMORAJ	The lord of justice.
DHUTI-CHADOR	The typical two pieces of cloth used by the Bengali males in a definite fashion.
DIKSHA	To be initiated by learning mystic and esoteric words (bij-mantra) for silent prayer.
DOI-PHOTA	The sacred mark deliverd by the Priest on the forehead of the devotee with curd.
DOLMANCHO	It is a room within the temple campus at Kalighat, where the rocking cradle of lord Krisina and his lady love Radha is placed.
DONDI	The sacrificial stick measuring four cubits in length It is made up of a bamboo and a marmelos twig.
DORIDRANARA-YAN SEVA	It is the feeding programme arranded by the temple authority which is found to take place once a day, within the precinct of the temple at Kalighat.
DURBA	A grass, particularly with five or seven blades used in Hindu worship.
DURGA	The goddess stands for force.
EKADOSHI	The eleventh lunar day of both light and dark fortnight.
FALGUN	The eleventh month of Bengali year corresponding to the period from mid February to mid March.
GAMCHHA	A sort of napkin.

GANESH	A god who helps in achieveing perfection. According to the ancient Hindu text 'Puran ' he is the son of goddess Durga.
GANGA	The presiding deity of the river Ganges.
GANGA-PUJA	Worship of the goddess Ganga, which takes place on the tenth lunar day of light fortnight in the month of Jaistha (May-June).
GARVA GRIHA	It is a place inside the temple-room where the image of the goddess Kali is kept at Kalighat. The place is very low and one has to climb down some stairs to reach that place.
GHAT	It is the landing place at the bank of river, pond etc.
GHONTA-TALA	It is a place on the 'Jor bangla' (with reference to the Kali temple at Kalighat) over which a big bell is fixed. Public throw loose coins into a big copper bowl kept below that bell.
GHOT	A small pitcher. Usually such a pot is found before a deity on which 'Sankalpo' is done prior to worship.
GHOTI	A small pitcher shaped metal water-pot (commonly brass made).
GOTRA	Among the Bengali Hindus, it is considered that each family has been founded by a saint and so with his name the lineage is traced.
GURU-PURNIMA	It is the day of the preceptors, once a year.
HARI	An urn-shaped pot.
HARIKATH	A wooden stand to which the neck of the sacrificial victim is placed at the time of immolation.
HOM	An oblation of fire, into which ghee is poured.
HOM-BEDI	It is an altar within the temple boundary at Kalighat for sacrificial fire.
HOM-PHOTA	The sacred mark which is put on the forehead by the ashes from the oblation of fire.
HORI	A manifestation of Visnu.
JAGODHATRI	Mother of the world.
JAG-PRODIP	A special earthen lamp used for 'Durga-puja' by the 'Shebait' at Kalighat Kali temple.
JAISTHA	It is the second month of the Bengali year corresponding to the period from middle of May to middle of June.
JAJMAN	The clientele i.e. on whose behalf a Priest offers worships.

JALPANI	It refers to a meal offered to the deity which is made up of fruits,sweets, beverages of marmelos (bel-pana), plain sugar drink (chinir sarbat) etc. In one word, it is the 'Naibidya' made of fruits.
JANMASTOMI	The eigth lunar day of the dark fortnight of the month Bhadra (Aug-Sept) is celebrated as 'Janmastomi' as lord Krisna was born on that particular day.
JHAP	It means jump from a height over the dangerous objects. It is a part and parcel of 'Gajan' festival of the Hindus.
JHULONJATRA	It is a Hindu festival celebreated with Krisna and his lady love Radha. They are placed in swinging position in a cradle on this occasion.
JOY MONGOL-BAR	It is a kind of 'Broto' celebration in the month of Jaistha (May-June).
JOR BANGLA	It is called to the southern varandah of the Kali temple at Kalighat, facing the northern part of the 'Natmondir'. Actually the term signifies a particular type of architect design.
JOY DURGA	A manifestation of mother goddess (Durga).
KALABOU	It is worshipped during 'Durga-puja'. Plants e.g. paddy, arum, turmeric and kochu (a variety of arum) and also branches of trees like 'Jayanti' Marmelos, Pom-granate and 'Ashok' are taken. All these eight plants or branches are tied with a banana plant by a creeper of the plant 'Aparajita' keeping a pair of mamelos inside. Nextly the whole thing is enwrapped in a red bordered white sari in the fashion of a bride whose face remains covered by a veil. Locally this structure is called as 'Kalabou' or 'Nabopatrika' or 'Ganesher bou' (wife of the god Ganesh).
KALPO	A spiritual direction.
KAPALIK	Worshippers of the goddess Kali as well as Siva (Tantra followers)who generally prefer human sacrifice as a part of worship.
KARTIK	A god, who is the son of goddess Durga. It also refers to the seventh month of Bengali year corresponding to the period from mid October to mid November.
KHARA	A large falchion used in immolation.
KHICHURI	A hotch-potch, prepared by boiling rice and pulse with spices.
KRISHNA	An incarnation of Narayan, who was one of the chief characters of the epic 'Mahabharat'.

KRISNA-EKADOSHI	The eleventh lunar day of dark fortnight.
KSHAN	Some specific auspicious time of a lunar day.
KULACHAR/ KULO-PROTHA	The traditionally practised lineage norms. 'Kula' comprises all the lineage persons - horizontally and vertically of either father's or mother's side.
KUNDUPUKUR	A sacred pond in Kalighat. (For details vide Chapter I).
KUSUNDIKA	A scriptural performance following the marriage, found among the brahmin Caste. This is observed on the second day morning of marriage.
LAXMI	The goddess of wealth.
LUCHI	A flour-puff, fried in ghee.
MAGH	The tenth month of the Bengali year corresponding the period from middle of January to mddle of February.
MAHALAYA	The new-moon day immediately preceding the autumnal worship of goddess Durga.
MAHAPITH	A 'Pith' of supreme importance.
MANOSIK	A contractual prayer to a deity in which the devotee promises for certain offering, if the prayer is fulfilled.
MAYER GHAT	The landing stairs of the Ganges, facing the western gate of the Kali temple at Kalighat.
MOHONTO	Head of a monastery or a convent or a temple.
MONGOLAROTI	The ceremonial waving of light before a deity at dawn.
MONOSHA/ MONSHA	The goddess of snakes. The word also means a Cactus plant.
MONOSHA-TALA/MONSHA-TALA	It is the abode of the goddess Monosha within the campus of Kali temple at Kalighat.
MUL-SANYASHI	Head of a 'Sanyashi' group, who is found to lead in the Kali temple at Kalighat on the occasion of 'Gajan'.
NAIBIDYA	It is the essential offering in a Hindu worship. Chief ingredients are the moistened sunned rice displayed on a wooden or metal dish in a pyramidical fashion. Batasha i.e. small round sweets, fruits etc. are placed over that.
NAKULESWAR-TALA	Abode of Nakuleswar, the self-originated Siva at Kalighat, Calcutta.
NAM-SANKIR-TON/SANKIRTON	Chorus song for glorifying a diety.

NARAYAN	A manifestation of Visnu, who sustains the creation. Commonly this god is represented through 'Salgram sila' i.e. a particular black stone-piece.
NATMONDIR	The platform adjacent to a temple from which the diety inside the temple can be visited.
NAVOMI	The ninth lunar day of either fortnight.
NAVORATRI	The successive nine lunar days from first to ninth of the light fortnight. It comes twice a year, once in Autumn and once in Spring.
NIJO-MANDIR	It refers to the temple of the goddess Kali at Kalighat.
NITYA-PUJA	It refers to the worship which is regularly performed in the mornings, at Kalighat Kali temple.
NOA	An iron bangle. It is essentially used by the married Bengali Hindu women, until their husbands die.
PADOPADMA	The august feet.
PAITA	The holy thread slung over the shoulder in the fashion of a cross-belt by the upper Caste of Hindus, especially Brahmins. First time it is worn after a sacrament in child-hood.
PALA/SEVA-PALA	It is a system where 'Shebaits' partake the responsibility to serve and worship the goddess Kali at Kalighat, by turn.
PALADAR	Authorized person for handling a 'Pala' for the day.
PANCHOMI	The fifth lunar day of either fortnight.
PANCHAMRITA	It refers to the mixture of five sweet edible substances collectively namely curd, milk, clarified butter, sugar and honey.
PANCHO-GABYA	Five articles delivered from the cow e.g. curd, butter, milk, cow's urine and cow-dung. According to Hindus, mixture of these is very sacred and it's eating indicates body purification.
PANJA	A decree by some authority.
PANJABI	It is a variety of shirt (very loose in fitting) worn by the Bengaless.
PAYESH	A sweet dish, prepared by boiling rice in milk with sugar and other ingredients.
PERA	A kind of locally available sweet made of posset and sugar.

PITH/PITHO-STHAN	In reference to the old legend 'Daksha yajna' (for details vide Chapter II), 'Pith' is a sacred place containing a mutilated part from the body of 'Soti' (Soti-ango). There are differences of opinion among the scholars regarding the actual number of 'Pith' or 'Pitho-sthan'. Commonly people recognize fifty-one such places. In each 'Pith', spirit of 'Soti' is worshipped with a special name and that is invariably accompanied by a self-originated Siva called 'Vairav'. However, in some cases ambiguity lies with the determination of exact location.
POUS	The ninth month of the Bengali year corresponding the period from middle of December to middle of January.
PRODIP	An earthen lamp. Cotton wick and oil are used to lit this.
PRONAM	An act of making obeisance by lying prostrate or bending down and touching a spot or one's feet.
PRONAMI PAISA	Money or loose coins, those are offered to a deity at the time of making obeisance.
PROSAD	To partake the food offered to a deity. It is a symbol of acquiring god's grace.
PROSADI-FUL	Grace of the deity when obtained through the offered flowers.
PROTIPAD	The first lunar day of either fortnight.
PUJA	A worship.
PURAN	An ancient Hindu scripture. They are eighteen in number and each has several sections. It is believed that 'Puran' reflects the roots of earlier tradition. All the 'Purans' are not of same antiquity. They were written probably between early centuries of Christian era to sixteenth century A.D.
PUSHPANJOLI	The offering of a handful flower to a deity.
RADHA-KRISNA	A god and his lady love, worshipped by the people of Vaisnava Sect.
RAMNAVOMI	The ninth lunar day of light fortnight of the month Chaitra (Mar- April). It is the birth-day of Ramchandra and regarded as sacred to the Hindus.
RATHOJATRA	It is the Hindu festival popularly known as 'Car festival', where Juggerneut (supreme lord of the world) goes in a chariot for a sea-bath. The starting day is called 'Sojarath' and seventh day or the returning day is called 'Ultorath'.
SADHOBA	The married woman whose husband is alive.

SAIMBHU	In each place where mutilated part of Soti's body (Soti-ango) had fallen, there a Siva has automatically revealed himself. These self-originated Siva is called Saimbhu i.e. not created by man.
SAIVA	Worshippers of lord Siva as the members of a Sect.
SAKHA	A type of bangle made up of conch-shell.
SAKTA	Worshippers of power (in the form of Durga or Kali) as the members of a Sect.
SAKTI	Power.
SANAI	A wooden wind-instrument (Musical) like a flute.
SANKALPO	Concentration for a purpose Determination with a purpose is required prior to any worship or sacrifice.
SANKHO/SAKH	A sound producing conch.
SANKRANTI	The last day of any month.
SANTI-JOL	The sacred water which is sprinkled after the worship for the welfare and peace of the family.
SANYASH	A primitive Saivite rite followed by the abandonment of worldly enjoyment and taking a life of religious mendicant for a period.
SANYASHI	A person who follows 'Sanyash'.
SAPTOMI	Seventh lunar day of either fortnight.
SATYANARAYANA	An incarnation of lord Visnu.
SAYAN	Man consider a time for the sleep of the deities in their own form. Performances at that scheduled time is called 'Sayan'
SHEBAIT	Present owner of the Kalighat.
SITOL	It refers to the evening food of the diety.
SITOLA	Presiding goddess of the diseases like Pox, Measles etc.
SNAN-JATṘA	It is a date fixed by the Hindu almanac which is auspicious to bathe the deities.
SONDHYAROTI	The act of greeting deity by waving a lamp in the evening.
SONI	A diety - a planet who is believed to be a son of god Sun. It is considered that for its bad position, utter distress is created over an individual.
SOSTHI	A goddess bestowing children. The term also signifies the sixth lunar day of either fortnight.

SOSTHI-TALA	Abode of the goddess Sosthi within the precinct of Kali temple at Kalighat.
SOTI-ANGO	Mutilated body part of Soti, the mythical figure
SRABAN	The fourth month of the Bengali year corresponding to the period from mid July to mid August.
TAHOBIL/TAPIL-ER-JAYGA	It is a rectangular altar at the north-west corner of the temple campus of Kalighat Kali temple. Heads of sacrificial animal are sold from this spot.
TAMROKUNDO	It is a big copper bowl for putting coins, kept at the 'Jor-bangla' under a big bell hung over there.
TANTRA	Tantras are neither the ancient authentic religious scriptures of Aryan race, nor it is accepted throughout India. Rather they are a class of works on saiva and Sakta systems of religion created by the Bengalees. They came into vogue at the closing phase of Sanskrit literature and traced to an age before the birth of Mahomed. Some Tantras are reputed but they possess no fixed number because of their multiplying nature - new Tantras are often interpolated.
TANTRA-DHAROK	The person who holds the Tantra book and gives directions at the time of 'Durga-puja' in Kali temple at Kalighat.
TARPAN	A form of ancestor worship followed among the Hindus (for details vide Chapter VI).
TOPOR	A conical cork-hat which is specially found on the head of Bengali Hindu groom at the time of marriage.
VAIRAV	Consort of goddess Kali.
VAIRAVI	Consort of 'Brohmochari' i.e. female ascetics. In a similar fashion she is not supposed to be married.
VAISNAVA	Worshippers of Visnu, as the members of a Sect.
VIENGHAR	It is the room for making 'Pera', the sweets which are typically used by the public for the worship of goddess Kali at Kalighat.
VISNU	The second person in Hindu Trinity who is entrusted with the task of conservation of life upon the earth.
UPANAYAN	A ritual ceremony of Brahmins which means the wearing of a holy thread.

NAME OF THE PEOPLE IN REFERENCE TO THEIR HOMELAND :

BENGALI	Inhabitants of the State 'West Bengal'.
BIHARI	Inhabitants of the State 'Bihar'.
GUJARATI	Inhabitants of the State Gujarat'
HINDUSTHANI	Folk People of the States like 'Bihar' and 'Uttar Pradesh',
MARWARI	Inhabitants of 'Marwar', a region of the State 'Rajasthan'.
NEPALI	Inhabitants of the country 'Nepal'.
ORIYA	Inhabitants of the State 'Orissa'.
PUNJABI	Inhabitants of the State 'Punjab'.
RAJASTHANI	Inhabitants of the State 'Rajasthan'
SOUTH-INDIAN	Inhabitants of southern part of India i.e. the States like 'Karnataka', 'Tamil Nadu', 'Kerala' etc.

Pithosthans according Gupta Press Panjika

SERIAL NO	NAME OF THE PITH	PROBABLE LOCATION	MUTILATED BODY PART	NAME OF THE GODDESS	NAME OF THE VAIRAV
1	Hingula	Afganisthan (Present day Pakistan)	The central pore of the palate	Kottori	Bhimlochan
2	Sarkara or Karabir	Sind (present day Pakistan)	Three eyes	Mahisha-mardini	Krodhish
3	Sugandha	Sikarpur, Barishal (Present day Bangladesh)	Nose	Sugandha	Trambak
4	Amarnath	Kashmir	Upper part of the throat	Bhagabati or Mahamaya	Trisandheswar
5	Jwalamukhi	Himachal Pradesh	Tongue	Ambika	Unmatta
6	Jalandhar	Punjab	Left mammary gland	Tripurmalini	Bhishan
7	Baidyanath	Deoghar, Bihar	Heart	Joy Durga	Baidyanath
8	Nepal	Near Pashupatinath temple	Both the knees	Mahamaya	Kapali
9	Manabkshetra	Manash Sarabar, Tibet	Half from the left hand	Dakshini	Amar
10	Birajakshetra	Puri, Orissa	Navel	Bimala	Jagonnath
11	Gandoki	River Gandoki, Nepal	Right cheek	Gandoki chandi	Chandopani
12	Bahula	Ketugram, Burdwan	Left arm	Bahula	Bhiruk
13	Ujani	Kogram, Burdwan	Right elbow	Mangal chandi	Kapilambar
14	Chattogram	Present day Bangladesh	Half of the right arm	Bhawani	Chandrasekhar
15	Tripura	Dist. Tripura	Right foot	Tripur sundari	Tripuresh
16	Trisrota	Jalpaiguri	Left leg	Bhramari	Iswar
17	Kamrup	Assam	Vagina	Kamaksha	Umananda
18	Prayag	Allahabad, U.P.	Fingers from two hands	Lalita	Bhabo
19	Jayanti	Ambiguous	Left shank	Jayanti	Kramadiswar
20	Kalighat	Calcutta	Fingers from right feet	Kalika	Nakulesh or Nakuleswar
21	Kirit	Kiritkona, Murshidabad	Crown	Bimala	Sambarta
22	Baranashi, Manikarnika	Benaras, U.P.	Hair lock	Bishalakkhi	Kal
23	Kanyasram	U.P.	Back	Sarbani	Nimish
24	Kurukshetra	Haryana	Right ankle	Sabitri	Sthanu or Aswanath
25	Manibandha	Ajmer, Rajasthan	Wrist	Gaitri	Sarbananda

(Contd...)

SERIAL NO	NAME OF THE PITH	PROBABLE LOCATION	MUTILATED BODY PART	NAME OF THE GODDESS	NAME OF THE VAIRAV
26	Srihatta	Present day Bangladesh	Neck	Mahalaxmi	Sambarananda
27	Kanchidesh	Bolpur, Kankalitala	Skeleton	Devgarva or Bedgarva	Ruru
28	Kalmadhab	Four miles form Puri, Orissa.	Left buttock	Kali	Asitanga
29	Sonnad	Origin of the river Narmada.	Right buttock	Narmada	Bhadrasen
30	Ramgiri	Bilashpur, M.P.	Right mammary gland	Shibani	Chando
31	Brindaban	U.P.	Hair	Uma	Bhutesh
32	Suchidesh	Ambiguous	Upper row of teeth	Narayani	Sanghar
33	Panchasagar	Mayurbhanj, Orissa	Lower row of teeth	Barahi	Maharudra
34	Kartoatat	Bank of the river, Kartoa (present day Bangladesh)	Ear	Aparna	Baman
35	Sriparbat	Ambiguous	Right ankle	Sunanda	Nando
36	Bibhash	Tamluk, W.B.	Left ankle	Bhimrupa	Sarbananda
37	Prabhash	Ambiguous	Belly	Chandrabhaga	Bakratunda
38	Vairab parbat	M.P.	Upper lip	Mahadevi	Lambakarna
39	Magadh	Bihar	Right shank	Sarbanandakori	Bomkesh
40	Janasthan	Ambiguous	Chin	Bhramari	Bikritaksha
41	Godavari tir	Andhra Pradesh	Left cheek	Biswamatrika	Dandapani
42	Ratnabali	Ambiguous	Right shoulder	Kumari	Sib
43	Jugadya	Khirgram, Burdwan	Thumb from right foot	Jogadya	Khirkhandak
44	Mithila	Ambiguous	Left shoulder	Mahadevi	Mahodoy
45	Nalhati	Birbhum, W.B.	Lower part of throat	Kalika	Jogish
46	Bakreswar	Birbhum, W.B.	Space between the eyes	Mahishmardini	Bakranath
47	Iswaripur	Jassore (present day Bangladesh.)	Hand ornament (Panipadma)	Jasoreswari	Chando
48	Attahash	Ambiguous	Lower lip	Fullora	Biswanath
49	Nandipur	Sithia, Birbhum	Neck-chain (Har)	Nandini	Nandikeswar
50	Lanka	Ceylon sea shore	Anklet -chain with bell (Nupur)	Indrakshi	Rakkhaseswar
51	Birat	North Bengal	Fingers from left leg	Ambika	Amrito

(This chart actually follows the *Tantra* named 'Pranatoshini')

Index

Acharanirnaya Tantra, 16
Adya-Sraddha, 102
Akkhoy-tritia broto, 87
Ambubachi, 93
Ananta chaturdossir broto, 89
Annaprasan, 106
Aryan & non-Aryan fusion, 121

Bagdi, 47
Baisakh, 27
Bangiya Siksha Parishad, 34
Barer-puja, 97
Baro-Haldar, 28
Bason Majar Lok, 46
Bastujag, 113
Basudev, 20
Beggars, 61
Bhadra, 78
Bharat chamber of Commerce, Calcutta, 34
Bharat Sevasram Sangha, 34
Bhari, 45,63
Bhattacharjee Masai, 40
Bhog, 69
Bidyarambha, 112
Bighas, 17
Bigha, 2
Bipattrini broto, 89
Birla-gate, 93
Biswakarma, 94
Biswambhar, 71
Brahmomuhurto, 64
Briddhi-Sraddha, 102
Brohmochari, 2
Broto celebration, 86
Buddha-purnima, 95
Burrabazar, 61

Calcutta University, 34
Chaitra, 5, 82
Chakraborty, Bhawanidas, 2
Chanchor, 73,74
Chhat-puja, 97
Chhar-brahman, 43
Chhataks, 2
Chhoto-Haldar, 28
Chitrakar or Putua Community, 59
Chondi-path, 81
Chowdhury of Barisha, 1
Chowdhury, S.K. Roy, 3
Chowkidar, 48,49,50
Churakaran, 107
Clandestine marriages, 105

Common offerings made on
 the fulfilment of Manosik, 114
Common reasons for which Monosik
 are offered, 114
Community of beggars, 118
Conch-Shell cutters, 60
Cottah, 2
Council of Shebaits, 33

Dakshina, 87
Dalal, 44
Dasakarme Parodorshi
 Brahman, 44
Dasohara & Ganga-puja, 97
Dasa Karma, 99
Dasomi, 80
Dauhitras, 40
Dhannya, 76
Dhuli, 47,66
Dolmancho, 74
Dondi Kata, 115
Doridronarayan seva, 70
Durba, 76
Durga-puja, 29,41

East India Company, 17

Falgun,32
Female desires, 9
Financial resources, 53

Gajan, 83
Gamchha, 84
Ganesh, 93
Gangasagar, 93
Garva griha, 3
Ghonta-tala, 51
Gotra, 20
Govinda Ghosal Lane, 21
Govt. Sanskrit College
 Calcutta, 34
Groho-santi, 114
Guhya Kali, 16

Haldar, 20
Harish mongol barer
 broto, 87
Harkath-Tala, 10
High Court of Calcutta, 31
Hinduism is higher form
 of religion, 121
Hindu mythology, 1
Historical enquiry, 116
Hom-bedi, 4, 13
Hure-saja pala, 29

Ideal forms, 99
 vivaha, 99
 garva dhan, 99
 punsaban, 99
 simantayan, 100
 panchamrita, 100
 niskraman, 100
 namkaran, 101
 annaprasan, 101
 churakaran, 101
 upanayan, 101
Itu-puja broto, 90
Jadu Bhattacharjee Lane, 21
Jaistha, 32
Jajmans, 43
Jamai-sosthi broto, 88
Janmastomi broto, 89
Janmastomi, 77, 97
Jhap, 83
Jharudar, 53
Jhetel, 52
Jor-bangla, 4, 51

Joy mongol barer broto, 88

Kalighat Kali Mandir Shebait Sabha, 38
Kalighat Temple Committee, 31,32
  account of, 33
  rules & regulations of, 34-38
Kalika Puran, 15
Kalikshetra, 16
Kali-pith, 16
Kali-puja, 29,51
Kamar, 46
Kangsha Banik or Bell-metal worker, 60
Kapaliks,10
Kashari para, 60
Kashyap, 20
Khata mohorat, 93
Kula Guru, 40
Kului mongol barer broto, 90
Kundupukur, 13, 53

Lineage norms, 86

Madhyanna dol, 74
Mahabhagbat Puran, 15
Mahanil Tantra, 16
Mahasaptomi, 80
Male desires, 9
Mali, 48
Mandal, Udyog Narayan, 12
Mangolaroti, 7
Market & professional groups around the temple, 56-58
Marriages with financial difficulties, 104
Marriages without financial difficulties, 105
Mayer-ghat, 5, 85
Meaning & significance translated in English, 141-50
Mejo-Haldar, 28
Misra-brahman, 41
Monosha ghot, 78
Monosha-puja, 8,41,67,68,78,95
Monosha-tala, 7,8,78
Mukherjee, Swapan, 12
Mulasosthi broto, 90
Mul-sanyashi, 84
Mundamala, 54

Naibidya, 41,64
Nakuleswar-Tela, 5,8
Nandotsav, 78
Natmondir, 4,74,82
Navomi-puja, 67
Naw-Haldar, 28
Nepal Bhattacharjee Lane, 2
Nigam Tantra, 16
Nilsosthi broto, 91
Nitya-puja, 50
Nijaswa or Gharer Pala, 28

Observation & conclusion, 116
Occasions of public, 85
Occasions of Shebait, 72

Panchodevota, 64
Panchamrita, 106
Panda, Sudarshan, 5
Padma (lotus), 7
Parba-Sraddha, 102
Patkuroni, 46
Patuas of Kalighat, 59
Peon, 52

People in reference to
their homeland, 151
Period of Maratha invasion, 20
Phool-mali, 48
Pinde-dan, 111
Pithamala Tantra, 16
Pith, 17
Potit choturthi, 110
Pot tradition of Kalighat, 59
Pronami, 12
Puranic age, 15
Purohit darpan, 110
Radha-Krishna temples, 4,11

Rahasya-puja, 75
Rakshakali-puja, 76
Ramnavomi, 45
References, 137-40
Regional norms, 86
Register of the names
for genealogies, 123-36
Roy, Kasinath, 4
Sabitri chaturdossir broto, 88
Sacrificial spot, 116
Sadhbhakshan, 106
Saja pala, 28
Salgram sila, 64
Sanai-wala, 49
Sankata broto, 91
Sapindakaran, 102
Saptomi, 80
Saraswati-puja, 112
Sastayan, 113
Sathibrahman, 10,11,42
Satyanarayan, 94
Satyanarayan-puja, 98
Sejo-Haldar, 28
Simantayan, 106
Sitola-puja, 8,41,67,82,,96
Siva-puja broto, 87
Siva-temples, 14
Sivaratri broto, 91
Sivaratri, 7
Snanyatra, 4,18,76
Soa panch anna, 112
Solo anna, 58
Solo-dan, 110
Sondhi-puja, 81
Sosthi-puja, 96
Sosthi-tala, 7,8
Saimbhu, 1
Special performances in
other sacred spots, 95
Supreme Court of India,
New Delhi 30

Tantra-dharok, 80
Tarpan, 94
Temple organization, 2
Temple personnel, 40
Thakur, 45
Til Kanchan, 110

Vedic period, 122
Victoria Memorial ?
Calcutta, 17

Worshippers of left seat, 6
Worshippers of Right seat, 6
Worship to the Goddess Kali, 92

Yajna, 15

Zamindar, 3

MAPS AND ILLUSTRATIONS

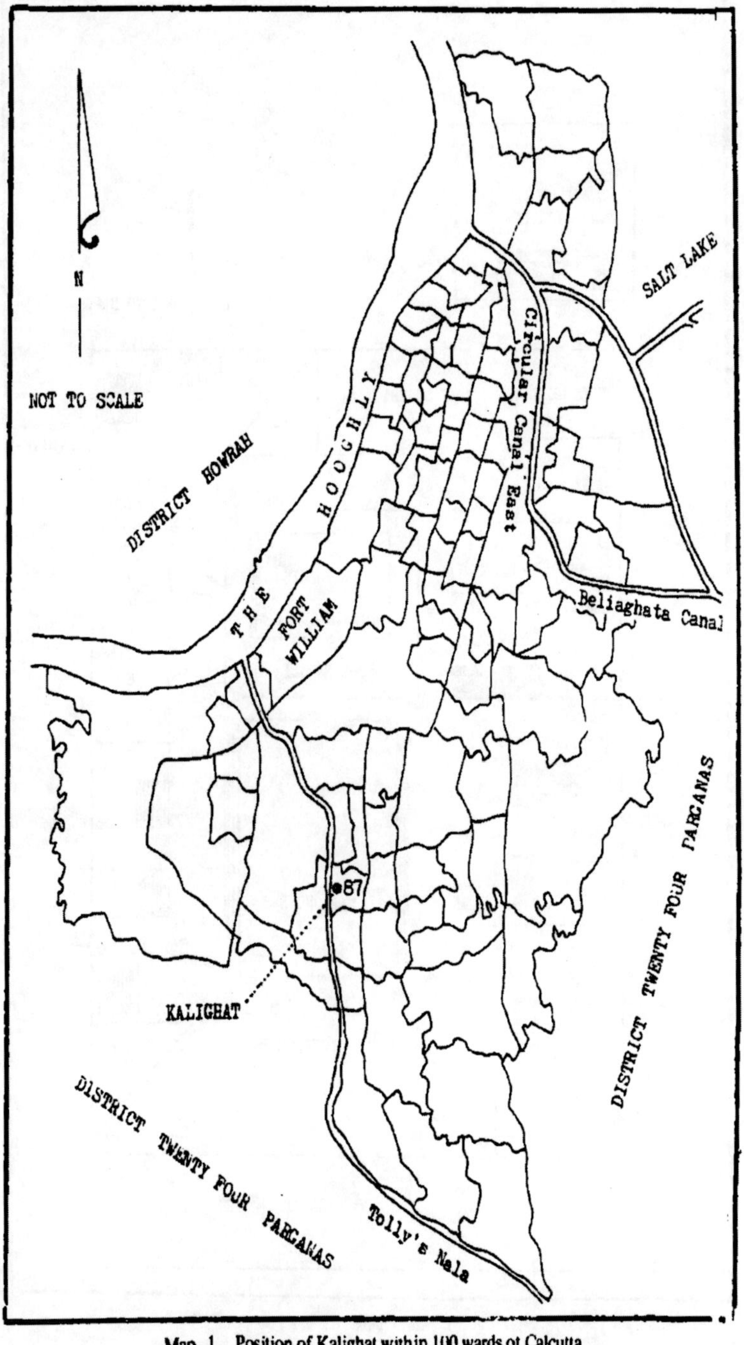

Map 1. Position of Kalighat within 100 wards ot Calcutta

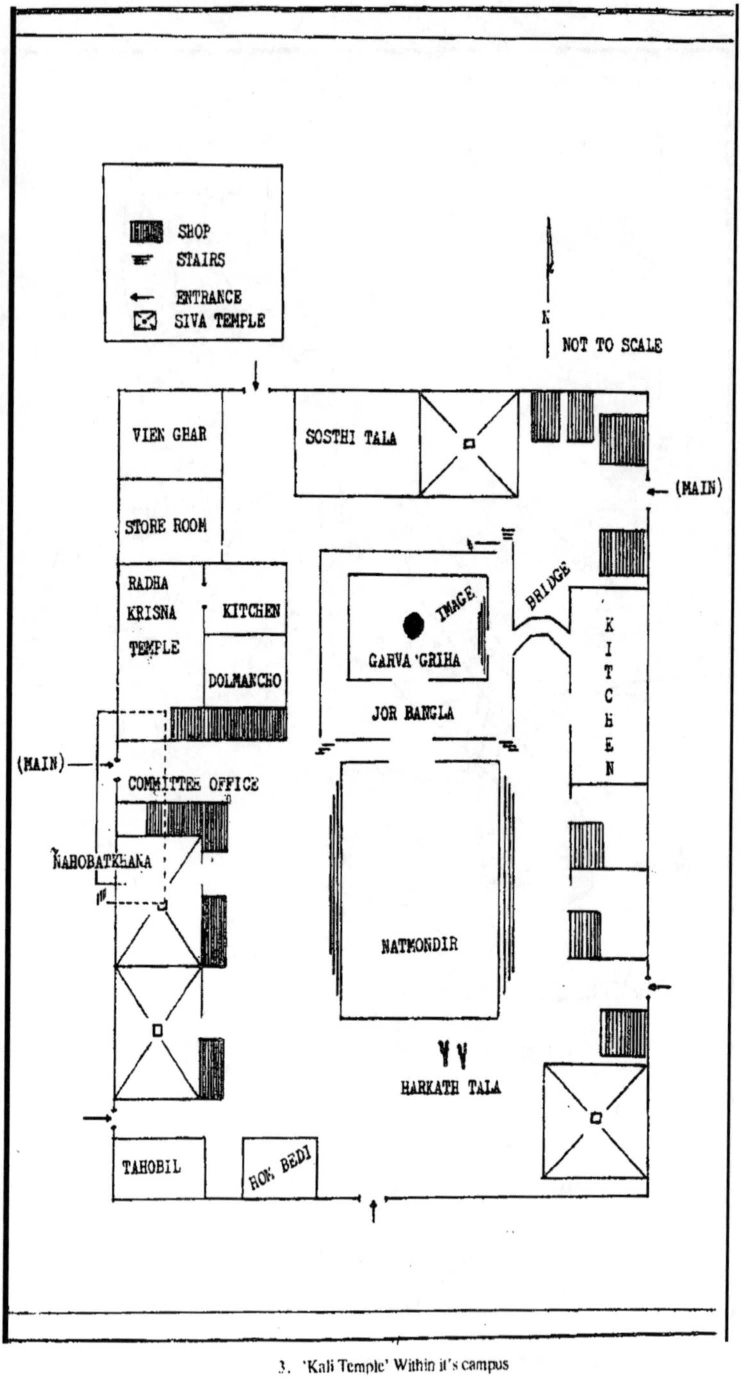

3. 'Kali Temple' Within it's campus

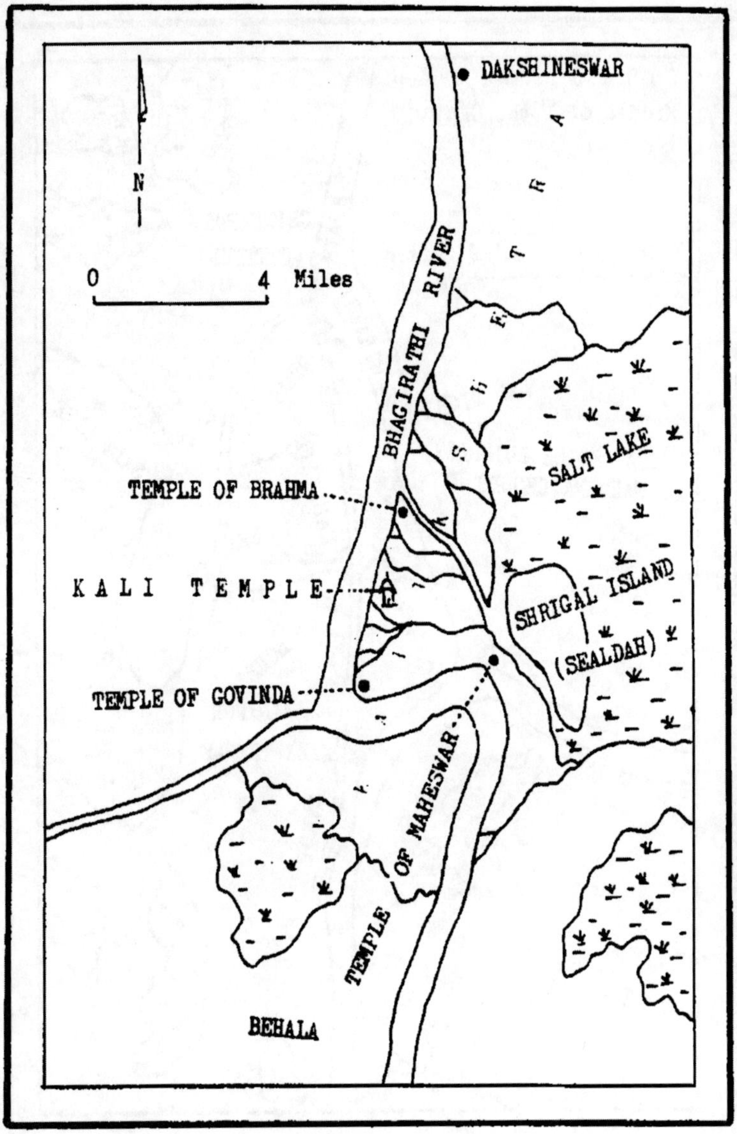

4. Kalikshetra (Calcutta : 12th. Century)

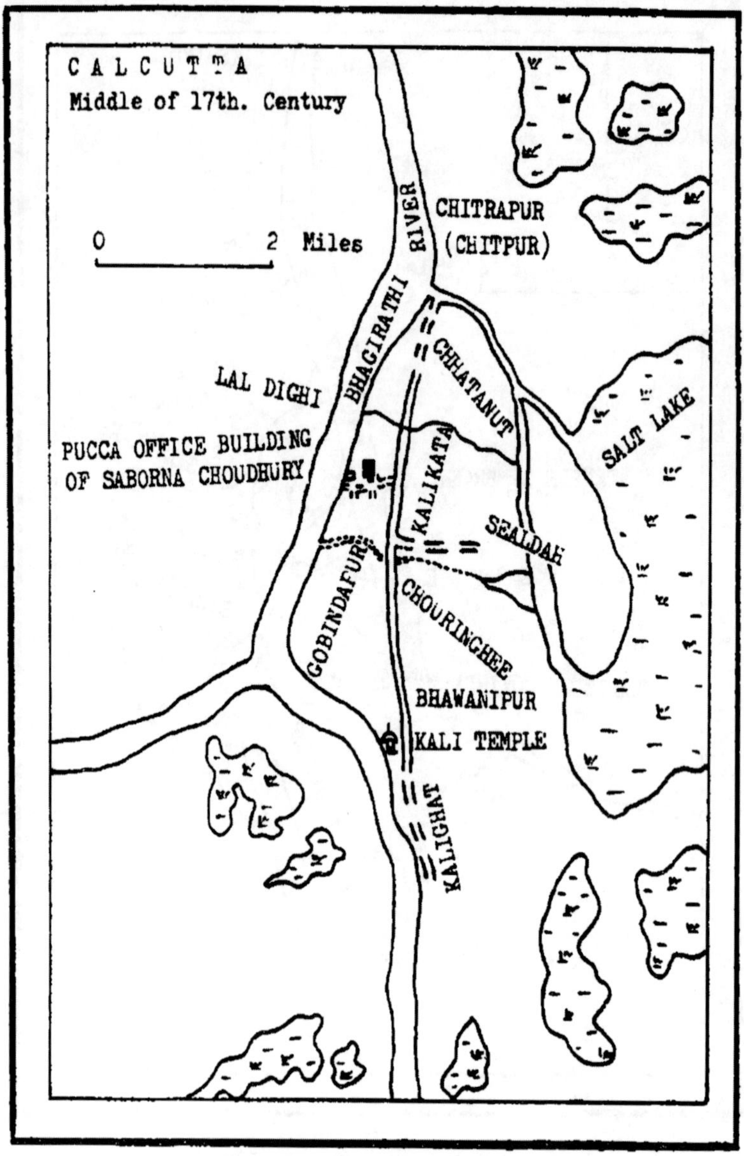

5 a Calcutta (Middle of 17th. Century)

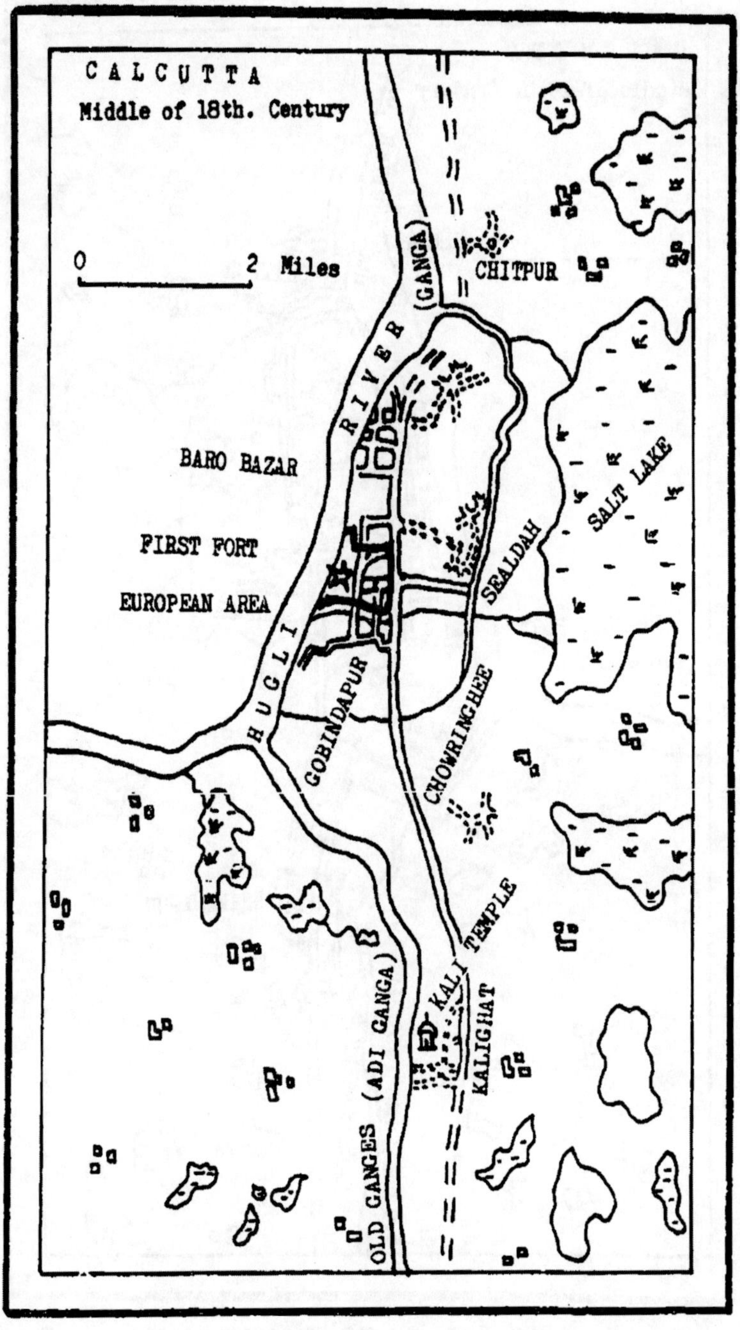

5.b Calcutta (middle of 18th Century)

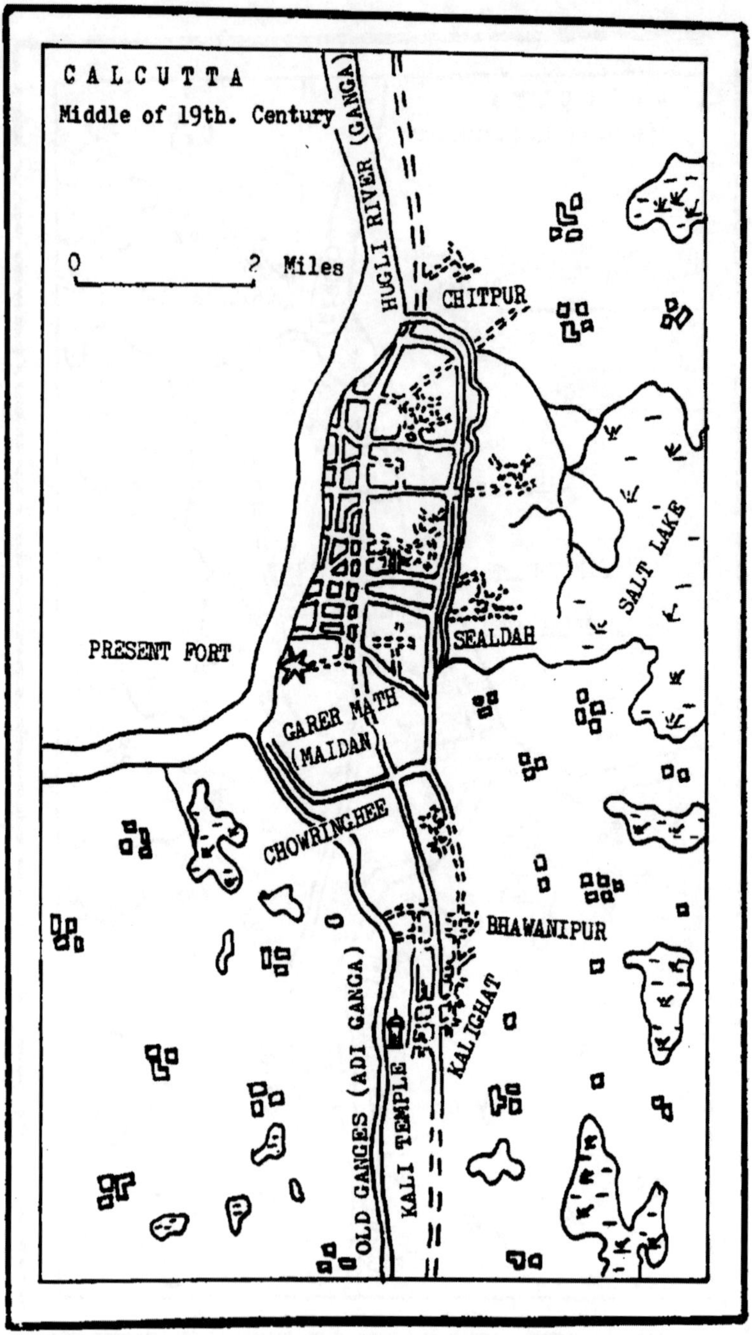

5.c Calcutta (middle of 19th Century)

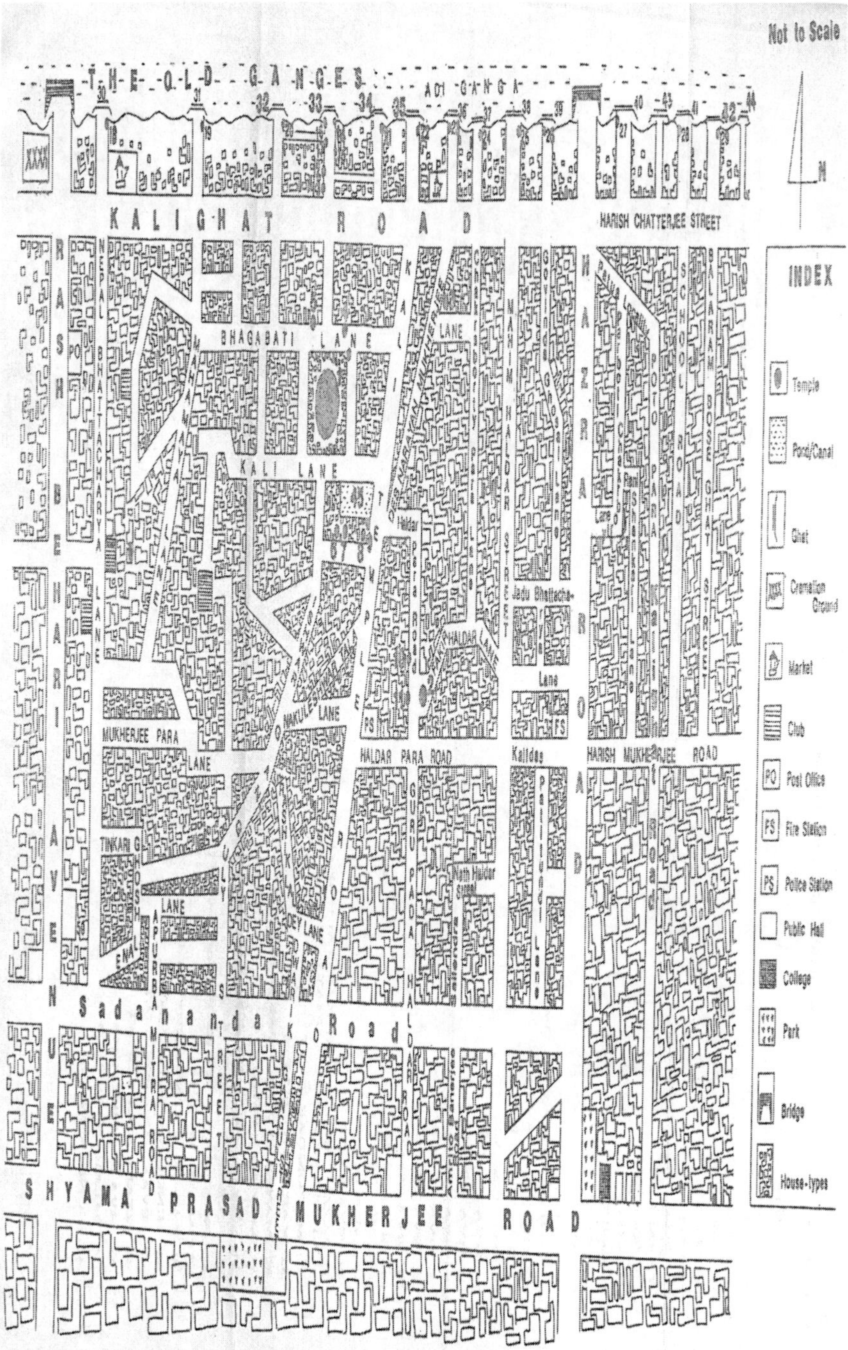

2. Area of present day Kalighat

EXPLANATION OF NUMBERS DEPICTED IN THE MAP NO. 2

1. KALI TEMPLE (MAIN)
2. NAKULESWAR TEMPLE
3. PANCHANAN TEMPLE
4. RADHAKRISNA TEMPLE
5. LOKNATH TEMPLE
6. ANNAPURNA TEMPLE
7. SITOLA TEMPLE
8. RADHAKRISNA TEMPLE
9. TARAKNATH TEMPLE
10. SITOLA TEMPLE
11. LAXMI NARAYAN TEMPLE
12. SONI TEMPLE
13. SONI TEMPLE
14. PANCHANAN TEMPLE
15. SITOLA TEMPLE
16. SONI TEMPLE ALONG WITH SABITRI IDOL
17. SONI TEMPLE ALONG WITH SABITRI IDOL
18. SIVA TEMPLE
19. SIVA TEMPLE
20. SIVA TEMPLE
21. SIVA TEMPLE
22. SIVA TEMPLE
23. SIVA TEMPLE
24. SIVA TEMPLE
25. SIVA TEMPLE
26. SIVA TEMPLE
27. SIVA TEMPLE
28. SIVA TEMPLE
29. SIVA TEMPLE
30. BAZAR GHAT/NEPAL BHATTACHARYA STREET GHAT/BASTUHARA GHAT
31. MAZUMDAR GHAT
32. KARTIKER GHAT
33. MAYER GHAT/SADAR GHAT
34. MEYEDER GHAT
35. DEBNARAYAN BANERJEE GHAT
36. RAJRAJESWARI GHAT
37. AGHOR DUTTA GHAT/BENE GHAT
38. ANONYMOUS
39. TARAK CHOWDHURY GHAT
40. HINDU MISSION GHAT
41. SEVAK SANGHA GHAT
42. SITALA MATA GHAT
43. SIVA SAMBHU GHAT
44. BALARAM BASU GHAT
45. KUNDUPUKUR

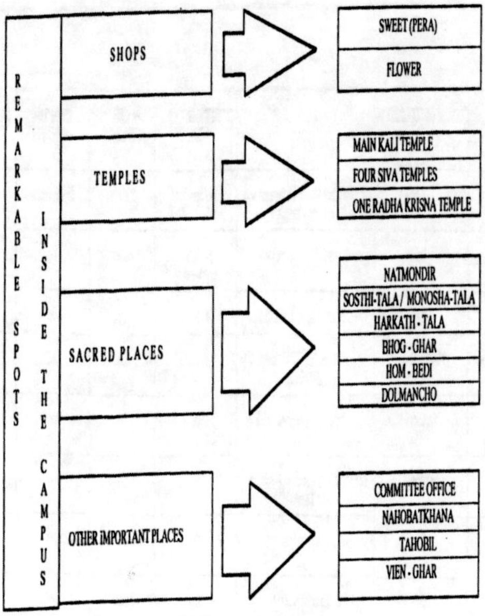

Chart 1.a Remarkable spots inside the campus

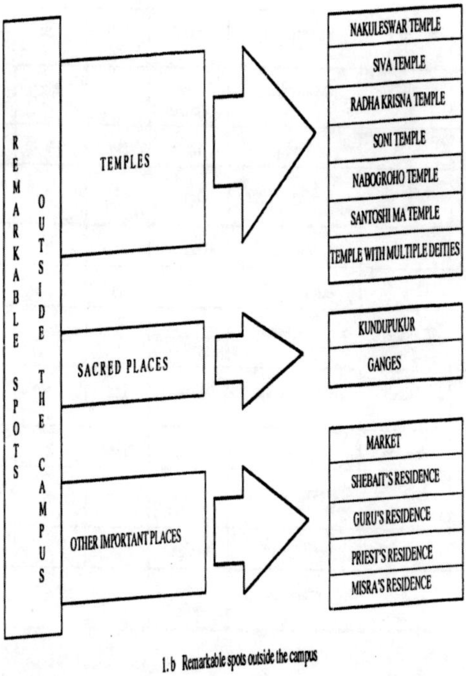

1.b Remarkable spots outside the campus

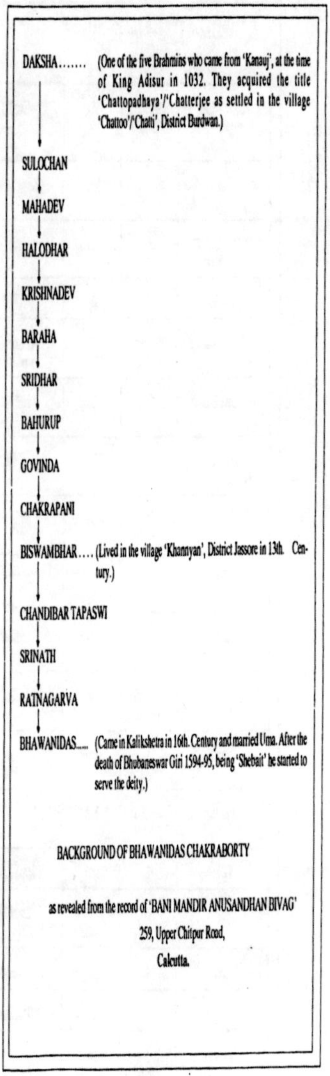

2. Background of Bhawanidas Chakraborty

A PROFILE ON TEMPLE PERSONNEL

DESIGNATION	NO. OF PERSONS	SEX	IDENTITY	NATURE OF OCCUPATION	JOB	WORKING HOURS IN A DAY FOR AN INDIVIDUAL	PAYING AUTHORITY	APPOINTING AUTHORITY	DRESS SPECIFICATION
Guru	1	Male	Bengali Brahman	Traditional	To initiate the baldar family members with mysterious formula	Not Specified	Shebaits	Shebait Family	Yes
Bhattacharjee Masai (Chief Priest)	4	Do	Do	Do	To worship the Goddess Kali	3 - Hours Approximately	Paladar	Do	Yes
Misra Brahman	8	Do	Do	Do	To attend the image of Kali	4 - Hours	Public	Do	Yes
Sathi Brahman	Numerous	Do	Bengali, Bihari, Oriya and Nepali Brahman	Non Traditional	To help Public in Puja Offerings	Not Specified	Do	Self	No
Chhar Brahman	Do	Do	Bengali Brahman	Traditional	To carry out personal orders of shebaits	Do	Do	Do	No
Dasakarme Parodorhi Brahman	Do	Do	Do	Non Traditional	To help public in specialised Worships and Rites	Do	Do	Self	Yes
Dalal	Do	Do	Not Specified	Do	To supply clients	Do	Do	Respective Shebait	No
Bhari	1	Do	Oriya Brahman	Do	To supply water	4 - Hours approximately	Paladar	PalAdar	No
Thakur	3	Do	Bengali Brahman	Do	To cook 'Bhog'	8 - Hours approximately	Do	Do	No
Jogare	No Specific Persons	Do	Do	Do	To assist the 'Thkur'	Do	Paladar / Thakur	Paladar / Thakur	No
Patkuroni	1	Female	Do	Do	To serve as a maid in the kitchen	Do	Paladar	Paladar	No
Basan Majar Lok	N O T S P E C I F I E D			Do	To clean the used utensils	1 - Hour approximately	Do	Shebait	No
Kamar	1	Male	Bengali Karmakar	Traditional	To immolate	Not Specified	Public	Do	No
Bagdi	23	Male and Female	Bengali Bagdi	Do	To help in the immolation	Do	Do	Do	No
Dhuli	1	Male	Bengali	Do	To beat the drum	Full working hours	Committee	Do	Yes
Mali	1	Do	Oriya Brahman	Do	To clean some special places	Do	Do	Committee	Yes
Sanai Wala	Team of 3 Persons	Do	Bihari	Non Traditional	To play Sanai	2 - Hours approximately	Do	Shebait	No
Chowkidar	8	Do	Bengali and Bihari	Traditional	To serve Paladars, who are Shebaits	12 - Hours	Shebait	Committee	Yes
Darwan	10	Do	Bihari and Nepali	Non Traditional	To guard the Temple	8 - Hours	Committee	Do	Yes
Peon	2	Do	Bengali	Do	To convey messages to and from office	7 - Hours approximately	Do	Do	Yes
Jhetel	2	Do	Bengali	Do	To carry out orders of office	Full working hours	Do	Do	Yes
Jharudar	2	Do	Bihari	Do	To clean the campus	2 - Hours approximately	Do	Do	No

Actual duty for this designation has changed

3. A profile on temple personnel

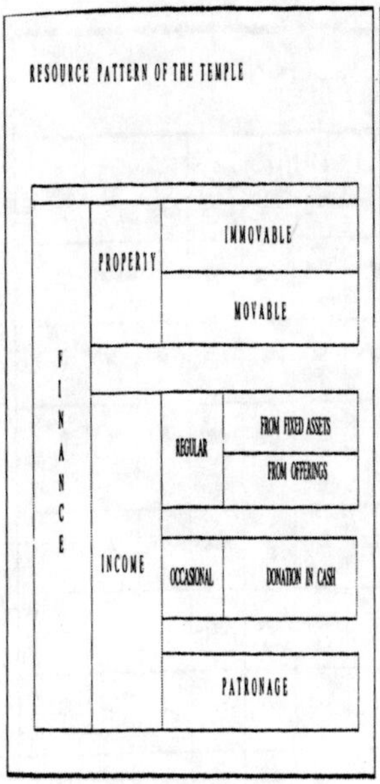

4. Resource pattern of the tempe

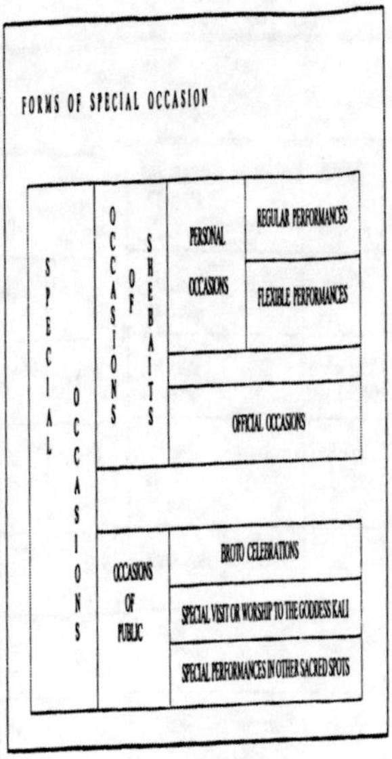

6. Forms of special occasion

REMARKABLE ACTIVITIES AT A GLANCE

APPROXIMATE TIME	PERFORMANCE	PERFORMER
4.00 A.M.	Opening of Doors	'Misra - Brahman'
4.10 A.M.	Cleaning and Decoration	Do
4.30 A.M.	Mongolaroti	Kanai Haldar
5.00 A.M.	Nitya - Puja	Chief Priest
6.00 A.M.	Worship of Public	'Sathi - Brahman'
No Specific Time	Boli	'Kamar' immolates with the help of a 'Bagdi'
3.30 P.M.	Bhog - Offering	Chief Priest
3.45 P.M.	Doridronarayan Seva	'Chowkidar's Serve, to the Beggars
4.30 P.M.	Worships of Public	'Sathi - Brahman'
6.30 P.M.	Sondhyaroti	Chief Priest
7.30 P.M.	Sitol	Do
7.45 P.M.	Worships of Public	'Sathi - Brahman'
11.00 P.M.	Besh	'Misra - Brahman'
11.30 P.M.	Sayan	Do

5. Remarkable activities at a glance

CHIEF OCCASIONS OF 'SHEBAIT' AND THE NORMAL ROUTINE

	NAME OF THE OCCASION	PLACE OF PERFORMANCE	DATE	AUSPICIOUS MOMENT	APPROXIMATE DURATION	PERFORMER	ORGANISED BY	SPECIALITY IN THE PERFORMANCE	NORMAL ROUTINE: MORNING DECORATION	NITYA PUJA	BHOG RAG	DORIDRONARAYAN SEVA	Sondhyarati	SITOL OFFERING	BESH	SAYAN
	Rakshakali Puja	Jor Bangla	8th/14th Day of Dark Fortnight in 'Baisakh'/'Jaistha'	Night	3 Hours	One Chief Priest	Commitee	Hom, Adhibash on Previous Evening	As Usual	As Usual	As Usual	As Usual	Absent	As Usual	As Usual	As Usual
	Shanjatra	Garva Griha	Full Moon Day of 'Jaistha'	Early Morning	4 Hours	Particular Five Persons of 'Baro Haldar' Lineage	Do	Sol Anga Bathed and Clothed	Very Late	Very Late	Late	Late	As Usual	Do	Do	Do
	Janmastomi	Radha Krisna Temple	8th Day of Dark Fortnight in 'Sraban'/'Bhadra'	Night	3 Hours	One Chief Priest	Do	Adhibash, Hom, Basudev taken to Kali Temple	As Usual	As Usual	As Usual	As Usual	Absent	Do	Do	Do
	Nandotsav	Verandah of Main Temple	The day after Janmastomi	Morning	$\frac{1}{2}$ Hour	Do	Do	Abhiseth of Basudev	Do	Sometimes Late	Do	Do	As Usual	Do	Do	Do
	Monosha Puja	Monosha-Tala	5th Day of Light Fortnight in 'Badra'	Noon	$1\frac{1}{2}$ Hours	Do	Do	Boli	Do	As Usual	Sometimes Late	Sometimes Late	As Usual	Do	Do	Do
DU	Sosthi	Sosthi-Tala	6th Day of Light Fortnight in 'Aswin'	Evening	$1\frac{1}{2}$ Hours	Five Priests	Commitee Stands for Haldars and	Bodhan	Do	As Usual	As Asual	As Usual	Late	Late	Do	Do
RG	Saptomi	Garva Griha	The Day after Sosthi	Morning	2 to 3 Hours	For Five	Daubitras Others are	Jagrodip Worship	Do	Do	Late	Absent	Absent	Absent	Absent	Absent
A	Astomi	Do	The Day After Saptomi	Any Time	Do	Different	Conducted by	Sondhi Puja	Absent	Do	Do	Do	Do	Do	Do	Do
PU	Navomi	Do	The Day after Astomi	Any Time	Do	Parties	Respective Parties	Boli, Kalyaner Puja, Dakshinanto	Do	Do	Do	Do	Do	Do	Do	Do
JA	Dasomi	No Worship	The Day after Navomi					Sidur Khela	Do	Do	Early	Do	Do	Late	Early	As Usual
	Sitola Puja	Natmondir	8th Day of Dark Fortnight in 'Chaitra'	Noon	3 Hours	Many Priests	Commitee	Bhog, Brahman Bhojan	As Usual	Do	Late	Late	As Usual	As Usual	As Usual	Do
	Chanchor	Dolmancho	8th Day of Light Fortnight in 'Chaitra'	Night	3 to $3\frac{1}{2}$ Hours	One Chief Priest	Shebaits (Communally)	'Myra' is Burnt, a procession is arranged	Do	Do	As Usual	As Usual	Absent	Do	Do	Do
RA	Purbahnna Dol	Do		Dawn	$1\frac{1}{2}$ Hours											
MN	Madhyanna Dol	Do	Day After Chanchor	Noon	$1\frac{1}{2}$ Hours	Do	Do	Abhiseth of Radha Krishna	Do	Do	Late	Late	Sometimes Late	Sometimes Late	Do	Do
OV MI	Abhisekh	Do		Early Evening	1 Hour											
GA	Kata-Jhap	In Front of 'Mayur Ghat'	One Day before 'Boti-Jhap'	Evening	2 Hours	Bagdis of	Commitee	Ful Korano at Kali Temple, Jhap	Do	Do	As Usual	As Usual	Sometimes Late	Sometimes Late	Do	Do
JAN	Boti-Jhap	In Front of Nakuleswar Temples	Last Day of 'Chaitra'	Evening	3 Hours	the Temple		Ful Korano at Kali Temple & Nakuleswar Temple	Do	Do	Do	Do	Do	Do	Do	Do
	Nishi Puja Rahasya Puja	Natmondir and Siva Temples	New Moon of Each Month	Mid Night	3 Hours	Different Priests but separately	Shebaits and Priests (individually)	Hom, Bhog	Do	Do	As Usual	Do	As Usual	As Usual	Late	Late

7. Chief occasions of 'Shebait' and the normal routine

'BROTO' – THE NATURE AND FEATURES

MONTH	NAME OF THE BROTO	SPECIFICATION OF DATE	TIME	PERFORMER	PLACE OF PERFORMANACE	OBJECTIVE
Baisakh (April - May)	Siva Puja Broto	No	Morning	Unmarried Girls	Natmondir	To get a husband as good as Lord Siva
	Akkhoy Tritia Broto	Third Day of Light Fortnight	Do	Both men & women	Natmondir, Siva Temples and other suitable places	To pass the life happily and to achieve eternal peace after death
	Harish Mongol Barer Broto	Tuesdays	Do	Married women	Natmondir, shops with space, road corners	To overcome all grives of this world
Jaistha (May - June)	Joy Mongol Barer Broto	Tuesdays	Do	Women	Do	To check all the misfortunes of this world
	Jamai Sosthi Broto	Sixth day of Light Fortnight	Do	Mothers	Natmondir	For the well being of the Children
	Sabitri chaturdossir Broto	Fourteenth day of Dark Fortnight	Evening	Married women	Mayer Ghat	For long life of husband
Ashar (June - July)	Bippattarini Broto	Tuesday & Saturday (Between 3rd to 9th day of Light Fortnight)	Morning	Both men & women	Natmondir, shops with space, road corners	To prevent all the dancers of the family
Bhadra (Aug - Sept)	Janmastomi Broto	Eighth day of Dark Fortnight	Evening to Night	Do	Any suitable space outside the temple campus	To efface all sins
	Ananto Chaturdossir Broto	Fourteenth day of Light Fortnight	Morning	Do	Natmondir	Helps to escape from dangers
Kartik (Oct - Nov)	ITU Puja Broto (Starts)	Last Day	Do	Women	Natmondir, any suitable space inside or outside the temple campus	For riches and happiness
Agrahan (Nov - Dec)	ITU Puja Broto (Continues)	Sundays	Do	Do	Do	Do
	Mulasosthi Broto	Sixth day of Light Fortnight	Do	Mothers	Do	To keep the children free from diseases
	Kului Mongol Barer Broto	Tuesdays	Do	Women	Do	To stay away from scandal
Falgun (Feb- Mar)	Sivaratri Broto	Fourteenth day of Dark Fortnight	Night	Both men & women	Siva temples	To attain four results at a time – Dharma (Proper Attitude), Artha (Money), Kama (Passion) and Moksha (Liberation)
Chaitra (Mar - Apr)	Nilsosthi Broto	Last Day	Evening	Mothers	Do	For well being of the children
Any Month	Sankata Broto	Fridays of Light Fornight	Morning	Women	Natmondir	For Protection against dangers
	Santoshima Broto	Fridays	Noon	Do	Do	To achieve riches, happiness & peace in the world

8. 'Broto' - the nature and features

HINDU RITES OF PASSAGE AT KALIGHAT

NAME OF THE RITE		PERFORMANCE					
		RATE	TIME		EXPENSE		PLACE
			LOWER LIMIT	UPPER LIMIT	Lower Limit	Upper Limit	
DASAKARMA	Vivaha	Frequent	10 to 15 minutes	2 to 3 hours	Rs 10/- to Rs. 25/-	Rs 200/- to Rs 500/-	Rented room, any other suitable place
	Garvadhan						
	Punsaban						
	Simantayan						
	Panchamrita 'O' Sadhbhakshan						
	Niskraman						
	Namkaran						
	Annaprasan	Rare		3 to 4 hours		Rs 300/- to Rs. 400/-	Rented room or Natmondir
	Churakaran	Moderate	10 Minutes	20 minutes	Rs 5/-	Rs 10/-	Surrounding Areas of Monosha - Tala
	Upanayan	Frequent	One Hour	2 to 3 hours	Rs 100/-	Rs 300/- to Rs 400/-	Natmondir, Rented Room, any suitable space
SRADDHA	Adya - Sraddha	Frequent	20 Minutes to one Hour	3 to 4 hours	Rs 10/- to Rs 50/-	Rs 200/- to Rs 500/-	Rented room or bank of the Ganges
	Batsarik	Moderate	1 to $1\frac{1}{2}$ Hours	4 to 5 hours	Rs 50/- to Rs 100/-	Rs 200/- to Rs 500/-	
	Parba - Sraddha	Frequent	5 Minutes	10 minutes	Re 1/-	Rs 5/-	
	Briddhi - Sraddha						

9. Hindu rites of passage at Kalighat

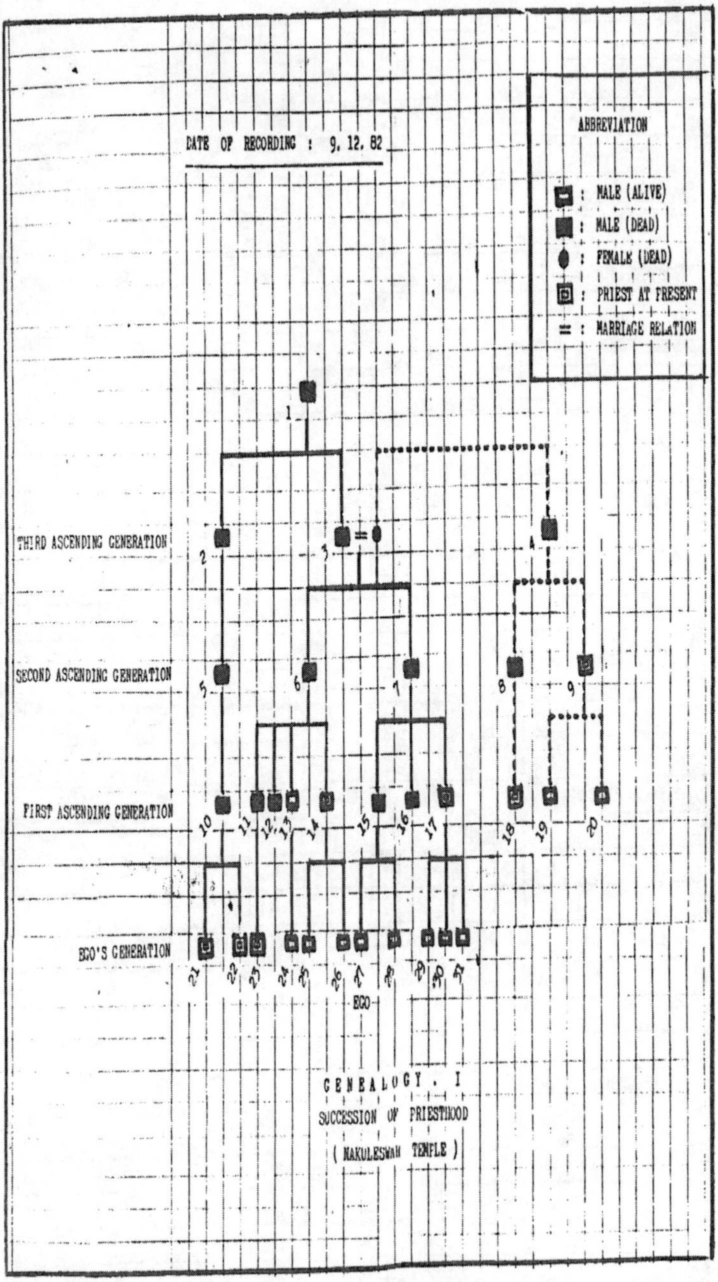

GENEALOGY . I

SUCCESSION OF PRIESTHOOD

(NAKULESWAR TEMPLE)

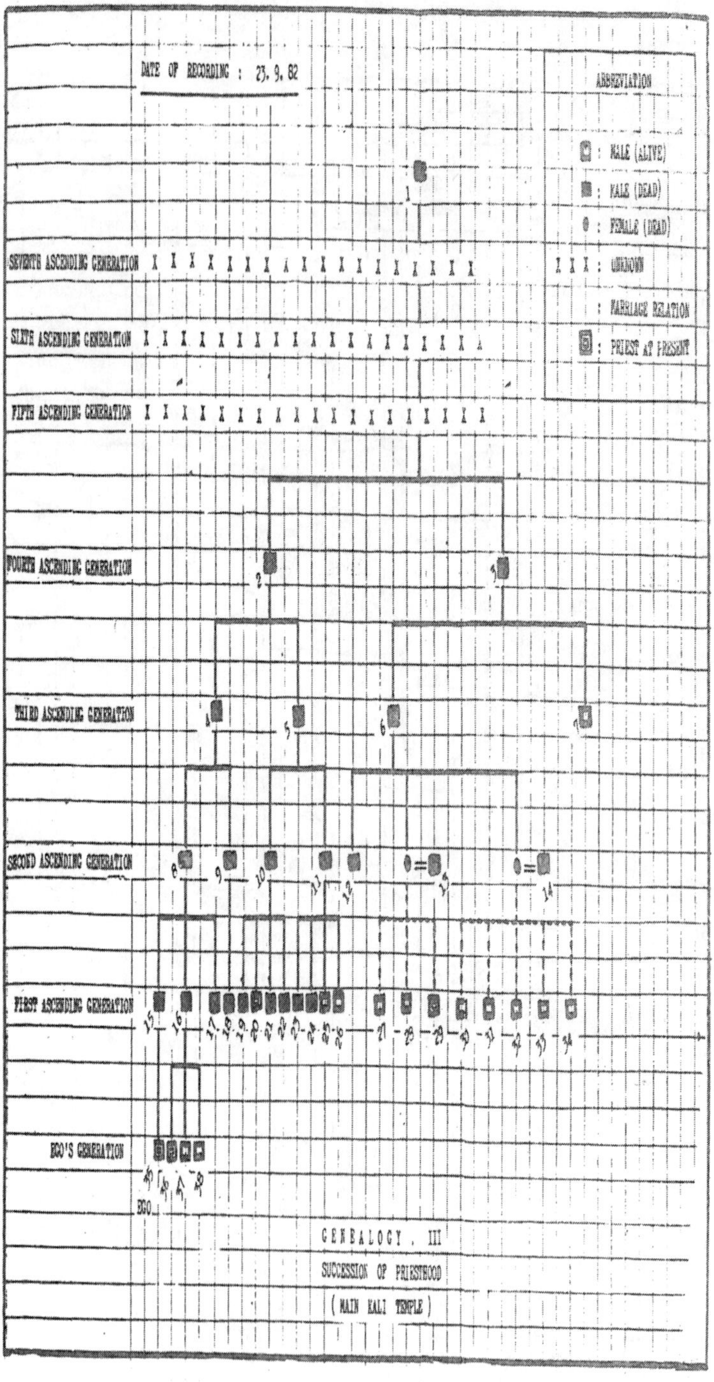

GENEALOGY . III

SUCCESSION OF PRIESTHOOD

(MAIN KALI TEMPLE)

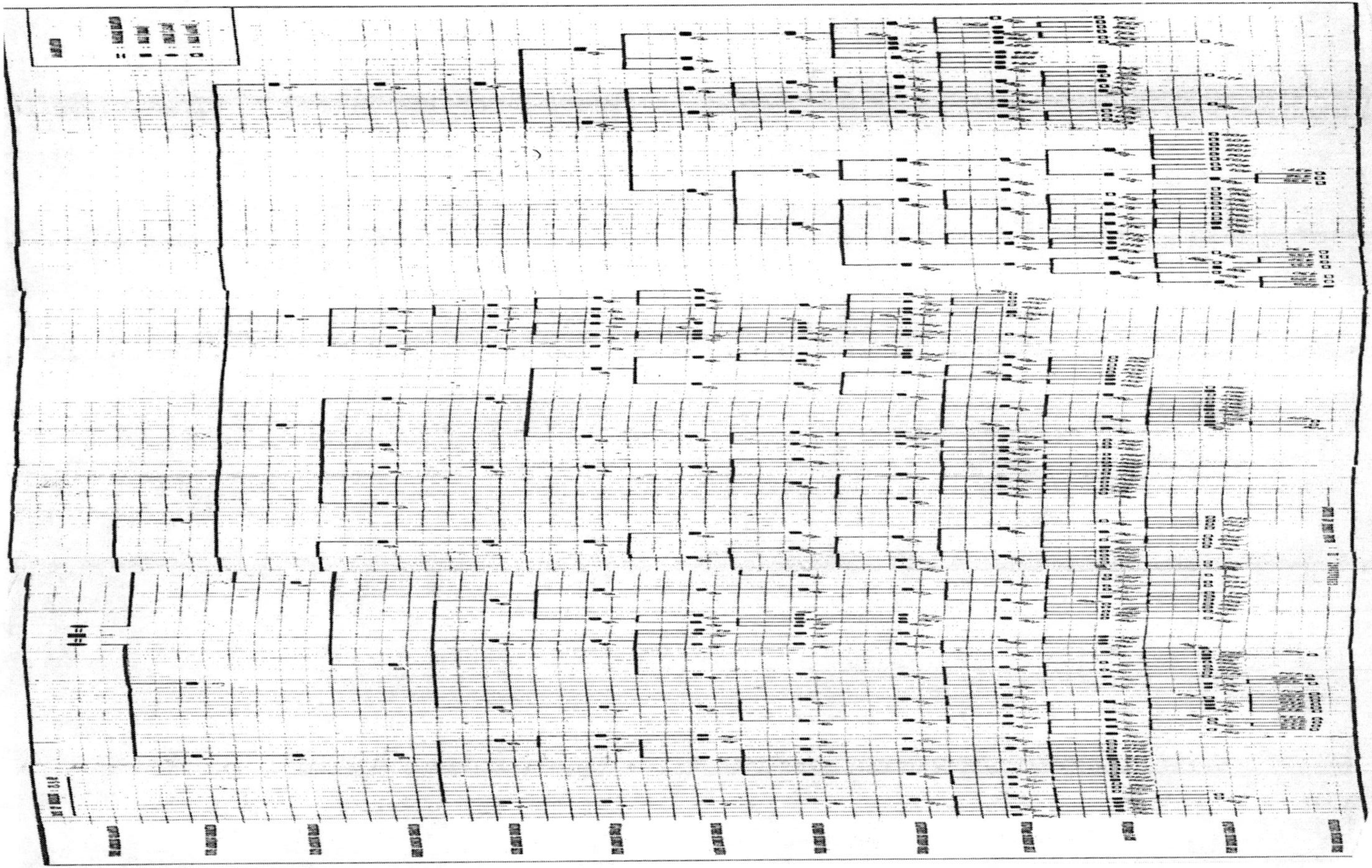